CONSUMER

ECONOMICS

CONSUMER ECONOMICS

JAMES F. NISS

Department of Economics
Western Illinois University

Prentice-Hall, Inc., Englewood Cliffs, New Jersey

Library of Congress Cataloging in Publication Data

Niss, James F.
    Consumer economics.

    1. Consumption (Economics)   2. Economics.
3. Finance, Personal.   I. Title.
HB801.N55   381   73–5995
ISBN 0-13-169441-3

© 1974 by Prentice-Hall, Inc., Englewood Cliffs, N.J.

Printed in the United States of America

10 9 8 7 6 5 4 3

PRENTICE-HALL INTERNATIONAL, INC., *London*
PRENTICE-HALL OF AUSTRALIA, PTY. LTD., *Sydney*
PRENTICE-HALL OF CANADA, LTD., *Toronto*
PRENTICE-HALL OF INDIA PRIVATE LTD., *New Delhi*
PRENTICE-HALL OF JAPAN, INC., *Tokyo*

Contents

Preface

Over the last several years the economics profession has become increasingly concerned about its ability to impart to students in basic economics courses the knowledge and analytical skills economists believe they should master. A part of this concern has expressed itself through the activities of the Joint Council on Economic Education in the form of workshops, materials development, and the development of standardized testing instruments. These activities have focused on the marginal changes which might be made in the course in order to improve student reception and student interest. Such changes include the problems approach, the current topics approach, the elimination of certain principles to provide a more manageable and meaningful number for the student's mastery and so on. Rarely have these proposed changes deviated to any great extent from the accepted norm as typified by basic principles books such as those written by Samuelson, McConnel, or Reynolds.

This book proceeds from a rather markedly different basic premise in that it is believed that students of economics will have a more intense interest in the course and will learn more easily the principles and analytical skills if the course is related to their daily decision-making processes. In order to make this connection to daily life, the basic principles of economics and the more important concepts of consumer education or consumer economics have been brought together, thus enabling the student to acquire both skills in economics and skills in making rational daily decisions regarding the allocation of his income. The basic purpose of the materials that follow is to indicate how consumer economics can become an integral part of the principles of economics courses and in so doing give the student badly needed information.

The second basic objective of the book is to provide a generalized outline for a basic principles of economics course including consumer concepts. The basic outline begins with a study of the current issues and problems in personal and societal economics. It then considers the methodology of decision making both for the consumer and for the economist. Basic questions of supply and demand, consumer purchasing of goods and services, housing, automobiles, and so on, are considered. Micro-economic considerations of the theory of firms and markets and the process of income distribution are given specific consideration for the potential of income earning power and the kinds of job opportunities which will be developing in various sectors of the economy. In general the suggested outline includes the basic topics usually covered in a one-semester or one-year principles course and adds to them budgeting, consumer purchasing, investments, insurance, and consumer credit. It uses these consumer topics to illustrate economic concepts and to allow for student application of economic concepts.

The bulk of the textual material developed is not generally found in basic economic texts. This material is an elaboration upon the basic outline and is designed to provide the student with sufficient insights into consumer economic concepts when used in conjunction with a basic principles book.

It is the desire of the author to provide the student and the instructor with materials which will enrich and expand upon the concepts in a basic economics course. The intent is not to supplement the basic economics course with a course in consumer economics. It is essential that persons not only become good consumers and good purchasers of consumer items, but that they also understand the ramifications of monetary and fiscal policies, of antitrust policies, of wage price guidelines, and so on. It is of little value if we are educated consumers, able to allocate our incomes wisely, yet we have a minimal understanding of economic policy questions and improperly exercise our restraint with regard to these questions through the voting mechanism.

The author wishes to thank Drs. Floyd Crank, Peter Senn, and M. Eugene Moyer for valuable assistance in preparation of the basic outline. Dr. Ross Lowe has assisted in preparation of the section on budgeting and has read other sections of the manuscript. Special note should be made of the work of Melvin Smith and Cyrus Richardson, who labored on sections three, four, and five. Special thanks are given to the three reviewers, from whose constructive comments this work benefited greatly. They are Professor Richard Shirey, Genessee Community College, Professor Francis Yeager, University of Houston, and Dr. Glenn Wilt, Jr., Arizona State University.

James F. Niss

CONSUMER
ECONOMICS

Decision-Making
Processes

Every day each of us is required to make hundreds and perhaps thousands of decisions. Some of the decisions are very small and inconsequential such as "Do I climb the stairs or ride the elevator?" Others are more important in that they require us to decide between spending time on academic endeavors or spending time in recreational activities. Others become even more important in that they are decisions regarding major events in our lives, such as: do we enter college or attend a trade school, do we enroll in a military program or attempt to find work in a civilian sector, etc. Decision making is an extremely important process, one which each of us faces countless times throughout our lives. In order to understand the process, we will look at some of the elements of making decisions in this section. The first decision-making process to be considered will be rational goal attainment; the second, the application of cost benefit techniques; and the third, the process of making decisions on the basis of impulse.

RATIONAL GOAL ATTAINMENT

Economists and businessmen assume that most decisions made by households and businesses fall into the category of rational goal attainment. This is not to indicate that the process of cost benefit analysis does not involve rational goal attainment. However, as we will note below, the process of cost benefit analysis requires the ability to quantify highly the benefits and costs obtained when one either acquires a product or carries out the decision process. Rational goal attainment can best be considered by establishing in approximate order the steps which a person or organization follows in reaching a decision.

ESTABLISHING DESIRED GOAL(S)

The establishment of a goal involves deciding what need or needs one wishes to satisfy. If a decision is to be made regarding the purchase of an item of clothing, the desired goal is to obtain or purchase the item for use. Consider, for example, the purchase of a coat. A coat could meet several supporting and, in some ways, conflicting goals. First, it probably would be needed for protection from the elements. Second, it could be desired in order to enhance the appearance of the wearer. Hence, as a goal is established for the purchase of this kind of an item the buyer is in effect saying, "I have a dual goal, the goal of protection and the goal of enhancing appearance." In many cases the order of these goals would be reversed, in that the person might desire the item of clothing first for appearance, and second, for protection.

ESTABLISHING CONSTRAINT(S)

As one desires to achieve a goal he must recognize that there are certain constraints or parameters within which he must operate. For example, consider a football player who wishes to carry the ball across the goal line in order to achieve six points for his team. One of the first constraints facing this player is that he must not step out of bounds. Second, he must not allow his knee to touch the ground. Third, he must continue to maintain forward movement. These are some of the constraints established by the rules of football. In economics and in consumer economics there are also constraints within which the decision maker must operate. Consider some of the more important:

Income. One of the first prerequisites of making a consumer purchase is that the purchaser have sufficient income or can borrow sufficient funds to purchase the item or items desired.

Time. An individual who wishes to attain a goal must not only have the income but must be willing to allocate time to selecting and purchasing the product in order to carry out the decision process. We all know that on weekends various supermarkets offer sales and loss leaders at prices lower than during the week. In addition, some stores have prices consistently lower than others. Therefore, if time were not a constraint, we could achieve our goal of purchasing a desired amount of food by going from store to store and buying only those items at a particular store carrying the lowest prices. This example, however, overlooks two factors. One is the factor of time—it requires time to travel from store to store. In addition, it overlooks the cost of traveling from store to store. Hence, the savings may be more apparent than real if one considers the time and travel cost involved in making these purchases.

Ability. If the goal to be achieved is a goal regarding life employment, occupational choice, or academic endeavor, the abilities of the decision maker must be considered. Obviously, if a person has relatively low manual dexterity, he probably will not decide to be a dentist or a watchmaker. On the other hand, if one has relatively low interests and abilities in academic subjects, he will probably not choose to become a doctor of philosophy. Likewise, the managers of a business firm will probably not choose to enter a market in which they have no experience and relatively little equipment adaptable and usable in that market.

The preceding are examples of constraints operating on decision makers. The reader is encouraged to make a list of constraints which have affected a recent decision.

COLLECTING DATA

Decisions cannot be made in a vacuum. The most admirable set of goals and constraints will not allow the individual or firm to reach an adequate decision if this decision is not based on the relevant information available. One certainly cannot obtain the best bundle of food purchases for the lowest cost without considering and gathering information regarding prices charged by various stores and prices charged at various times of the year. Hence, it is imperative that information regarding the product or products be developed in order to obtain the desired goal. The kinds of data required are as varied as the decisions. Some typical examples are discussed below.

Comparative cost data. Regardless of whether the decision one reaches concerns the purchase of consumer items such as food, clothing, or an automobile, or whether it is the purchase of an item for business such as plant equipment, or the introduction of a new product, it is necessary that cost data be collected. Cost data are an important part of the decision-making process in that it must provide the decision maker with data regarding the initial cost of undertaking the decision. This means, for example, that a person desiring to purchase a washing machine must know the initial purchase cost of a number of alternative brands and models of washing machines. Second, cost data should reflect the operating cost. Costs of operation of sixteen-foot refrigerators vary greatly with respect to both the type and brand name. Thus, it is important that one consider not only the initial cost but the monthly or day-to-day operating cost of a particular item. Last, there should be some attempt to investigate maintenance costs. The initial cost of a particular item may be relatively low; however, the required maintenance may be rather extensive after a period.

Hence, the total cost of undertaking a project or purchasing a product is the summation of the initial costs, the operating costs, and the maintenance costs. One cannot ignore any one of these if a complete picture of costs is to be made available.

Quality. Traditionally Americans have said "You get what you pay for." This is one of those little homilies which has a great deal of appeal but very little verifiable truth value. The quality of an item is not necessarily related to the price. If a person is to make a rational decision on a major item, it is necessary to investigate the quality of that item. Obviously the factor mentioned above, maintenance cost, and quality are in many ways related.

Sources of information. The consumer and the businessman have many sources of information available to them. Sellers can indicate the alternative prices at which they are willing to sell a product. In addition to information provided by sellers, there are a number of services which provide specialized price data. Prospective purchasers are able to obtain quality data from such organizations as the Consumers Union and the U.S. government. The federal government has recently published and has made available through the Office of Consumer Protection a listing of those items which the government has tested and specified as those which should be purchased by governmental agencies.

USING THE PRODUCT TO ASSIST IN GOAL ATTAINMENT

As one thinks of purchasing a commodity he must consider the extent to which this commodity will satisfy or achieve the goal. If one has the desire to obtain transportation services, the comparative shopping or cost data analysis process above would indicate that there are many ways of moving from one point to another. One may walk; take a taxi; take a bus; ride a bicycle; join a carpool; purchase an automobile; or, if the distances become greater, there are the options of plane and train travel. Each of these provides the transportation service from one point to another. However, each provides differing degrees of speed, convenience, and psychological satisfaction. In the American economy the ownership of an automobile has traditionally carried with it certain psychological benefits. Goods such as cars, clothing, and houses satisfy both a physiological and a psychological need on the part of the consumer or purchaser. With respect to consumer purchases, the psychological needs met by goods are often times as great or greater than the physiological needs satisfied. With respect to business firm purchases, however, the extent of psychological need satisfaction is often times more limited and therefore will not be as great a factor in the decision process.

In many cases, the individual or business unit must measure both objectively and subjectively the extent to which goods will meet or achieve the goals established in the first step of decision making. It is infinitely easier to establish quantitative criteria for the objective and physiological needs satisfied by goods and services than to establish criteria for the evaluation of psychological benefits. However, at some point the benefits must be determined and evaluated by the decision maker in such a way that the choices can be made and procedures can be established.

MAKING THE DECISION

The final stage of the decision-making process is the making of a decision based on the ability of the good in question in relation to its cost subject to the constraints to meet to the largest extent the goals established in Stage 1. This decision process culminates with the decision either to purchase or not to purchase a good or item or to carry out or not to carry out an expected procedure.

In reality the decision does not culminate the process; it is, however, the point at which one decides to carry out an activity. Following this decision most businesses and individuals evaluate the initial outcome and the results of the decision over a period of time in relation to the goals, the constraints, and the costs. This allows the individual to have a feedback of information for use in future decision processes regarding similar products or services.

COST BENEFIT ANALYSIS

In the discussion of rational goal attainment it was assumed that the decision maker would carefully analyze the various alternatives and establish a cost and benefit associated with each of these alternatives. This assumption is not necessarily true for many of the day-to-day decisions made by consumers, since these purchases often involve relatively small amounts for rather insignificant commodities. However, when the selection of housing is considered, or the building of a flood control project or a missile system, great costs are involved if the wrong decision is made. As a result of the potential for costly errors, the federal government and other branches of government and business have evolved a decision-making process called cost benefit analysis. The process of embarking on a cost benefit analysis of a project is very similar to the process described above as rational goal attainment.

The first step or stage of the process requires a specification of the goals or objectives to be achieved as the result of the program. One must be careful to express these goals or objectives in terms of achievable satisfaction. One does not purchase a house, for example, for its aesthetic appearance but rather for shelter and psychological comforts. Thus, the goal of this project is not the purchase of the house, but rather the attainment of shelter and other needs.

Second, the quantity of output or the total amount of satisfaction that can be received from the project must be measured. Hence, if one is talking about the purchase of food, he would consider the quantities of various proteins, carbohydrates, etc., that could be obtained in the purchase.

A third step in the cost benefit analysis decision process is to collect the data regarding the cost of the program or decision. This means that not only the initial cost data must be collected but the cost data over the entire life of the project under consideration.

Fourth, one must analyze and seek out potential alternatives which might be able to provide the same level of satisfaction or to meet the same goals either more cheaply or with less detrimental or environmental impact.

The last stage or step in this process is to analyze in a systematic way the data available so as to decide either (1) to carry out or not to carry out the process and (2) which alternative provides the greatest benefits at the least cost if the program is to be carried on.[1]

The process of cost benefit analysis has been used to a large extent by the Army Corp of Engineers in determining the desirability of completing various flood and water control projects. In the Department of Defense the entire concept of program budgeting—that is, budgeting over the entire period of the proposed program and not just over a part of it—and cost benefit analysis have been used extensively in evaluating alternative weapons systems.

The process does not differ markedly from the processes that we, as consumers, should follow as we make our day-to-day purchases. The major difference would be the magnitude of the decision process. Whereas the consumer tends to talk in dollars or thousands of dollars, governmental agencies tend to make decisions in millions and billions of dollars and, hence, the social cost of making an error is potentially much greater than the social cost of error on the part of the consumer.

NON-RATIONAL DECISION-MAKING PROCESSES

Each of us nearly every day makes a non-rational decision. That is, we either depend on habit to control our decision processes, or we make an impulse purchase of some commodity or item. One may be walking through the supermarket, for example, and pick up a can of smoked oysters. This is often times considered an impulse purchase in that there was not a conscious desire or plan to purchase the commodity prior to moving through the super-

---

[1] See H. H. Hinrichs and G. M. Taylor, *Program Budgeting and Benefit Cost Analysis* (Pacific Palisades, California: Goodyear Publishing Company, 1969) for a detailed discussion supplemented with cases.

market. However, some steps of the rational decision process may have entered in briefly as we looked at the can of smoked oysters. Impulse purchases tend to be non-rational and are conditioned by such things as social pressure, advertising, packaging, etc. One should not condemn completely the process of impulse buying since in most cases it only represents a small portion of income. However, the sum of these small portions of income for all of the people in the economy becomes considerable. Perhaps this is why such large quantities are spent on advertising—to encourage us to purchase on impulse.

Rational goal seeking means that we attempt to follow either a cost benefit analysis technique or in a more loose fashion a rational goal attainment process in order to maximize as best we can our satisfaction given the annual income which we have at our disposal.

The foregoing is intended to show the manner in which rational goal attainment procedures can be used to assist consumers in applying economic theory and economic concepts to the process of allocating and earning income. Each of us desires to attain a certain level of income. This level of income is determined by our abilities and our desires to enter the market system. Given these desires and income, each of us may well attempt to maximize satisfaction. The wanderer may desire very little in material satisfaction and therefore may be willing to engage only slightly in the world of work. The person desiring large quantities of physical comforts and psychological security in goods and services may engage vigorously in the world of work and may even attempt to marry a rich spouse. In either case, the process of attaining one's goals and achieving satisfaction requires that consideration be given to alternative costs and to alternative purchases.

MAKING DECISIONS FOR QUALITY OF LIFE

The rational decision-making process and the cost benefit process assume that the individual, the business firm, or the governmental unit will attempt to achieve the highest level of satisfaction or profit for the least outlay. These decision processes assume that the decision maker can evaluate the alternatives with the knowledge that the prices paid for goods and services reflect the true and total cost to society. In order for the individual and society to maximize satisfaction, it is necessary that the private cost—the market cost of goods—be equal to the social cost of the goods.

It might be helpful to consider an example to show the difference between private cost and social cost. In a midwestern community one frequently finds a food processing company processing peas and sweet corn. The food processor produces two "goods" and two "bads." The "goods" are the canned and frozen peas and corn. The "bads" are the water pollution of the river caused by decaying effluent from the process and the stench of the decaying pea vines and corn husks.

Until very recently, the cost of the firm's product to consumers included only the cost of labor, capital, and the raw materials used in processing. This is the private cost of the goods produced. Prior to the establishment of controls under the auspices of state and Federal governmental agencies, the cost of the "bads" would not be included in the private cost or market price of the goods produced; that is, the consumer paid only the direct costs of production, the private costs, and the residents of the town bore the cost of the air and water pollution.

The residents of the town bore a real cost; because of the aroma drifting from the processing plant, their houses were of lower value. They were required to air condition their homes in the summer; they found that their fishing and recreational opportunities on the river were limited. In effect, these people were subsidizing the persons who were buying the processed corn and peas. Thus the consumer was actually paying a private cost or a market price for the food processed which was lower than the total social cost. The market price includes only the outlays actually made by the producing firm, whereas the social cost includes the additional costs borne by other persons in the economy.

CONSUMERS' ENVIRONMENTAL CONCERNS

As a consumer, each of us desires to maintain a standard of living as high as is possible given the constraints of income and prices. As citizens, we also desire to see that we not only consume goods but that we also have a high quality of life. A quality life means many different things to different people. Each of us must consider what we desire as á quality standard to be achieved. The selection of our own quality standard can be rational from society's point of view only if the private cost, market price of goods and services, reflects the actual total cost to society. Thus, the price of peas and corn must be raised to include the cost of treating the waste by-products of the production process. When this is done, the market price will be more nearly equal to the social cost.

The cost of electric power will rise as low sulphur fuels are utilized. The cost of automobiles will rise as the anti-pollution devices are included. These increased prices reflect the fact that, increasingly, costs borne by society at large are being included in the market price.

The process of equalizing the social cost and market price frequently requires legislative action. Since the founding of our country, it has been assumed that the streams and air belonged to no man but rather belonged to all men in common. It was perfectly acceptable to utilize open sewers in the streams and belching smokestacks in the air as waste disposal mechanisms. When the United States had 50 million people and a per capita income of less than $1,000, this was a problem. Now that it has over 200 million people and per capita income of over $4,000, the problem has become a catastrophe. The rate at which pollutants are dumped into the air and water and the rate at which raw materials are depleted tends ot increase in proportion to the increases in population and per capita income. As long as each polluter considers the air and water his personal property to do with as he pleases, there is little inclination to begin abatement practices. Each will continue to pollute, transferring a part of his production cost to society at large. The consequences of this action will be that the social cost of production is greater than the private cost.

The rational consumer sees that the price of goods produced in conjunction with pollution, that is, the "goods" with "bad" by-products, will be relatively cheaper than goods produced without the pollution by-products. Society will tend to produce and purchase more of the goods which damage the environment and relatively fewer of the "clean" goods. Whenever the social cost is greater than the private cost, the total impact on society will be that too many of the pollution-creating goods will be produced and too few of the clean goods will be produced. Since the producer believes that he has a property right in the air and water, he will continue to pollute; and since the rational consumer bases decisions on private cost and tends to buy goods which create relatively large amounts of pollution, it is necessary for some branch of government to require that the cost of production include the cost of cleaning up the "bads" so the private cost more nearly equals the social cost.

The Environmental Protection Agency attempts to achieve this goal by establishing air and water standards. The establishment of these standards requires that business firms and individuals develop processes which do not emit pollutants. In meeting the standards, it is expected that the cost of production will rise. As this occurs, the market price should rise, thereby reducing the demand for products which have a heavy impact on the environment.

The Environmental Protection Agency must, of necessity, operate on a national scale. The first reason is that air and water pollution knows no geographical boundaries. The second and most telling reason is that if a single state or municipality attempted to impose air and water standards on people and industries within its political jurisdiction, it would soon discover that industries and people were moving out of the region. This would occur because the costs of production in other areas not enacting clean air standards would be lower than in the area which was attempting pollution abatement. Thus firms in high cost, clean air areas would lose business to low-cost firms operating in areas without pollution control regulations.

The desire to obtain a higher quality of life requires that legislation be enacted on a national and even a world-wide scale. As a result of this legislation, the market price will tend toward the social cost of goods and services produced. Then as rational decision makers we could choose between goods on the basis of price alone and would know that these prices reflected the total and true cost to society.

INDIVIDUAL DECISIONS FOR A QUALITY LIFE

We all can, whenever possible, choose goods, services or modes of life which have a lesser impact on the environment. It is possible to establish a very simple rule for choosing between products. This rule is: "Choose goods and services which have a low environmental impact whenever satisfaction and costs are equal." The impact can be considered in two areas: energy and raw materials required in production, and pollution generated in production and destruction. The consumer, whenever possible, should choose products or services which require relatively little energy and raw materials to produce and create few pollutants as they are produced and as they end up on the garbage heap. If each person consciously selects a mode of life based on these concepts, the level of pollution will decrease; and our energy and raw materials requirements will also decrease.

If society is to survive in an organization similar to that which we now have, it is necessary that factors such as these be given strong consideration in our decision processes.

The utilization of the low-environmental impact rule is relatively simple. Every day each of us consumes beverages from milk to soft drinks to alcoholic beverages in paper cartons, throwaway bottles or metal cans. The low-environmental impact rule would require that these beverages be purchased in containers that are returnable and reusable. Throwaway bottles and disposable cans require substantially higher amounts of energy and raw materials in their production. This production process pollutes the air and water and creates a substantial disposal problem. Each of us could help reduce environmental impact by purchasing beverages in returnable bottles rather than in throwaway containers.

As we choose recreational alternatives, the environmental impact rule can operate to assist in the selection of healthful and enjoyable recreational opportunities. When visiting a park, we can choose between walking along the trails or riding a trail bike through the woods and forests. If we walk, we move quietly without disturbing the animal inhabitants or our fellow hikers. The passage of people along a trail has some impact on the soil structure and encourages a limited amount of erosion. Now consider the trail bike. It whines through the woods disturbing both the native inhabitants and other persons who might be looking for solitude in the forest. Its tires have a more detrimental impact on the trail than walking, tending to cause greater erosion. This is the direct impact on the environment of the woods.

Also consider the impact on the environment in general. The greatest impact that the hiker might have on the external environment would be the resources required to produce his boots and trousers. On the other hand, the resources required to build and use the motor bike are substantial in that steel, rubber, gasoline, ball bearings, etc., are all required, having a large energy and raw material requirement as well as creating substantial pollution. If we follow our decision rule of considering the low-impact goods or services, we would choose to hike through the woods. Not only does this reduce the impact on the environment but, other things being equal, walking is cheaper than riding a motor bike. This same line of reasoning can be applied to skiing versus snow-mobiling, swimming versus water skiing, canoeing versus motorboating, and tent camping versus motor home traveling. In each case, the satisfaction or utility is not markedly different; but the environmental impact is very different.

The low-environmental impact rule can also be implemented by industry. The selection of aluminum over steel for industrial purposes is based on sound economic and engineering reasoning. However, from the point of view of environmental impact, the production of aluminum requires many times more energy than the production of steel. Industrial selection of non-degradable plastics has also lead to a potential plastic-pollution problem.

CONCLUSION

If the desired quality of life is to be achieved, it is necessary that two processes be carried out and interrelated. First, it is necessary that the social cost of producing goods equal the market price of those goods. Second, consumers and business firms alike must implement the low-environmental impact rule when selecting goods and services. These two processes, when utilized together, provide the means for moving toward a society which recognizes the environ-mental problem and chooses to charge those who are willing to pay for high-impact goods the full cost of producing those goods. More importantly, it is necessary for society to begin a conscious and forthright process of imple-menting the low-environmental rule in order to move away from heavy reliance on goods and things and to move toward a society based on a less destructive and more symbiotic relationship with the environment.

Budgeting

CHAPTER *II*

BUDGETING

Far too many families with adequate incomes operate financially on an emergency basis. They are forever short of cash, with their perpetually inadequate supply of this precious commodity being expended on "emergencies" such as a new suit for graduation, a new dress for a very special occasion, unexpected hospitalization, the need to entertain Aunt Maude who arrived in town unannounced, or a down payment on a new television set or washing machine when the old appliance fails totally at a most inopportune time.

Why does Family A, with an income of X dollars, live a harum-scarum financial existence—frequently borrowing to meet crisis after crisis, and often finding itself on a pauper's diet until the next pay check is received—while Family B, with the same X dollars in annual income, seldom faces a financial crisis and always seems to meet unexpected situations with relative calm?

Budgeting, or financial planning, is not a panacea for all problems involving money, but it does enable a family to make advance provision so that the purchase of clothing, entertaining at dinner, buying a new appliance, or even having a broken arm set, is not an "emergency" for which it is unprepared financially.

Well-run businesses and governmental units invariably operate on a budget, and the consumer would do well to consider the merits of a similar foundation for his own living.

STEPS IN THE BUDGETING PROCESS

The budget, a written financial plan, is based on family values, goals, wants, and priorities. Therefore, the *first step* in its preparation is the holding of a family council during which there is a candid discussion centering on what goals the family has and the order in which its wants are to be met. All members of the family, except the very youngest, should have a voice in this discussion; and the views of all should be treated with respect. It is extremely important that the support of all family members be secured at this stage, for their cooperation is essential if the budgeting process is to succeed.

The *second step* in budgeting is arriving at a realistic projection of income for the next budget period. Hoped-for wage increases, overtime pay, bonuses, and cash gifts from Aunt Maude should not be included unless there is substantial assurance that they are forthcoming. Only when a workable income figure has been arrived at is there a basis for planning expenditures. Some families are content to budget take-home pay, and others prefer to work with gross earnings.

The *third step* involves determination of how money was spent in the past, because past expenditure patterns are an index to future spending. Receipts, check stubs, and recollections of family members will be useful in reconstructing past expenditures. If a large percentage of expenditures cannot be thus accounted for, perhaps the establishment of a budget should be deferred for two or three months during which time a careful record is kept of how family funds are being spent.

TABLE 2-1

PERCENTAGE DIVISION OF FAMILY EXPENDITURES
FOR URBAN U.S. FAMILIES, 1969*

| | Level of Expenditures (Percent) | | |
Item	*Lower*	*Intermediate*	*Higher*
Food	27	23	20
Housing	21	24	25
Transportation	7	9	8
Clothing	9	9	8
Personal care	3	3	2
Medical care	8	5	4
Other family consumption (reading, recreation, education)	5	6	7
Other costs (gifts and contributions, insurance)	4	4	5
Occupational expenses	1	1	1
Social Security and disability	5	4	3
Personal taxes	9	13	17
Total	99	101	100
	($6,544)	($10,064)	($14,571)

*Family of 4 persons
Source: U.S. Department of Labor, Bureau of Labor Statistics.

When a family has resolved to live on a budget, however, it may not be willing to wait while it identifies past spending habits. In this case, the family could refer to one or more tables which reflect spending patterns of families in circumstances similar to their own. One such table, reflecting varying conditions, is reproduced here. It will be necessary, of course, to adjust these figures so they will be suitable for a specific family.

The *fourth step* in budgeting is the establishment of budget categories suitable for the family. There should be a sufficient number of budgetary divisions for each to be meaningful, yet a small enough number to facilitate the recording of expenditures. Six categories would obviously be of little value, while twenty-six would usually represent greater detail than necessary. Basic categories frequently found include Savings, Food, Clothing, Shelter, Transportation, Household Operation, Gifts and Donations, Personal Allowances, Travel and Entertainment, Medical and Dental, and Life Insurance. Many families would prefer to separate Gifts and Donations into two categories, and perhaps the same would hold true for Travel and Entertainment or for Medical and Dental.

Categories should be defined so that there is little chance of disagreement as to how an expense should be recorded. It is suggested, for example, that *Food* include food both at home and away; that *Clothing* include laundry, cleaning, and repairs, as well as purchases of new items; that *Shelter* represent rent or that part of the mortgage payment which is actually interest, while the increase in equity is recorded as *Savings;* that *Transportation* include cab and bus fare, auto operation, license fees and auto insurance; and that *Household Operation* include utilities and installment payments on household furniture and appliances. Personal Allowances should be recorded in total for each member of the family, with expenditures of these amounts considered a personal matter with no details entered on family records.

Some families use *Sales Taxes* and *Gasoline Taxes* as budget divisions; this practice, however, is of little value, especially if the purpose is to yield information for tax returns. Instructions included with Federal Income Tax forms provide tables which set reasonable deductions for these items, and the taxpayer is relieved of the need for dealing with minutiae.

The *fifth step* in budgeting is a crucial one—that of assigning dollar allocations to each budget division. This is, admittedly, exploratory and subject to later revision. However, tentative figures should be decided upon for each category on the basis of past expenditures or "average" figures for families in like circumstances, adjusted as the family deems reasonable.

The *sixth step* is the recording of expenditures as they occur and periodic reference to the records during the month to determine whether the family is "overspending" in any area. Most payments of any size will be paid by check and posting may be done from the checkstub record once or twice a week. Small cash expenditures should be noted on an index card or in a pocket secretary at the time the cash is paid out and the information transferred to the records at home when it is convenient to do so. One family member should be selected to assume primary responsibility for keeping budget records up to date.

The *seventh step* in budgeting calls for occasional revision of the budget as it becomes apparent that allocations are out of line with reality.

BUDGET RECORDS

Some families excuse their failure to keep a budget by stating that it is "not worth the trouble," and they may sincerely visualize the process as one of endless recordkeeping. On the contrary, a good budgeting system calls for a minimum of recordkeeping and even de-emphasizes this aspect. Recordkeeping is necessary, of course, as a device for determining whether the budget is being followed and therefore whether the plan is succeeding. The recording of expenditures should require no more than a few minutes a week, and there should be a prior understanding that no attempt will be made to account for every penny of income. At best, the family should be able to determine how *most* of each month's income was spent. Far more important than the painstaking recording of expenditures is the setting of goals and periodic determination of family progress toward those goals. The budget should have a disciplinary influence, but a family should never become its slave.

One family which has budgeted successfully for years simply assigns one page of a stenographer's notebook to a budget category each month and keeps that record as illustrated below for a two-month period:

	Clothing	
Budgeted for January		35.00
Dry cleaning	6.00	
Dress for Susie	15.00	
Shoe repair for John	4.85	
Belt for John	2.00	27.85
Carried forward to February		7.15
Carried forward from January		7.15
Budgeted for February		35.00
Available in February		42.15
Dry cleaning	4.25	
Shirt for John	5.00	
Shoes for Susie	6.00	15.25
Carried forward to March		26.90

FIGURE 2-1

Sample Family Budgeting Forms

Step 1. Establish family goals, desires and objectives in terms of goods and services.

1. Lifetime Objectives
  a. Home ownership
  b. Educational fund
  c. Retirement
  d.
  e.
  f.
  g.

2. Annual Objectives
  a. Travel
  b. Furniture
  c. New car
  d.
  e.
  f.
  g.

3. Monthly Objectives
  a. Food
  b. Clothing
  c. Recreation
  d. Medical
  e.
  f.
  g.

Step 2. Estimate family income.

Income Sources:
  a. Annual wages and salaries   _____
  b. Rental, interest and dividends   _____
  c. Other income
    (1) Gifts   _____
    (2) Borrowings   _____
  d.   _____
  e.   _____
  f.   _____
  g.   _____

Total Annual Income   _____

Step 3. Collect data on past family expenditures.

Category:	Jan	Feb	Mar	Apr	May	Jun	Jul	Aug	Sep	Oct	Nov	Dec
Food												
Housing, utility												
Clothing												
Transportation: Car												
Other												
Taxes												
Household furnishings												
Medical care												
Insurance												
Savings												
Contributions												
Debts												

Last Year's Expenses

FIGURE 2-1 (cont.)

	Family Budget for Monthly Allocation											
Step 4. Establish family budget categories. — Category:	Jan	Feb	Mar	Apr	May	Jun	Jul	Aug	Sep	Oct	Nov	Dec
Food												
Housing, utility												
Clothing												
Transportation												
Taxes												
Furnishings												
Medical care												
Insurance												
Savings												
Contributions												
Debts												
Emergency fund												
Recreation												
Tuition												
Books, newspapers												

Step 5. Allocate amounts to categories by month.

	Family Expenditures for Monthly Expenses											
Step 6. Record actual expenditures and compare them to budget estimates. — Category:	Jan	Feb	Mar	Apr	May	Jun	Jul	Aug	Sep	Oct	Nov	Dec
Food												
Housing, utility												
Clothing												
Transportation												
Taxes												
Furnishings												
Medical care												
Insurance												
Savings												
Contributions												
Debts												
Emergency fund												
Recreation												
Tuition												
Books, newspapers												

Step 7. Evaluate and revise budgeted allocations in light of actual expenditures and changing goals.

This family will attempt to build a substantial balance in the clothing account so that there will be adequate funds to buy "back-to-school clothes" in August and to take advantage of legitimate sales in purchasing needed items. Similarly, it builds a balance in the property tax and life insurance accounts so that, when these once-a-year items fall due, budgeted funds are available. The medical and dental account is used to accumulate amounts to pay for routine office calls and to meet hospital and surgical expenses not covered in their entirety by medical insurance.

Other budgeting procedures and forms are reproduced here, and much more elaborate sets of records are available for those who care to use them.

SUGGESTED READING

American Bankers Association, *Personal Money Management,* Banking Education Committee, 90 Park Avenue, New York, New York, 1970.

Cohen, Jerome B. and Arthur W. Hanson. *Personal Finance: Principles and Case Problems.* 3d ed. Homewood, Ill.: Richard D. Irwin, Inc., 1964. (Chapter 2: "Expenditures and Budgeting")

C.U.N.A. International, Inc., *Family Budget Service,* Public Relations Department, Box 431, Madison, Wisconsin.

Gordon, Leland J. and Stewart M. Lee. *Economics for Consumers.* 5th ed. New York: American Book Co., 1967.

Household Finance Corporation, *Money Management: Your Budget,* Money Management Institute, Prudential Plaza, Chicago, Illinois, 1967.

National Consumer Finance Association, *It's Your Money,* 1000 Sixteenth Street N.W., Washington, D.C., 1967.

Phillips, E. Bryant and Sylvia Lane. *Personal Finance: Text and Case Problems.* 2d ed. New York: John Wiley & Sons, Inc., 1969. (Chapter 2: "Budgeting")

Troelstrup, Arch W. *The Consumer in American Society: Personal and Family Finance.* 4th ed. New York: McGraw-Hill Book Co., 1970.

Unger, Maurice, A. *Personal Finance.* 2d ed. Boston: Allyn and Bacon, Inc., 1969. (Chapter 2: "The Personal Budget")

U.S. Department of Agriculture, *A Guide to Budgeting for the Family.* Washington, D.C.: Government Printing Office, 1965.

———, *Helping Families Manage Their Finances.* Washington, D.C.: Government Printing Office.

———, *Managing Your Money.* Washington, D.C.: Government Printing Office, March, 1964.

Techniques
of Choice Making

CHAPTER *III*

ANALYSIS OF CONSUMER CHOICE

Two hundred years ago the average American lived on a self-sufficient farm. He and his family produced most of the things the family required. Life was a struggle for the basic necessities of existence—food, shelter, and clothing. Little was bought and little was sold. The frontiersman, unlike today's consumer, had few complicated economic decisions concerning the allocation of his income.

In contrast, however, today's consumer exists in a highly developed market society. We work for others and usually produce nothing for our direct consumption. In terms of economics this individual is far more efficient and productive because of his great economic specialization and has a far higher material standard of living than the frontiersman. Because of this specialization, however, the consumer has thousands of economic decisions to make which would never have occurred to a frontiersman. Accordingly, the consumer must decide how to best allocate his scarce resources: his income, energy, and time.

The decision as to how to allocate income into the various areas is a fundamental problem for the consumer. There are many different methods for allocation of income. Among the methods are the following: (1) Many consumers use an emotional approach when allocating their income. These consumers buy whatever appeals to them on the spur of the moment. (2)

Another common method of allocating income is emulating the neighbors. (3) A third method is a simplified application of economic analysis in financial decisions.

Generally, the emotional approach provides the individual with the worst of all possible methods. Income is spent on whim; it is neither a systematic nor rational method of allocating personal resources. In the long run such a consumer is usually dissatisfied with his buying decisions. He does not obtain the goods he really desires and is always short of money.

The person who simply models his expenditures on the basis of how others spend their income runs the risk that others' decisions may not really reflect his consumer needs. For example, some consumers buy a second car, not because they need it, but simply because everyone else on the block has purchased one.

The third method seeks to establish a rational plan to allocate resources using a simplified form of economic analysis. Such a method helps the consumer establish what his real goals are and helps to develop a plan to achieve these goals. Such a method will generally be found superior to the first two methods because it allows the individual to form a rough plan to achieve his desired ends instead of a random expenditure of resources which may or may not achieve his goals.

The fundamental problem confronting the consumer is the same problem which confronts nations and societies as a whole. The problem is that we all have unlimited wants but only limited resources. Because of scarcity people cannot have everything they desire, so the problem becomes one of allocating personal resources in such a way as to get the most from the resources at hand. How well this allocation is performed largely determines how well an individual will achieve what he desires, at least in a material sense. This is the economic concept of maximizing. The problem for the consumer is then to maximize his re-sources—his time, energy, and money.

In both business and personal life economic theory assumes that people wish to maximize utility. Utility is simply the satisfaction or usefulness that a person derives from his limited resources. Business tries to obtain maximum profit from sales while consumers attempt to use their resources in such a way as to obtain the greatest possible satisfaction.

Consider a typical consumer's problem. The consumer is considering two possible purchases but has only the resources for one. On one hand he would like to purchase a $500 color television set, but on the other he would like a $500 vacation in Florida. If you were in the consumer's place, which alternative would give you the greatest satisfaction from your scarce resource ($500)? No one can answer this question except you—the consumer. Utility is a personal concept; it is vague, impossible for anyone but the individual to measure. What provides great utility for one person may provide little for another.

Despite the fact that utility is an impossible phenomenon to measure and predict precisely it does provide the consumer with a tool, a rule of thumb, upon which to base his economic decisions.

When a consumer is considering the purchase of some item, he consciously or unconsciously calculates the added utility that the item will bring him. The cost of a product can be looked at in two ways, dollar cost or opportunity cost—what a person is giving up to buy the item. Opportunity costs are simply the true costs of the item to the consumer. The opportunity cost of a $2,000 water ski boat may be the cost of a trip to the Bahamas. The opportunity cost of a $20 meal in a restaurant is sixty gallons of gas for the car. In other words, since people cannot have everything they want, they must give up something to obtain another item.

Consider the opportunity costs involved if you were considering the purchase of the following:

1. a $6,000 sports car
2. a $300 stereo
3. a year of college
4. braces for a child's teeth for $1,500
5. a fine, expensive funeral for a beloved grandparent

Opportunity costs are expressed in terms of alternative uses of the scarce resource. After considering the alternative uses of resources presumably the thoughtful consumer who wishes to maximize his utility will pick the alternative which provides the greatest satisfaction.

Consider, for example, the funeral for the grandparent in terms of opportunity costs. The consumer who is paying for the funeral has no choice; he must pay for the funeral, but he does have some control over the cost. He must decide whether to have an inexpensive $1,000 funeral or to pay for a prestigious $8,500 funeral. If the consumer were to consider the opportunity costs involved in such a purchase, they might be as follows. The opportunity costs of the expensive funeral might be three new cars, four years of college for the consumer's son, one round-the-world vacation, twelve short vacations, or the down payment on a $40,000 house.

Such a procedure allows an individual to consider what must be given up (in dollars, or in other goods and services) to obtain or buy the item under consideration. Once the true cost in terms of other items is established, he can decide whether he is maximizing utility by obtaining the goods or services in question.

A consumer who bases buying on impulse or emotion, however, does not consider alternatives because this makes a potential purchase painful; it forcefully shows what he must give up to have what he wishes. The emotional consumer does not like to feel constrained by having to give up anything. He is a grown version of a child in a candy store.

The emotional consumer, when considering the expensive funeral, might pick the funeral without considering an alternative use of the resource and might defend his decision by saying "You cannot think about people (living or dead) in terms of money." Yet this same person may be in great need of expensive medical treatment, or his children may need money for college. Thus, the consumer's great personal needs which, if satisfied, would provide much utility, may be foregone for an expensive funeral for the grandparent, which in the long run may provide less utility for the consumer than other expenditures.

The rational consumer may choose the most expensive funeral or the least expensive funeral after weighing the utility derived from all other alternative uses of the resource. He might say, unlike the emotional consumer, "I have considered the alternatives to the expensive funeral and after such consideration feel that this expenditure gives me greater satisfaction than any other possible uses of the money." In effect the rational consumer is putting a price tag on the emotional satisfaction, status, and other benefits provided by the expensive funeral and is deciding that it gives him greater utility than any alternative use of the resource. The emotional consumer who decides upon the spur of the moment that a big expensive funeral is what he wants may later regret the expenditure. The rational consumer has given the expenditure careful considera- tion and will probably not regret his decision later. The rational consumer has maximized, and the emotional consumer may not have maximized, the utility from his scarce resources.

THINK IT OVER:

1. What would you think if the rational consumer had decided that he preferred a round-the-world trip and an inexpensive funeral for his grandparent instead of the expensive one? Would you approve of such a decision?
2. Many couples are hopelessly in debt and yet continue to spend wildly. Why do they act this way?
3. Why can economists look at funerals and consider them to be like any other good or service which the consumer can purchase?

MANIPULATION OF CONSUMER DEMAND

The demand curve of an item is composed of consumers' evaluations of the price in terms of utility provided by the item. Generally the lower the price the greater the quantity demanded.

However, in the real world this notion, while often true, assumes that people have a basic knowledge of the market prices for the item. A gas station will not stay in business long if it charges forty-five cents per gallon of gas when the common rate is thirty-two cents. Consumers know that the gas at forty-five cents per gallon will not provide any more utility than the gas selling for thirty- two cents. Seeking to maximize utility from their scarce resources, they will purchase gas at the lower price. Consumers do seek to maximize utility when they have a good knowledge of prices and the quality of goods.

On the other hand, when it comes to the purchase of less common items, the consumer is at a great disadvantage because he lacks knowledge of the prices and quality of various goods.

As an example of how lack of knowledge hinders consumers' efforts to maximize utility, consider the Compac brand of vacuum cleaner. The price of two-horsepower canister vacuum cleaners varies from $70 to $90 at local retail stores. All of the cleaners are quite similar in characteristics and quality. The Compac brand, which is sold only door-to-door, carries a price which ranges from $300 to $375. It is a machine essentially similar to the others mentioned.

The Compac is sold by high pressure door-to-door salesmen. These salesmen are extremely persuasive and present demonstrations calculated to give the impression that the machine is "different" from any other model on the market, thus serving to limit possible consumer price comparisons. The features which are touted by the salesmen are largely fictitious. How can this machine be sold to consumers at such a great differential from the general market price? If consumers do try to maximize as economic theory contends, why do they buy this machine?

The forces in the market, chiefly competition, tend to keep the quality and price similar for all the machines except the Compac. People do shop and compare the various brands. If one machine were priced much higher than other similar models, people would not buy the high-priced machine because they do compare. The door-to-door salesman, however, is able to sell his machine for $200 more because many customers are not aware of the approximate market price and features of other machines. The price the salesman quotes is often assumed by the consumers to be the market price for all cleaners.

The goal of the door-to-door salesman can be seen on the graph (Figure 3-1). Many consumers are aware of the approximate price of cleaners (they

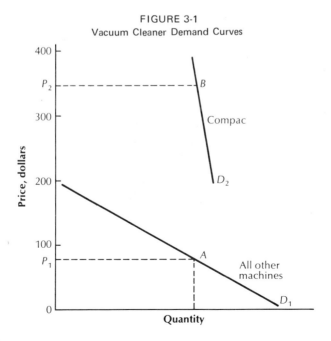

FIGURE 3-1
Vacuum Cleaner Demand Curves

compare and shop around), and they can be seen as point A on demand curve D_1. If the price of the machines were increased, they would buy fewer machines; if the price were lower, they would buy more. Thus, most consumers behave as economic theory would suggest they will.

The job of the door-to-door salesman is to persuade people to pay more than the price at point A shown on the demand curve D_1. To do this the salesman attempts to create fictitious quality differences. If the consumer can be persuaded that the machine is different or better, he will be willing to pay more and be less eager to compare the machine with competing machines.

To make the price seem lower the salesman may misstate the price or promise a ten-dollar kickback for each friend who buys the machine which the consumer recommends. With such techniques the consumer is moved from the normal demand curve for cleaners and shifted to another curve D_2 (point B). Thus, consumers pay more for a machine which is similar to the ones sold at a much lower price. Because of misstatements, trickery, promotion of false and misleading features and promises of kickbacks (which the company does not intend to honor), the consumer pays far more for the machine than similar and competing models found in stores.

If these consumers could compare all the machines lined up in a row with each of their prices attached, none would feel that the Compac was worth three times the price of competing machines. Because of high pressure door-to-door sales tactics and deception bordering on fraud, a segment of the buying public pays a higher price than necessary. If consumers had good knowledge of all products and prices, they probably could not be deceived or manipulated by salesmen.

Such machines in most states (as with most major door-to-door items) are sold on a contract basis. Once the consumer has signed a contract to buy the machine he cannot change his mind. Thus, the consumer who buys the Compac at that moment feels that he (or she) is getting a good buy only to discover a day or two later that he has paid a much higher price for the machine than could have been obtained for a similar machine from a store.

To help consumers who buy from door-to-door salesmen on the spur of the moment and who later wish to change their minds, several states including Illinois, have adopted a "cooling off" period of two to three days. Should the customer change his mind during this time, he can, by notifying the seller, void the agreement. At this time the Federal Trade Commission is considering such a legal safeguard for consumers who, on the spur of the moment, are susceptible to door-to-door salesmen and later regret buying from them.

A consumer can usually save by avoiding door-to-door sales. Prices are generally much higher for merchandise purchased from such sources than from conventional sellers.

The consumer would be wise to be particularly wary of door-to-door sales in the following areas: (1) home improvements, (2) silverware and cutlery, (3) vacuum cleaners and sewing machines, and (4) recreational land.

Do consumers behave as economic theory suggests? Economic theory assumes that consumers are rational and therefore seek to obtain the greatest utility from their limited resources.

Visit a supermarket and spend fifteen or twenty dollars. When you return home examine your purchases and ask yourself, "Was I rational? Did I maximize utility?"

By maximizing utility the consumer is simply assumed to be using his resources in a way which allows him to achieve his desired consuming goal. Thus, a consumer who spends resources in a way which does not match his goals is not a utility maximizer. Some of the reasons a consumer may not spend in a manner consistent with his goals are:

1. Advertising pressures
2. Peer or social pressure
3. Fraud or deception
4. Lack of product information (price and quality)

The consumer may find that such pressures as the above keep him from spending his resources in the way that allows him to realize his goal. Often the merchant is able to increase the consumer's spending by such means. The food store is a good place to observe such techniques. Stores have found that it is possible to persuade consumers to buy more than they intended. A few examples illustrate how this is achieved.

Many stores endeavor to sell more by pricing items in such a way as to make them seem less expensive. One of the standbys is to assign prices ending in the number 9. People will often buy an item priced at thirty-nine cents yet refuse to consider it at forty cents. Another way stores stimulate the consumer's buying is to use multiple pricing. Soap may not sell well at thirteen cents per bar; but if the bars are priced at three for thirty-nine cents, many consumers feel that they are saving money and stock up—especially if there is a big sign drawing their attention to the "discount price." At times stores sell the multiple item at a price higher than that of the same item sold on an individual basis. Occasionally one will find such multiples as gelatin dessert marked "five for sixty-nine cents." The consumer concludes that this is a real bargain unless he stops to calculate the per package price. In this case gelatin was selling for eleven cents per individual package (same size). One reason that such a device works is that people hold the often true notion that it pays to buy in quantity, but such truisms are often exploited by merchants.

The consumer who is aware of the store's desire to stimulate impulse buying with such tactics has a better chance of resisting such expenditures and of holding his budget down.

Many stores display food at the ends of aisles, near cash registers, and in places of heavy traffic. At such locations the consumer is likely to see displays, carts, and counters piled high with merchandise. Often these displays feature signs which say "everyday low prices" or "special." Many consumers see these signs and displays and assume that the items are on sale. The careful consumer would be wise to check the normal locations for such items and to check the price. Often such "specials" are not sales at all. But since the consumer is not exactly sure of prices, he tends to assume that the "special" is a sale and to stock up on the item. One buyer found facial tissue on "special" at an impulse display (at the end of an aisle). The sign read "key buy" and the tissue was priced at thirty-five cents for a box of 200. This was not a sale at all but was the usual price for the item. In the tissue area of the store, similar products were priced as low as twenty cents for the same quantity. Yet many consumers bought several boxes at the impulse "key buy" display thinking that this brand tissue was being sold at reduced prices. One wonders how many boxes of the tissue would have been sold if the "key buy" sign had not been posted.

Consumers attempting to reduce food expenditures also ought to be aware of "tie-ins." For example, strawberries featured in a display may really be on sale, but next to the strawberries the shortcake and whipped cream or topping appear at inflated prices. The consumer is attracted to the sale and then pays more than necessary for associated products (the tied-in goods).

Generally prices of staples like coffee, flour, and sugar show little difference in price from store to store. The reason is that consumers have a good idea of the general price level of these basic items and have a basis on which to compare. Should one store charge consistently higher prices for these items, it is likely to lose its customers. On the other hand, items which are not staples, such as frosting, cookies, cosmetics and similar items, vary greatly in price from store to store. As a rule of thumb the prices of non-staple items are much more volatile from store to store. This dual pricing of staples vs. non-staples suggests that consumers do act rationally, as demand theory suggests. But when consumers lack knowledge of prices or are unsure of normal or average prices, they do not act in a discriminating way. Thus, as one would suspect, the price range of non-staple items is much greater from store to store than with staple items.

The following survey to test this notion was taken September 20, 1967, at four supermarkets in Elgin, Illinois. A ten-pound bag of Gold Medal All-Purpose Flour ranged in price from $1.15 to $1.16. On the other hand, a non-staple item, Hershey's Cocoa, ranged in price from a high of thirty-nine cents per half-pound box to a low of thirty cents, a percentage difference of over 25 percent. Other items followed this general pattern.

If the consumer is to have some basis for comparing prices and acting in his economic self-interest, he must have knowledge of goods and the quality of those goods. The merchant, on the other hand, will likely sell more merchandise at higher prices if the consumer does not have such information. Merchants sometimes deliberately act to confuse the consumer by making comparisons difficult. One area in which this occurs is the meat section of the supermarket. Often ordinary cuts of meat are given special names such as "supreme" steak, which is really chuck steak. The object of new and exotic names is to give the consumer the impression that he is buying special quality and to prevent comparison. When exotic names are given, the price is usually increased—from four cents to $1.40 per pound, according to one observer. Thus, the consumer is likely to pay more for meat unless he insists upon relying on government meat grades and upon buying meat by its common name.

What is the significance of the merchandising techniques described so far? By using these and other tactics retailers often manipulate the consumer, the result being that he is buying more (and often more expensive) food than he intended when he went shopping. In Figure 3-2 the economic effect of this manipulation can be seen. When the consumer goes shopping, his demand for food goods might be like D_1 (at price level P_1 he intends to purchase Q_1 quantity of food). However, because of fictitious sales, tie-ins, and similar tactics the consumer finds that he is buying more than he intended. The store with various ploys has been able to shift the consumer to demand curve D_2 and Q_2 quantity of goods. Figure 3-2 shows that the consumer has purchased more goods at the same price than he intended to purchase.

The effect of impulse shopping may be a little different. Few people go to the store intending to buy cookies. Yet because of clever placement and packaging many people buy them on impulse. Due to the low utility gained from cookies the consumer would perhaps only consider putting it on the food list if the price were low (Figure 3-3, P_1, D_1). But when the consumer arrives at the store, the attractive display packaging and product spotter signs entice her to

FIGURE 3-2

Manipulation of Consumer Demand

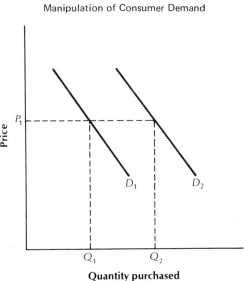

Quantity purchased

FIGURE 3-3

Buying on Impulse

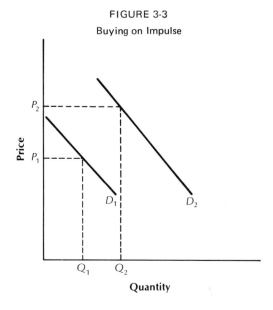

Quantity

buy at P_2, D_2 on the spur of the moment. The store finds that consumers will buy more of the high-profit cookies only when the desire to impulse shop is stimulated. Thus, the store is able to shift consumers from the original demand curve D_1 to D_2, resulting in selling more cookies at higher prices. The store's profit is improved by encouraging such shopping.

How does this type of activity relate to economic theory? If the consumer is rational, as economic theory supposes, he should try to maximize. If the consumer is rational and is a maximizer, why does he allow himself to be tricked or guided into buying things he does not really strongly desire?

Economic theory assumes that all products of a category are identical in size, quality, and appearance. Given the identical nature of these items the consumer would buy, if rational, the one that costs the least. As any shopper knows, in the real world comparisons are not that easy. Products come in many sizes, qualities, and appearances. Therefore, comparison on a meaningful basis is difficult. Given these basic differences it becomes easy for the merchant to add to the confusion with merchandising techniques which make rational consumption difficult at best.

Consumer organizations are pushing for changes in the law which would make rational food shopping easier. Some of these proposals are: (1) enforcement of standardized package sizes and weights (for example, packaging detergent in one-pound, five-pound, and ten-pound packages instead of many odd-sized packages and weights) (2) restriction of sales to *bona fide* sales, and (3) simplification of grades and terminology in the sale of meats.

These are but a few of the suggestions which would assist the consumer in becoming more rational in shopping. The basic notion is that the consumer, if given a simple and easy basis to compare, will be able to buy the needed goods at a lower cost, thus allowing the family's resources to be more wisely utilized.

THINK IT OVER:

1. Do you think that you are a rational shopper?
2. If you were a store owner, why might you be tempted in the summer to rename chuck steak "Supreme Bar BQ Steak"?
3. If you did think that you would rename the steak, upon what basis did you decide?
4. What is the economic reason for renaming the steak and raising the price?

The theory of demand has been examined. It can be seen that, based on the notion of utility, only a few consumers will purchase an item at a high price (because only a few get enough utility to justify the purchase); but at lower and lower price levels more people will gain enough utility from the item to be willing to purchase it. Thus, if the price is high, economic theory suggests, only a few will be demanded. The lower the price the greater the quantity of that item which will be demanded. In other words, consumers try to stretch their shopping dollars; more people are willing to buy when the price is low. The consuming public, when they have good knowledge of prices and goods, tend to act this way. When consumers do not have knowledge, they are more easily manipulated by sellers.

SUGGESTED READINGS

Economics Readings

McConnell, Campbell R. *Economics.* 5th ed. New York: McGraw-Hill Book Company, 1972. (Chapters 4 and 24)
Samuelson, Paul A. *Economics.* 8th ed. New York: McGraw-Hill Book Company, 1970. (pp. 57-65)

Personal Economics Readings

Baker, Stephen. *Visual Persuasion.* New York: McGraw-Hill Book Company, 1961.
Blackwell, Roger D. *Cases in Consumer Behavior.* New York: Holt, Rinehart, and Winston, 1969.
Caplovitz, David. *The Poor Pay More.* New York: Free Press of Glencoe, 1963.

Commerce Clearing House, *Fair Packaging and Labeling Act, with Explanations,* New York, 1966.

Cross, Jennifer. *Supermarket Trap.* Bloomington, Ind.: Indiana University Press, 1970.

Engel, James F. *Consumer Behavior Selected Readings.* Homewood, Ill.: Richard D. Irwin, Inc., 1968.

Margolius, Sidney, *Buyer Be Wary.* Public Affairs Committee, 381 Park Avenue South, New York, New York.

Markin, Rom J. *The Psychology of Consumer Behavior.* Englewood Cliffs, N.J.: Prentice-Hall, Inc., 1969.

Public Affairs Committee, *Funeral Costs and Death Benefits.* 381 Park Avenue South, New York, New York.

Tucker, William T. *Foundations for a Theory of Consumer Behavior.* New York: Holt, Rinehart and Winston, 1967.

Wanson, Chester R. *Buying Behavior and Marketing Decisions.* New York: Appleton-Century-Crofts, 1968.

Wilson, Harmon and Elvin Eyster. *Consumer Economic Problems.* Chicago: South-Western Publishing Company, 1966.

Buying Goods and Services

CHAPTER *IV*

APPLICATIONS OF THE THEORY OF THE FIRM

PRIVATE-BRAND GOODS VS. NAME-BRAND GOODS

Most consumers live by the economic assumption of maximizing utility. Consumers try to get the most from their limited resources, chiefly their consuming dollar. With the claims and counter claims for various products and many brands in the market place, such a task is complicated. To simplify such decisions many consumers have developed rules to guide their shopping such as "quality always pays in the long run," or "you get what you pay for." Unfortunately these rules often leave much to be desired if the consumer is trying to maximize his satisfaction. One has only to examine such publications as *Consumer Reports* or *Consumer Bulletin* to discover that these adages, while sometimes true, are hardly iron-clad rules. Many times items higher in price or name-brand items will be found to be inferior to less expensive and non-name brand goods. Reliance on brand names or price as a criterion of consumer choice leaves much to be desired. Price and brand in reality give little assurance as to quality and even less assurance of getting the most for the consumer's shopping dollar. If brand name and price are not good guides to getting the most utility from the consumer's dollar, what is?

31

Consumer testing services are of much help in providing information as to the quality and price of items. Experience on the part of the consumer and his acquaintances is also of value in obtaining products that deliver the most quality and satisfaction for the least expenditure. In addition to these obvious sources of help, an understanding of the economic processes should be of great assistance to the consumer when he is evaluating the purchase of goods.

One area in which the consumer faces difficult consuming decisions is the area of determining whether to buy private-brand items or name-brand goods. The choice is difficult because private brands (store's own products) are usually from 10 to 30 percent lower in price than well-known nationally advertised brands. Some consumers shun store brands for fear of poor quality, while others buy only store-brand goods to save money. Neither extreme represents a rational economic approach to the problem.

The consumer who understands the economic principles of private brands and understands the reasons for the price differential is in a position to make a far more rational choice than the uninformed consumer. One area in which private brands abound is the supermarket. Most large chain stores offer at least one and sometimes two "private brands" in addition to nationally known major-brand foods. Examples of three private brands found in the Midwest and their parent stores are:

Lady Lee	Eagle Stores
Eagle Brand	Eagle Stores
Kroger	Kroger Stores

Why do stores carry such brands instead of relying on nationally known brand-name goods? Two possible reasons are:

1. Private brands are lower in price than name brands. A store can hope to attract more customers by offering a lower-priced line of merchandise than its competitors.
2. Profit margins on private-brand items may be as high as on national name brands, or higher.
3. Consumer loyalty may become associated with private brands.

Many consumers assume that private-brand products are inherently lower in quality than nationally known brands. This is not always the case (depending upon the item and the store). Many private brands are the same quality and are often identical in every respect to major brands.

The question may be asked, if an item is the same as a name brand, why can it be sold for a lower price under a private brand? Some reasons are:

1. Store brands do not have to cover the costs of advertising, wholesalers and other overhead, thus reducing the cost to the retailers.

2. By contracting with a producer for a very large private-brand order, the retailer may receive a substantial discount.

3. A large private-brand order may allow a producer to utilize more efficiently his plant than if he had to depend upon the sales of his own national brand.

4. A large long-term contract to produce a store's private brand reduces the risk associated with changing market conditions that the producer would face if he had to sell a national name brand.

5. Some private brands are lower in quality when compared with name brands. In this event raw material costs involved in such production are lower than production under a name brand.

These reasons help account for the cost difference between name brands and private brands. By restricting this examination to goods which are of equal quality, an analysis of the economic principles of private brands can be demonstrated.

In an analysis of the concept of supply, the assumption is made that the producer desires to operate at his least cost level of output. The reason is clear. To produce at any other level would increase the manufacturer's costs per unit. Clearly, while serving as a useful device to illustrate the concept of decreasing costs of production, this assumption does not reflect the problems faced by many producers. Many producers, because of over-capacity, perhaps caused by a low level of consumer demand or recent plant expansion, cannot operate at the optimal level of output (see Figure 4-1, point B). Rather, they are at a higher level of cost and are producing less than at their least cost level (Figure 4-1, point A). Such producers realize that, if they could produce at point B, their costs would be reduced. The problem that the producer faces is not how output can be increased, but how additional output can be sold.

In order to sell additional output, the producer in this illustration has two options:

1. He could lower the price of his name-brand goods.

2. He could contract with a large chain and produce the needed output under the store brand rather than his own brand.

Either method would allow his output to be increased, thus lowering average cost of production. The producer does not want to reduce the price of his own brand goods. Such a reduction in price would likely offset any possible gain in his profit caused by the lower cost of production. Would he not also reject producing under a private brand for the same reason? Before answering this question an examination of a firm's cost structure may be of some help to the reader.

All producers have two kinds of production cost, Fixed Costs (FC) and Variable Costs (VC). Fixed costs are the costs which do not change with the level of production. Such costs may include debt on capital equipment and

FIGURE 4-1

Attempt to Achieve Efficient Plant Utilization

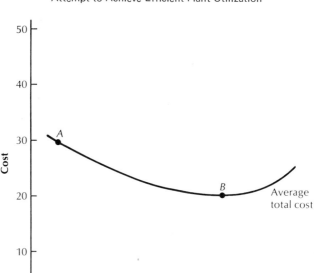

plant, insurance, light, heat, and taxes. Variable costs, on the other hand, change as output changes. Variable costs include chiefly raw materials and labor.

Even if nothing is produced, the fixed costs continue unabated. Fixed costs per unit produced can be obtained by dividing fixed costs by quantity of goods produced.

$$\frac{FC}{Q} = \text{Average fixed cost.}$$

Notice (Figure 4-2) that the more goods produced, the smaller the AFC becomes.

Consider how the costs affect a producer. Assume a California food processor has fixed costs at a fruit processing plant of $1 million a year. If the plant has zero output, these costs continue unabated. Should the plant produce 10 million units, his fixed costs remain $1 million.

However, the average fixed cost (fixed cost per unit produced) declines rapidly as output increases. The greater the output, the lower the AFC (average fixed cost). Remember that fixed costs (FC) do not change, but the amount of fixed cost per unit produced (AFC) declines as output increases.

While average fixed cost declines continuously as output increases, the same cannot be said of variable costs. Up to a point variable costs per unit do

FIGURE 4-2

Firm Average Fixed Costs

not change much; these costs can be controlled. If a producer is only going to manufacture a few units he purchases little raw material and hires a small work force. As output is expanded, more workers will be hired and more raw material purchased. Thus, VC (variable costs) do not change significantly as output increases up to some point. At some level diminishing returns begin to occur, caused perhaps by crowded and inefficient plants. Thus variable costs are driven up.

How does this relate to private brands? The manufacturer sees his economic self-interest being served by producing private brands in addition to his own brand-name product if it reduces AFC. He could increase his sales and thereby decrease AFC by reducing the price of his product. But reducing the price could cause dollar sales to fall, offsetting the decreased costs and could leave the firm's profit or losses unchanged.

At this point a large national chain store approaches the fruit processor and offers to buy 10 million cans of fruit, but only if the processor will give a 20 percent reduction in price. He is unlikely to give such a discount to the chain on his own name-brand product. To do so would result in all other chain stores demanding a similar discount, an unacceptable alternative from the producer's viewpoint.

Wishing to increase output, the processor offers to produce the fruit at the specified discount under the store's own brand name. The packer bases his decision on the following cost data (fixed costs only).

Output	Fixed Cost	$AFC = \dfrac{FC}{output}$
0	1,000,000	
10,000	1,000,000	$100.00
100,000	1,000,000	10.00
1,000,000	1,000,000	1.00
10,000,000	1,000,000	.10
20,000,000	1,000,000	.05

Fixed cost does not significantly decline past this level of output. Now let us assume variable cost as constant. Over a reasonable range of output the AFC can be seen to change as output increases (see Figure 4-3):

FIGURE 4-3

Fruit Producer's Average Fixed Cost and Average Variable Cost

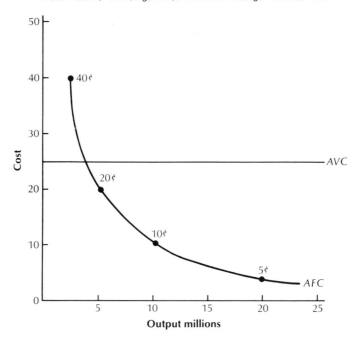

The processor reasons that by accepting the chain store's offer he will be able to increase his output and cut his average costs from ten cents per unit to five cents. This plan has the virtue of allowing him to retain the old and higher

price on his own brand name, while cutting his average fixed cost by 50 percent per unit. The store brand, even if it is produced at no profit, allows his total profit to increase because of the reduction in AFC on his own brand-name output.

The following table shows AFC, VC, selling price and profit per unit produced. The chain store order is assumed to produce no profit directly—it is sold at cost. Examine the impact of the chain store's private-brand order:

TABLE 4-1

Before Private-Brand Order

Output	AFC	VC	Total Cost	Selling Price	Profit	Total Profit
10,000,000	10¢	19¢	29¢	30¢	1¢	$100,000

Name-Brand Production and Private-Brand Order

Cost Breakdown on Brand Name:						
10,000,000	5¢	19¢	24¢	30¢	6¢	$600,000
Private Brand Production:						
10,000,000	5¢	19¢	24¢	24¢	0	0
Total Production:						
20,000,000	5¢	19¢	24¢			$600,000

It can be seen that the reduction in AFC has a great impact on profit. The increase in profit resulted even though no profit was made directly on the private-brand order. The contribution to profit of the firm was only indirect— through reduction in the firm's AFC, made possible by the added output resulting from the private-brand order.

Who benefited from the private-brand production? The packer benefited by increasing his profits (or reducing his losses). The chain benefited by selling its own private brand at a lower price, thus gaining more customers. The consumer gained by obtaining food at lower prices. The buyer, seller, and producer all gained from the private-brand production. But one group lost. These were the persons who bought the firm's branded product. They, in effect, were providing a subsidy to the firm's profits.

The production and retail sales of private brands is based on sound economic logic. Utilization of such goods can save the consumer money as well as produce greater profits for the producer and retailer. Whether or not private-brand purchases make economic sense to a particular consumer depends upon the utility gained from the private brand as compared to the utility gained from purchasing name-brand items. The key to the problem is the amount of utility gained from the purchase of an item, compared to any other use of the resource. Clearly, the resource ought to be deployed in such a way as to maximize the consumer's utility.

The consumer, however, to maximize utility, must decide what he really wants from his resources. Should his goal be buying the maximum number of goods and services from a limited income, private brands will help him get more goods because they are usually less costly. Should the consumer decide he wants to obtain status and assurance of quality (provided by name brands), he must be willing to obtain fewer goods at higher prices.

NON-FOOD PRIVATE-BRAND GOODS

Private brands exist not only in foods, but in furniture, appliances, automobile tires, and many other durable and nondurable goods. For example, Sears sells electric typewriters under its own private brand. These machines are mechanically identical or similar (depending on the model) to the Smith-Corona brand-name typewriters made by SCM Corporation. Almost any item that is commonly produced can be found selling under private brands as well as the major name brands, usually at a considerable reduction in price.

From a consumer's standpoint is private merchandise a good buy? This is a hard question to answer since it depends upon the consumer's values and tastes as well as the particular item in question.

Some people buy goods not only for the services provided by that item but because of some other service provided, such as status, prestige, and the pleasure of owning a brand-name item. In this case the pleasure presumably is great enough to justify buying the brand-name good as opposed to the private brand.

People may also buy name brands for such other reasons as confidence in the brand, better service and a feeling that a producer will be more apt to stand behind his product under his own brand name than behind goods produced by him under a private brand for others. As long as a consumer recognizes that he is paying more for the real or imagined superiority of the name-brand item, he is being rational and should not be faulted for maximizing the utility from his scarce resources. On the other hand, a person who buys name-brand goods and pays more for them when there is no quality difference—simply because of a blind faith in brand names or because of adages such as "you get what you pay for" —is not economically rational.

Sears, by guaranteeing financial support and a certain level of purchases, reduces the risk to Whirlpool and cuts the firm's costs. Whirlpool can count on a steadier demand for its products than if it had to depend exclusively on the fluctuating sales through independent retailers. Because its costs are reduced it can offer Sears a lower price than would otherwise be possible. Since Sears can obtain the machines at a low cost level, it can sell the machines in large quantity and often at a discount price. Thus there are numerous reasons to account for the existence of private brands. Often such reasons are rooted in efforts by producers and retailers to reduce costs and improve profits.

THINK IT OVER:

1. Who, if anyone, is hurt by private-brand production?
2. Suppose that the demand for the brand-name product in the example concerning the fruit processor increased to 20,000,000 units for the producer's name brand (optimal capacity of the plant). Should the producer renew his contract with the chain store to produce the private brand or produce solely under its own brand name?
3. Why did the producer's profit increase by 600 percent when it began private-brand production in addition to its own name-brand production, even though no direct profit resulted from the private-brand order?
4. Suppose a theater is operating at less than one-third capacity. How might the theater increase its total profit using an approach similar to the one discussed in the example?
5. When would it make economic sense for a producer to sell products under a store or private brand?
6. At what point would the economically astute producer discontinue production under private brands and concentrate on name-brand production?

APPLICATION OF ECONOMIC THEORY TO CONSUMER PURCHASES

Changing conditions in agriculture, the law, advertising, manufacturing, and management quickly outdate information on specific buying techniques. For this reason the consumer should obtain such specific information not from a text book, but from monthly or yearly consumer publications. However, knowledge of the basic economic issues involved in any purchase will aid in forming rational buying practices. This section deals with the broad general method of utilizing economic concepts to make decisions concerning nondurable and durable goods. The consumer who understands basic economic reasoning has a guide to help form his buying decisions. With such an understanding he gains perspective which will help him to utilize specific buying information found elsewhere.

For example, specific buying information or "buymanship" will help one to avoid buying a car from a company which is known to have produced a high percentage of "lemons." Using economic reasoning helps the consumer analyze the car market in general and the true costs of driving a particular car in light of the changing economic conditions. Thus if there is a sluggish year in the auto industry, economic reasoning would suggest that substantial price reductions could be gained if bargaining were used. The specific information printed about the car one year earlier when economic conditions were better might suggest that a higher price be paid than would be necessary now. Use of general economic reasoning can assist in personal economic decisions, especially when utilized with current specific information such as that provided by Consumers Union and *Consumers Bulletin*. Specific information provides "facts," and economic reasoning provides a guide or framework for evaluating potential decisions.

The method of applying economics as a tool in personal consumer decision making will be illustrated in the following sections:

1. Non-durable goods
2. Durable goods
3. Housing

It should be stressed that what is important is the method. The specific facts will become dated, while the method or approach will remain a serviceable guide to the consumer. While only a few areas are examined, this does not mean that economic reasoning cannot be applied to other topics of consumer interest. The same methods do apply. Once the consumer understands the reasoning process he can apply a similar approach to any particular area he wishes. The particular topics chosen are only intended as an illustration of the economic process, rather than as a specific buying guide for goods of all types.

CONSUMER PURCHASES OF NON-DURABLE GOODS

Much of the consumer's income is spent on non-durable goods. Non-durable items are goods which are rapidly consumed and must be replaced. Clothing and food must be constantly replaced, regardless of the state of the economy. For this reason the demand for non-durable items remains relatively constant. Consumers may change their buying habits as income rises and falls, but the total consumption of non-durable goods does not change significantly as the state of the economy fluctuates.

The consumer faces many decisions as to how to allocate his personal income. He must buy the goods required to sustain life, make life comfortable, and give pleasure. Briefly, the hierarchy of goods and services which most consumers must obtain includes food, shelter, clothing, health, medical care, and leisure goods. The particular *mix of goods* and services a person buys is dictated by necessity and preference. For example, every person requires some minimum level of food intake (both in quality and quantity) to continue living. Once enough food is obtained to sustain life a consumer turns to fulfilling his next need or desire. For example, after food most people would desire clothing. Once the clothing needs are met a person would desire shelter. After shelter other needs would be met.

Since most families face scarcity, that is, their real or imagined needs are greater than their ability to obtain them, consumers must make choices. They must allocate their scarce resources in such a way as to maximize utility. The particular mix of goods and services chosen by the consumer depends upon the consumer's evaluation of the utility derived from a good compared to the utility obtained from alternative goods.

A person who has little money will find that he gets greater utility by shopping very carefully, taking much time to obtain food bargains. By so doing his income is stretched and he can buy other items he needs, thereby obtaining a higher level of utility than before. On the other hand, a person who is well off may find that the money saved by shopping carefully is so slight that it is not worth the trouble because his time is worth more than the possible savings. The person with a relatively high income gains more utility by conserving his time than his money. The person of moderate income could be expected to have different shopping habits and techniques than others with more or less income. Yet despite the different habits all can be maximizing utility from their scarce resources.

Consider how this formulation of utility will affect a consumer's selection of stores and how the consumer determines if a certain store meets his particular needs. Does it matter where the cost-conscious consumer shops?

Stores and Prices. To answer the question "Does it matter where you shop?" a survey was conducted among three chain stores in a local area. A typical market basket of goods was drawn up and goods were priced at various stores on the same day. From the prices of the different baskets yearly food budgets were computed. This highly limited survey indicated that some stores were consistently lower in price than others. The actual results were as follows:

Store	Annual Cost
A Foods	$1,214
B Foods	$1,222
C Foods	$1,323

The survey showed that the most expensive store was about 9 percent more costly than the least. This survey was repeated each year for three years to see if any change occurred. Little change was noted in the relative difference. All items compared were brand-name goods of identical size chosen at each store on the same day. What accounts for the consistent price differential between the three chain stores?

The store C Foods is a local chain. It is much smaller than the other two organizations. Presumably it does not have the same ability to buy in large enough quantities to get large discounts from its suppliers, as do the larger chains. Unable to compete on a price basis, the store offers greater services such as check cashing, bill-paying services (utility bills), and personal service. It even provides such extras as free coffee for its customers. The store's customers tend to be affluent. The generally higher prices do not seem to bother these customers.

On the other hand, A Foods is a large midwestern chain of supermarkets and specializes in a discount style of operation. Its size presumably allows it to obtain greater discounts on items than the smaller stores (economies of scale). The store tends to have a narrower range of brand-name products than other stores. It also gives considerable space and emphasis to its own private-brand goods. The store's private brands range from powdered milk to bleach. These store-brand goods range from 5 to 30 percent lower in price than the nationally known brands the store stocks. The private-brand goods were not compared in the survey of prices. The store offers no trading stamps, very little service, and no extras such as utility-bill paying services. The store, for these reasons, has a lower overhead than the smaller chain.

It is no surprise that the prices tend to be consistently lower than those found in the other food stores in the town. Because of its prices, this store tends to have chiefly moderate-income customers who are very price conscious.

The B store in this area tends to be somewhere in between the two chains previously discussed. Its prices tend to be a bit higher than A, but considerably lower than the C store. The store appears to offer a few more customer services and a slightly greater range of products and brands.

At which store would a rational maximizing consumer shop? If the consumer is concerned only with the lowest possible prices, he would shop at A store. If he were concerned only with convenience, atmosphere, and personal service, he would shop at the C store. Customers who desire low prices, but more services, would choose the B store.

The question the consumer must answer for himself is what he really wants. A consideration of the opportunity costs may help the consumer decide the question.

The opportunity cost of obtaining the least possible cost of food is personal service and convenience. On the other hand, the opportunity costs of obtaining a large amount of service is higher food costs. The opportunity cost must be measured against alternative uses of the scarce resources. If the alternative uses of the resource are more important to the consumer than the extra service, the rational consumer would elect a lower level of service in exchange for some other use of the resource (shopping dollar). For example, a family that is on a limited budget may see the opportunity cost of shopping at the higher-priced store as costing them a vacation trip, a color television or additional recreation. So long as they value the alternative uses of the resource greater than they value the services received, they would not choose to shop at the high-cost, high-service store.

A family of greater affluence might consider the difference in cost between the high-cost, high-service store and the low-cost, low-service store in a different light. These customers might feel that any other alternative use of the resource is less important than pleasant shopping with personal service. Thus the potential savings in food costs which could be applied to some other use is of less utility than the time saved and pleasant shopping conditions encountered.

THINK IT OVER:

1. Which group is showing a rational economic behavior: the affluent group who shop for service, or the less affluent group who are willing to forego extra service to save food dollars?
2. Since the goods which were compared in the survey above were identical and only prices differed, at which store would you shop? (Be sure to estimate your opportunity costs).
3. What are the economic trade-offs made when considering the opportunity costs involved in the preceding question?
4. Set up an investigation of comparative prices in your home town.

Shopping Food Sales. It has been shown that there is often a significant difference in price of identical merchandise from store to store. Some consumers attempt to save money on food and other purchases by making special efforts to shop for sale items at many stores. Many consumers have wondered whether such efforts are economically justified or merely an act of self-deception. How can an answer be determined? One way is to consider all costs that face the consumer, both explicit and implicit, and to compare these costs against the savings from such shopping. If the savings are great enough to cover the shopper's explicit and implicit costs, such as travel and value of time and effort, then such activity would be economically justified. If not, the special effort expended to obtain the savings is not justified.

In order to test the proposition that a family could save money by making a special effort to shop sale items at several stores, a limited survey was undertaken. An assumption was made that the consumer would visit several stores and buy only the items on sale at each store. The regular price was noted, the quantity a typical consumer would purchase for a household was estimated and the savings were tallied. The savings were then weighed against the consumer's implicit and explicit costs.

A consumer who shopped for the sale items listed in the survey in the same quantity specified would have saved $5.18.

The explicit costs for taking advantage of this sale would be transportation expenses. The three stores were located at several points around the town. To drive the various distances to the stores would have been a total round-trip distance of about 20 miles. The survey assumed that the consumer would be driving an intermediate-size sedan, one year old. The Department of Transportation, Federal Highway Administration estimates that such a car costs fifteen cents per mile to drive (including depreciation, oil, license and insurance).

CONSUMER PURCHASES

Store One	Size	Reg. Price	Sale Price	Sav.	Qunt. Pur.	Savings
Instant Maxwell House Coffee	2 oz.	.47	.39	.08	2	.16
Kraft Margarine	1 lb.	.43	.30	.13	5	.65
Grade A Eggs	1 doz.	.49	.42	.07	2	.14
Campbell Cream of Mushroom Soup		.17	.13	.04	10	.40
Easy-Off Oven Cleaner	16 oz.	1.20	.95	.25	1	.25
				Savings		1.60
Store Two						
Bacon Reg. Slice	1 lb.	.53	.49	.04	2	.08
"SOS" Steel Wool	18 pads	.43	.40	.03	2	.06
Cascade Dishwasher Detergent	1 lb.	.99	.91	.08	2	.16
C & M Magic Frosting Mix	1 lb.	.21	.17	.04	4	.16
Creamette Brand Macaroni	3 oz.	.14	.12	.02	4	.08
1¼ lb. loaf of bread	1¼ lb.	.39	.33	.06	3	.18
				Savings		.72
Store Three						
"Formica" Brand Floor Shine	32 oz.	1.27	.99	.28	1	.28
Carnation Evaporated Milk	13 oz.	.21	.17	.04	10	.40
Kraft Grated Parmesan Cheese	8 oz.	.93	.86	.07	1	.07
Bisquick		.47	.44	.03	2	.06
Kleenex "Boutique" tissue		.26	.20	.06	4	.24
Banquet Chicken Pie	8 oz.	.18	.11	.07	10	.70
Westpack Frozen Peas	10 oz.	.18	.12	.06	5	.30
Swanson Frozen Apple Pie		.76	.49	.27	3	.81
				Savings		2.86
				Total Savings		$5.18

Thus, savings on food less cost of travel are:

$5.18 (savings)
- 3.00 (cost of travel)
$2.18 (saved)

Shopping sales on this basis appears to be economically a sound practice, but is it? If you were working for someone else on a part-time basis, what wage would you require on a per-hour basis? By looking at the cost or value of your spare time in this way it becomes possible to consider the value of your time an implicit cost and to make a true estimate of the savings realized.

Even spare time has a value or cost. To ignore such a cost gives a false or illusory sense of savings. The "wage" earned by the consumer from shopping the sale can be computed by dividing time spent into savings realized:

$$\frac{\text{Savings}}{\text{Time}} = \text{savings per hour or "wage"}$$

The savings realized by purchasing the food at sale prices was $2.18 (after transportation expenses), while the time spent was about two hours, thus the wage earned or savings per hour is:

$$\frac{\$2.18}{2 \text{ hours}} = \$1.09$$

Whether the consumer feels that the savings per hour, or "wage," earned by shopping the sales is worth the effort will depend upon what he feels his spare time is worth. The consumer's alternative use of spare time versus money saved will serve as a criterion or yardstick against which activity can be measured.

The time required to "earn" the savings through shopping could be used at other activities. For example, perhaps the consumer could save more by sewing clothes for the children or by tuning up the car. If any such alternative use of time will return more money per hour, it would be irrational to forego these opportunities to earn less by shopping the sales.

An unemployed consumer's time is worth little; the wage earned by shopping the sales may be the most productive use of spare time. An affluent mechanic who could use his spare time far more productively would be foolish to work for less, e.g., shopping at food sales. To honestly determine savings one must include the implicit value of time. To ignore the value of time is to overstate the savings.

THINK IT OVER:

1. Assume that you could save the amount indicated on page 44. Because you are more centrally located, the total distance you must travel to realize the savings is only five miles, and takes one hour. How much will you earn on a dollar-per-hour basis by shopping the sales?

2. On the basis of the wage which you would earn in Question 1, would such an activity represent the best use of your spare time?

3. To determine the true value or cost of your spare time, it has been suggested that a rule of thumb is to consider the minimum wage you would be willing to accept if someone offered you a part-time job. Do you think that such a rule is valid?

4. Why is it important that a consumer consider the cost of his time when evaluating money-saving activities performed during his leisure hours?

5. Many people build kits. If you can save thirty dollars by assembling a kit in your leisure time (total time twenty hours), is such an activity justifiable? If so, on what basis? (Pleasure or a money-saving activity.)

6. If you indicate that you would build the kit to save money, would you also build the kit for someone else (that is, selling it to them for cost plus $30)? If you are willing to do this, your spare time is worth how much per hour?

7. If you were willing to build the kit for your own use but were unwilling to build it for others on a cost plus $30 basis, what is your economic rationale for building the kit? (There are some.)

CONSUMER PURCHASES OF DURABLE GOODS

When a firm is contemplating investment in capital goods such as a new plant or new machinery, a number of factors are considered before the investment is made. One of the main factors considered is the annual rate of return on the investment. The return on the capital invested in the machinery ought to be greater than any other alternative use of the investment. One way to measure the return is to consider how much the money would earn if left in the bank. Assume that a person was going to invest $2,000 in a machine. He knows that he could simply leave the money in the bank and earn 5 percent or $100 per year interest on the money. The machine should earn at least this amount plus an amount for replacement in order for it to be an economically sound investment.

When the consumer invests his capital (consuming dollars) he can use the same type of yardstick to determine if the contemplated purchase is an economically sound investment.

Some consumer purchases are sold on the basis of being a good investment. These items can with some precision be evaluated as the firm would evaluate its investments to determine if they are economically sound. Consider a few items which are advertised as investments: the home freezer, storm doors and windows, insulation, aluminum siding and many other items. Are such "investments" really as good as their promoters claim? Does it pay the consumer to buy these items?

Purchasing a Home Freezer. One way to find out whether such an investment is economically sound is to consider costs, as does a firm. Such an accounting considers both implicit and explicit costs. For the sake of illustration the home freezer is a good example. The home freezer is advertised and sold in major appliance stores and mail order houses on the basis of saving the consumer money as well as providing convenience. Statements such as "it pays for itself out of money saved on food bills" or "cut food costs" are used in ads. If such claims are true when all costs were considered, then the freezer would be a sound investment which the wise consumer ought to consider purchasing.

The freezer selected for illustration is a middle-of-the-line (not the most nor the least expensive), sixteen-cubic-foot freezer. It is a GE CA16DE, 16 CF model sold at $262. It is a manual defrost model.

In order to determine if the investment is sound, costs must be computed.

There are two types of cost, explicit and implicit. Explicit costs are the direct costs involved in the operation. Such costs would include:

		Cost Per Year
Depreciation (cost per year), assuming a fifteen-year life	$\frac{\$262}{15} =$	$17.46
Maintenance over life, estimated at $30	$\frac{30}{15} =$	2.00
Power consumption (estimated by Central Illinois Power Co., 83KW at 3 cents per KW = $2.50 per month		30.00
	Total explicit cost per year	$49.46

Implicit (opportunity) cost must be computed on the basis of what the resource (money) would have earned if put to another use. As a basis for comparison consider that the $260 has been left in a savings account earning 5 percent. This shows how much interest is lost when an investment is made in capital.

Cost of freezer	$262.00
Interest rate	5%
Interest for one year	$ 13.10

Had the capital been left in the bank, it would have earned $13 per year forever.

Total costs (explicit and implicit):

	Per Year
Explicit costs	$49.46
Implicit costs	13.10
Total costs (per year)	$62.56

If the freezer is to be considered "economical," that is, a good investment, it must save the consumer at least $62 per year in food costs.

Assume that a family of four has purchased the freezer. In the past they have spent $1,800 per year on food. They intend to stock their freezer from supermarkets when food is on sale. However, only about 30 percent of their food costs are related to items that are usually frozen (meats, vegetables, etc.). If one-third of the food can be frozen in the freezer, the portion of their food budget which they can expect to utilize in the freezer is $540 ($1800 × 30%). By shopping only sales and stocking their freezer with those items, the family finds it can save an average of 20 percent on the portion of the food budget which can be frozen: $540 (freezeable food) × 20% (savings due to sale) = $108 savings on food.

Is this freezer economical for this family?

Total savings per year on food	$108
Total cost of freezer per year	62
Savings	$ 46 per year

On a monthly basis the savings is $3.83. When considering this example one must remember that the family tried to systematically shop for and stock the freezer from sales (an unrealistic assumption for most people). Do you think the savings were worth the trouble? No allowance was made for food wastage. Food that is kept frozen for long periods of time does deteriorate. How would such wastage be computed into the yearly cost of freezer operation?

Whether the freezer saves the consumer money is, at best, debatable. The Department of Agriculture and Consumers Union have calculated that the savings which are generated by the freezer annually are small. The Department of Agriculture views the freezer as a convenience rather than a money saver. Do you agree?

Whether the investment in a freezer or any other good is a "good" investment is determined by the costs vs. money saved. Consider the following changes and calculate whether the freezer in the preceding illustration is a good buy or not. Assume each question changes only one variable; variables otherwise remain as given.

1. The interest rate paid on savings falls to 2 percent.
2. Electric power costs increase to five cents per KWH.
3. The freezer can be expected to last only twelve years.
4. The purchase price of the freezer is reduced by a sale to only $150.

As each variable is changed the freezer may become more of a cost saver or it may become less economical.

Whether an investment should be undertaken or not depends upon costs. As costs change rational decisions change. If the consumer is aware of a way to evaluate costs in relation to investments, he will be able to adapt to changing conditions and obtain the most from his resources.

THINK IT OVER:

1. Would it pay to insulate your home if the price of gas were to drop to 10 percent of its current price?

2. Which is better: an investment in a $10 watch that looks good and keeps time well but only lasts for three years or an investment in a fine expensive watch that will run forever but costs $100? The key to this problem is the current interest rate. Assume no maintenance required on either watch.

3. When would an investment in storm windows be worthwhile from an economic standpoint, if the cost is $1,000 and the life is 20 years? Including lost interest on invested capital, what would be the minimum fuel savings per year that would be required to make such an investment economical?

The Consumer and his Auto.   The typical American consumer's love affair with the automobile is legend. When the consumer buys a car he is buying more than just transportation. He may be buying status, masculinity, or an extension of his ego. Few consumers decide to purchase a car simply on the merit of providing low-cost transportation. However, despite the emotional attachment to an auto, the rational consumer can make an effort to determine the true costs of auto buying and operation.

Economists assume that the consumer is a rational being and therefore makes consuming decisions in a rational manner. Most consumers would act according to this assumption, provided they had perfect knowledge of price, quality, and reliability, and provided that deceptive sales practices were not employed by dealers. In the real world the consumer does not have such a wealth of information. Most consumers have little knowledge in the economic sense on which to base their decisions. Thus, the consumer does not meet the economists' basic assumptions.

How often do consumers see advertisements for autos that give precise price information concerning operational equipment, financing, etc? Instead of hard facts auto makers and dealers promote the glamour, speed, power and luxury of their product. The various producers compete against one another in every respect except price. Even special promotions and sales are expressed in terms such as "Ford White Sale" or "Bonanza Week at Your Chevy Dealer."

One cannot be expected to make rational economic decisions based upon such information. Auto companies and their dealers are unwilling to provide consumers with true costs, profit markups, and estimated costs of the care on a per-mile or yearly basis. The consumer must obtain the information himself from other sources. Fortunately the consumer does have access to information which will greatly assist in the selection of an auto. Such information is available from sources such as Consumers Union *(Consumer Reports Magazine)*,

Consumer's Bulletin, various car publications on the newsstands, credit unions, banks, and the U.S. Department of Transportation.

True Costs of Car Operation. Basically car costs can be determined in the same way as any other capital item. Costs can be divided into two main areas. One area is fixed costs, (FC) which include depreciation, license and registration fees, and insurance. These costs continue even when the car is not driven. The variable costs (VC) are costs which vary depending upon how much the car is driven. Variable costs include gas, oil, tires, and maintenance expenditures. The more the car is driven, the greater will be the variable costs.

The two costs, when added, (FC + VC) give the total cost per year of the auto. However, most consumers would find such total expense information of little value. A more useful expression of costs for comparison purposes is the total cost per mile. To arrive at this figure the total cost is divided by the number of miles driven in a year. The costs for an average car would be computed on the basis of 10,000 miles per year.

$$\frac{FC + VC}{10,000 \text{ miles}} = \text{Total cost per mile.}$$

Anyone can estimate the cost per mile of his car, but there is no real need to do this since consumer, automobile, insurance and governmental organizations have made various estimates of car costs on a per-mile basis. The following cost estimate was based on a 1970 sedan costing $3,374 with an assumed ten-year life span of 100,000 miles. It assumes the car is driven 14,500 miles the first year.

First Year Estimated Variable Cost:

Garaging, Parking & Tolls		1.43¢ per mile
Gas and Oil		1.84
Maintenance		.51
Tires		.12
	Total VC	3.90¢ per mile

First Year Estimated Fixed Cost:

Depreciation		6.59¢ per mile
Insurance		1.44
Taxes and Fees		2.28
	Total FC	10.31¢ per mile

The total cost per mile (FC + VC) for the first year will be:

Fixed Costs	10.31¢ per mile
Variable Costs	3.90
	14.21¢ per mile

This may appear to be an excessive figure, but one should remember that most people consider the cost of the car on a cash-out-of-pocket basis (mainly gas and oil). Such a computation clearly makes the car appear far less expensive per mile than is the case.

The estimated cost for the ten-year life span of the car is as follows:

Ten-Year Average Variable Cost:

Garaging, Parking & Tolls	1.80¢ per mile
Gas and Oil	1.89
Maintenance	1.55
Tires	.39
Total VC	5.63¢ per mile

Ten-Year Average Fixed Cost:

Depreciation	3.19¢ per mile
Insurance	1.72
Taxes and Fees	1.35
Total FC	6.26¢ per mile

The ten-year average total cost per mile of 11.89 cents is only slightly less than the first-year cost of operation. Almost the entire difference can be accounted for by a decline in depreciation cost that is not equaled by an increase in maintenance.

The more miles the car is driven per year, the lower the cost per mile will be. This is because the fixed costs are being spread or averaged over more miles.

This effect can clearly be seen in the estimate shown below. The estimate was based on a medium-sized sedan. The estimate is on a total cost-per-mile basis

(FC + VC = ATC per mile).

Note that the estimated minimum cost appeared at about 25,000; presumably if the car were driven more miles, the costs would begin to climb above the minimum because of increasing VC, due to the need for more repairs, tires, adjustments, tune ups, and other maintenance expenses. The contribution to total cost changes when more miles are driven per year. If the car is only driven a few miles a year, most of the cost is from fixed costs and depreciation. If the car is driven many miles per year, the cost per mile in variable costs is greater than fixed costs.

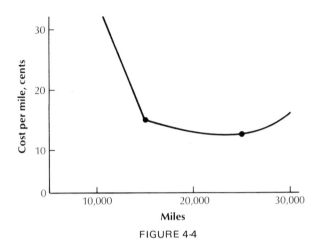

FIGURE 4-4

Cost Per Automobile Mile Per Year

Purchasing a Used Car vs. a New Car. Many people assume that a used car will be less expensive to purchase and operate than a new car. This is based on the assumption that a used car, having decreased in price due to depreciation, is a good buy. Depending on the price of the used car and its condition, this may or may not be true. As a rule of thumb, however, used cars represent no real cost saving over a new car (for an average used car, when all factors are considered). Even in the 10th year, when depreciation is less than 2 percent of the original cost, the cost is still about twelve cents per mile. There comes a point at which the dwindling depreciation is more than offset by the higher cost of maintenance. Beyond some point costs do not decline no matter how far a car is driven. Depreciation does decrease as an expense as the car is driven more, but this is more than offset by increased repairs and maintenance. Driving a used car to save money is of questionable economic validity. Of course there are exceptions to the general rule; but, on the average, when all costs are computed, there is very little cost difference between used and new car costs. A person who is a skilled do-it-yourself mechanic might save some money on the used car as compared with the new car by making his own repairs. (In effect he would be working for himself; his wages would be savings on repairs.)

A note of caution is in order for those considering the purchase of a used car. Many people on a limited budget face a hard decision. They could buy a new compact car or a low-mileage second-hand luxury car. Often people in this situation are tempted to purchase the used luxury car, which appears to be a better buy since it is big and has many extras such as air conditioning, stereo, and power seats and windows. The compact car appears small and stripped by comparison.

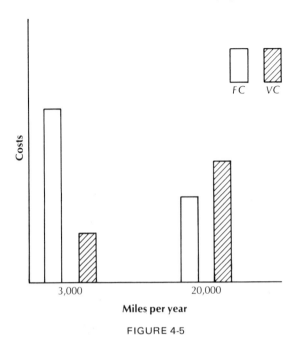

FIGURE 4-5

Examples of Fixed and Variable Automobile Costs

The problem resulting from the purchase of the used luxury car is that it is extremely costly in gas, tires, and repairs. Thus, the variable costs are very great compared with the new compact auto. If reliable transportation is the consumer's goal, an inexpensive new car rather than a used luxury auto will be the best solution.

Buying a Car. One area in which a real savings can be made in the purchase of the car is in making the "deal." The reader will recall that it is assumed that the consumer will make the best possible economic decision; that is, he will act in his own economic self-interest when purchasing any item. To be able to act in one's economic interest requires knowledge, and the information needed to act in one's own economic self-interest when buying is not obtainable from advertisements or from dealers. Prices, for example, are supposed to be listed on the window sticker but this figure is fictitiously high. The actual purchase price may be $200 to $1,500 less than the posted price.

Lack of price information from the dealer and the fictitious price stickers help promote dealer profits. If many consumers can be persuaded to pay more for their cars than the dealers' minimum acceptable price, the dealers will improve their profits.

We can speculate on the effect of the auto dealers' disguised pricing:

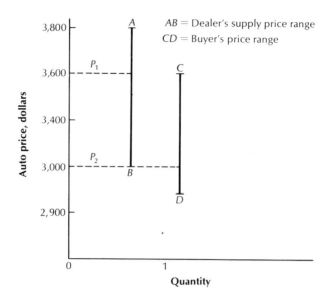

FIGURE 4-6

Bargaining over Automobile Price

The diagram shows the economic behavior of the auto dealer and buyer.

Point A   This is the manufacturer's suggested retail price, the so-called "sticker" price. The dealer would like to sell the auto at this price.

Point B   This is the lowest price at which the dealer will sell the car. This may be as low as $100 over dealer cost according to Consumers Union.

Point C   This is the highest price most consumers are willing to pay for the auto.

Point D   This is the price the consumer would like to pay for the car if possible.

It should be noted that neither the buyer nor the seller is apt to obtain the price he desires. After hard negotiations, the price must fall between P_1 and P_2. The exact price is indeterminant (cannot be predicted) and depends upon the bargaining skill of both the buyer and seller. Price sources are available indicating the actual wholesale price and the minimum markup that can be expected if a consumer bargains with skill. Armed with facts the consumer will be more likely to pay less, thereby moving toward point B.

It is important to visit several dealers and to tell them you are shopping around for a car. Have the dealer write down the cash price for the auto as well as the price of the options, taxes, and delivery charges. At this point it is best not to indicate that you have a car to trade in; by doing so you prevent the dealer from quoting an inflated trade-in allowance which will simply be added into the price of the new car. This will only add to the confusion in the bargaining process.

Make the rounds of dealers several times. This should force them to negotiate with you in earnest. This is important since it forces each dealer to make progressively better offers. Remember, the dealer wants to sell the car; but he would much prefer to sell it to you at a higher price than at a lower price.

The negotiating process takes time, but like good wine it cannot be rushed. If the consumer is not in a rush, is skilled, and has the facts, he can usually save a substantial amount.

Consider the following case, which illustrates the negotiating process. In February of 1968, one individual decided he wanted to purchase a new 1968 Rambler Rebel station wagon, model 550. The car was a standard size, six-cylinder standard transmission.

The first round of shopping was on a cash basis, all options included in the price, as well as taxes, delivery charges and license. Three dealers in a fifty-mile radius were compared. The following prices are as quoted by the dealer with each visit.

	Dealer 1	Dealer 2	Dealer 3
Round 1	$3,100	$2,970	$2,900
Round 2	$2,700	$2,560	$2,600
Round 3	$2,700	$2,495	$2,550

After two weeks and three rounds of negotiation (ten hours actual shopping time) the low price of $2,495 was accepted by the buyer. This price was only achieved after hard bargaining. This price corresponded closely with information provided by a credit union. The credit union provided the wholesale price plus minimum expected dealer profit. After this point one could not expect the price to be reduced by further negotiation.

Perhaps at this point the reader may feel that it is just too much trouble to get the best possible "deal" on an auto. "After all, what are a few dollars?" the consumer may ask.

Return to the case illustrated. A consumer accepting deal #1 would have paid $3,100 (less financing and insurance) for the car in question. After ten hours of negotiation with three dealers, the customer in the example bought from dealer #2 at a final price of $2,495. Compared with the first deal, the consumer saved $605. The magnitude of this saving can be given perspective if computed as a wage earned by the consumer for negotiating. The savings yielded a wage of $605/10 hr. = $60.05 per hour. Thus, the time taken to negotiate makes economic sense because most people could earn more per hour in savings than they could working at any other job.

After obtaining the best possible price many consumers fail to obtain the best possible financing. Auto dealers often prefer to sell the car as a package (car + credit + credit life insurance). Dealer financing is very costly compared to bank or credit-union financing. By the same token insurance purchased as part of a package "deal" from the dealer is usually more expensive than that from conventional insurance sources. Financing through a bank or credit union is usually obtainable for all but the very worst credit risks, since the car is the collateral for the loan.

A number of factors will affect your bargaining power and hence the discount you can obtain when purchasing a new car:

1. The strength of the economy has a great deal of influence on the level of demand for autos. A period of slack consumer demand naturally enhances your bargaining power.
2. The degree of popularity of the particular make and model of auto you desire also affects price. Large discounts may be made to sell a car of low acceptance by the public.
3. Year-end, left-over cars may be bought at bargain prices. (Make sure that the price being paid is less the total first year's depreciation.)

Since most car prices are negotiable, the dealer tries to maximize the price of each sale to obtain maximum profit. There are several methods employed by dealers which are used to gain an advantage over the consumer, and the consumer should be on guard for these tactics. If the consumer is aware of these tactics, he can take a defensive posture to preserve his negotiating position.

1. One tactic dealers often employ is known in the automobile trade as the "Hot Box." Customers are taken into small booths to discuss the "deal" with the salesman. At some point the salesman excuses himself, leaving the customers alone (usually husband and wife). Generally the customer uses this opportunity to discuss the particulars of the proposed deal with his wife. Many times the booth has a listening device planted in it. The goal is to allow the salesman to listen in on the customer's conversation and thereby gain an idea of the terms that are acceptable to the customer. The dealer may find that the consumer may settle for a far higher price than the minimum price the dealer may be willing to accept. Thus the dealer makes greater profits than would be likely without such a technique.
2. Stalling. Salesmen are aware that a tired customer is less apt to drive a hard bargain. Accordingly many dealers give long test drives or spend hours rewriting deals. When sufficiently tired, the consumer's resistance falls, and he may consent to a deal that he would have rejected hours earlier.
3. Pressure to "Buy Now!" A dealer may infer that a deal made today will not be acceptable twenty-four hours later. With some exceptions this is

not the case. The salesman knows that if the consumer can be rushed, he will pay a higher price than if given time to think and compare prices. A well-known consumer rule is a wise one: when making an important decision, wait for twenty-four hours before committing yourself.

The costs of buying a car have been examined, as well as the costs of used vs. new cars. It can be seen that a car is expensive to own; but if the consumer exercises a little care and is aware of the costs, he can minimize those costs and yet obtain the car he desires. The consumer who purchases a car with such information and care is apt to make a far more rational decision than the consumer who purchases a car on a blind, trusting emotional basis.

SUGGESTED READING

Economics Readings

McConnell, Campbell R. *Economics.* 5th ed. New York: McGraw-Hill Book Company., 1972. (Chapters 26-29)

Samuelson, Paul A. *Economics.* 8th ed. New York: McGraw-Hill Book Company, 1970. (Pp. 441-442, 447, 453-465)

Personal Economics Readings

"Beef Baiters Meet the Press," *Consumers Reports,* June, 1968, pp. 306-307.

Cassidy, Ralph Jr. *Competition and Price Making in Food Retailing.* New York: The Ronald Press, 1962.

Consumer's Digest. Published by Consumer's Digest, Inc., Chicago. (See November and December issues for automobile price buying directory.)

Dichter, Ernest. *Handbook of Consumer Motivations.* New York: McGraw-Hill Book Company, 1964.

Erickson, Lawrence W. and Barbara Simi. *Family Financial Education for Adults.* Silver Springs, Maryland: Council for Family Financial Education.

Fox, Harold W. *The Economics of Trading Stamps.* Washington, D.C.: Public Affairs Press, 1968.

Household Finance Corporation, *Your Automobile Dollar,* Money Management Institute, Prudential Plaza, Chicago, Illinois.

Jackson, C. R. *How to Buy a Used Car.* Philadelphia: Chilton Book Co., 1967.

Margolious, Sidney. *The Consumer's Guide to Better Buying.* New York: Pocket Books, Inc., 1963.

——. *How to Make the Most of Your Money.* New York: Meredith, Inc.

——. *Responsible Consumer.* Public Affairs Committee, 381 Park Avenue South, New York, New York.

Milton, Arthur. *How to Get a Dollar's Value for a Dollar Spent.* New York: Citadel Press, 1964.

Mowbray, A. Q. *The Thumb on the Scale: Or the Supermarket Shell Game.* Philadelphia: J. B. Lippincott, 1967.

Padenburg, Daniel I. *Economics of Food Retailing.* Ithaca, N. Y.: Cornell University Press, 1968.

Rich, Stuart U. *Shopping Behavior of Department Store Customers.* Boston: Harvard University Business School, 1963.

Schoenfeld, David and A. A. Natella. *The Consumer and his Dollars.* Dobbs Ferry, N.Y.: Oceana Publications, 1966.

Wingate, Isabel, Karen R. Gillespie and Betty G. Addison. *Know Your Merchandise.* New York: McGraw-Hill Book Company, 1964.

Consumer Credit
as an Extension of
Current Income

CHAPTER *V*

CONSUMER CREDIT AS AN EXTENSION OF CURRENT INCOME

We have studied the economy from the point of view of producer, consumer, government, and investor, and we have attempted to view the various roles which the individual consumer can play in the determination of distribution of scarce resources. In our coverage of the consumer, we have seen the problems he faces in current consumption; the methods by which he is paid for his services; the impact of the distribution of incomes on society; and the means at his disposal for protecting his life style. Now we will view the methods by which the consumer can use credit to extend his current income and delineate some of the problems and choices the consumer faces in this area.

It will be useful to present some examples of situations in which credit is used by people to extend their incomes. We will look at a high school graduate headed for college, a young married couple, a middle-aged family and a retired couple.

When a student completes high school and prepares to enter college, he or she is often faced with the problem of financing future education out of rather meager current income. Despite the fact that the student often has an income of less than $2,000 he will, through the use of credit, be able to live on an income level of $4,000 or $5,000. The student is capable of using credit because it is expected that the college education will provide him with greater future income than if he were to terminate his education at the completion of high school. Credit in this case is used to transfer *future* income to *present* consumption.

Often a young married couple will have costs which exceed their current income levels. The expenses of buying housing and furnishings, medical services and early expenses of child rearing tend to exceed the average young married couple's income. To circumvent this problem the young married couple is able to utilize various forms of consumer credit to expand their buying power. Their real dollar income may be substantially below the standard at which they are living.

As a family moves to the middle-aged level, the distance between their ability to pay, or their income level, and their cost of living is closing. The use of credit by this age group is usually limited to the purchase of durable items such as washer-dryer combinations, food freezers, cars or recreational items. Because of payment procedures it is necessary for this group to use credit as a means of adjusting shortages of cash (income) at one time against surpluses of cash at some other time.

For the retired couple the use of credit is almost negligible. Because they have reached that period in their lives when their expenses are least and their assets are highest, the retired couple is often a supplier of credit, through their savings, rather than a user of credit. The use of credit to extend their incomes is usually in the area of health services, where the retired couple is apt to meet a great expense at a time when their incomes are low on a monthly, dollar basis.

The use of consumer credit to extend the purchasing power of a household or an individual is a relatively new concept. Traditionally the rule of thumb was that if a person could not pay cash he should not purchase the good or service. This concept has been associated with the Puritan or work ethic and has been prevalent throughout our history.

This philosophy flourished in a much less complex period of time in the development of the American economy. People in the United States in the seventeenth and eighteenth centuries had very low effective demand for consumer durable goods. More often than not, these types of goods were not available to the early settlers whose low incomes were used to meet the bare necessities of life. As the economy of the United States began to develop, people began to have surplus money available for various purposes. When churches began to establish insurance companies, people began to have a place to save. As society became more complex, the need for other types of savings facilities brought forth the development of the banking system, savings and loan institutions, credit unions, and consumer credit firms.

As the economy developed, the portion of income expended on necessities declined in proportion to that used for discretionary spending. Borrowing had its beginnings when a person was faced with an act of God, such as fire or crop failure. Then it was permissible for an individual to borrow, and often his friends helped him in this crisis situation. It was still taboo to borrow for "frivolous" items such as a new buggy or Sunday clothes.

It was not until after World War II that the wide use of consumer credit came into being. As can be seen in Graph 5-1, consumer credit has grown rapidly in the last twenty years. Consumer credit in 1970 is almost eight times that of the level of consumer credit in 1950—$127 billion in 1970, as opposed to $15 billion in 1950.

This rapid expansion of consumer credit over the past twenty years has been the result of the rapid rise in disposable income and increasing demand for goods. The demand for credit has increased in all the basic categories except repair and modernization loans. The demand for cars, consumer durables, and personal loans has increased with increases in the ability and desires of consumers to obtain additional goods.

In the last fifteen years, commercial banks have shown a greater willing-

GRAPH 5-1

Types of Consumer Installment Credit Outstanding

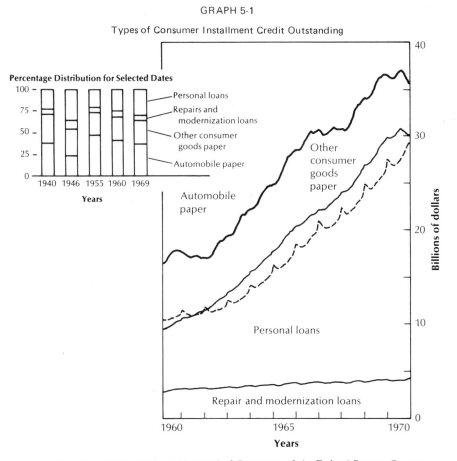

Percentage Distribution for Selected Dates

Years

Years

Source: *Historical Chart Book, 1970*, Board of Governors of the Federal Reserve System, p. 61.

ness to enter the consumer credit market. They have expanded their share of the market at the expense of sales finance companies and retail outlets as can be seen in Graph 5-2. The consequence of these changes in market shares has been lower credit costs for consumers, as commercial banks tend to have lower finance charges.

GRAPH 5-2

Major Holders of Consumer Installment Credit

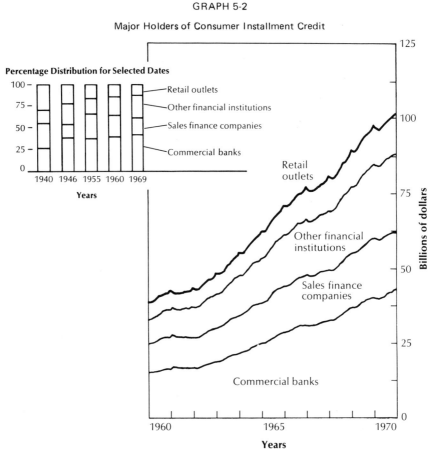

Source: *Historical Chart Book, 1970*, Board of Governors of the Federal Reserve System, p. 62.

Despite the increased use of credit and the increased ability to use credit due to larger disposable incomes, there still remains a strong reluctance on the part of some people to use credit to their best advantage. People who follow the Puritan ethic approach to consumer credit establish a set of rules for wise money management such as: "I don't buy anything on credit!" "Whenever I receive a credit card in the mail, I cut it up and return it to the sender." "I pay cash for everything, and that is the most economical way to operate." "If you mess around with credit, you will have nothing but trouble."

Probably most of us have heard comments such as these at some time in our lives. This view is often expressed by new immigrants to the United States or first-generation American citizens. Crucial to their view of credit is the idea that the wise money manager is thrifty and works hard. But what is thrift?

Webster's Dictionary defines "thrift" as "economical management; frugality"; and when we look up the word "frugal," we find that it means "economical in the use of resources; saving; provident." To be sure, savings is a very important concept in the area of money management but only part of the picture. The saving of money and the paying of cash are not good in and of themselves. This is only one of the methods by which the modern individual or household can meet its present and future needs. Wise money management is also the use of consumer credit at favorable or sometimes even unfavorable rates to meet cash requirements for worthwhile or necessary purchases.

THINK IT OVER:

1. What would the impact on society be if everyone followed the "Puritan Ethic" approach to credit?
2. Do you expect any basic changes in the use of consumer credit in the near future?
3. What is wrong with the approach "I pay cash for everything because that is the most economical way to operate"?
4. How does consumer credit affect the demand for goods and services produced in our economy?
5. How could the wise use of credit raise your living level?

FACTORS WHICH AFFECT THE USE OF CONSUMER CREDIT

Much of the literature in the field of consumer credit attempts to set hard and fast rules governing the individual use of consumer credit. This is usually a mistake, since each individual deals with a particular set of circumstances which affect his decision process. He must first determine his specific needs with regard to consumer credit. Rather than developing specific lists of do's and don'ts, we will try to investigate the various factors which might affect the use of consumer credit by any individual.

Discussion of the economic and non-economic factors affecting the use of consumer credit by the individual or household must include the following points:

1. Borrowing involves the implicit assumption of a pledge to return.

2. The borrowing capacity of an individual is limited by his expected ability to repay and by his reputation for repayment.
3. Borrowing involves risks and consequences for both the borrower and the lender.
4. Indiscriminate borrowing may lead to unfortunate consequences.
5. Changing economic conditions will have an effect on the utilization of credit and the payment procedure.

When an individual or household makes the decision to borrow, it is the beginning of a two-way street. Borrowing will involve the payment of the loan out of future income. Borrowing from a friend usually carries no additional costs in the repayment, so if two dollars is borrowed all that is expected in repayment is two dollars at some time in the future. When a person borrows from a professional lending agency, the repayment procedure involves not only the repayment of the amount which was borrowed, the principal, but also an additional percentage charged by the lender for the use of the funds, the interest. Interest charges vary with the type of institution, the amount of the down payment, the length of time and the amount of the loan. A "good" interest rate will vary with the economic conditions and with the individual goals of the borrower. In the early 1950's a person might have been advised to never pay more than 5 percent interest for a housing mortgage; but if that advice were followed in the 1970's, no housing would be built or sold, since the interest rates have reached 8 percent and higher. When a borrower is considering the amount which he will have to pay in the form of interest for the funds which he borrows, he should remember that all of the costs of the loan should be included before coming up with the percentage rate charged. Thus if there is a two-dollar service fee or a fifty-cent insurance fee, these items have to be added in as a cost of borrowing.

The ability of an individual to repay his debts is one of his major assets as he attempts to obtain credit. This is a difficult asset to obtain; and, once it is achieved, it is wise to do as much as possible to maintain a good repayment record. Part of the difficulty in obtaining a record of good repayment is the fact that many companies will not give an individual credit unless he can prove that he has a good payment record. Naturally, if an individual cannot get credit extended to him, he will have difficulty establishing his ability to make payments on time. For this reason, young couples or couples new to a community sometimes buy on a credit basis even when they are capable of paying cash—so they can establish themselves as good credit risks. Then, if the need or opportunity to use credit arises, they are able to demonstrate that they have had a good payment record in the past and that they are a safe risk for the lender.

The amount of interest which a consumer is apt to be charged is closely related to the risk involved for the lender. On a home mortgage, the interest rates tend to be the lowest because there is usually a large down payment involved. If payments are missed and the mortgage is defaulted, the lender can repossess the house and resell it to recoup any losses he may have suffered. On the other hand, the interest rates on retail sales accounts are much higher—18 percent and more on most service station and department store charges—because a higher risk is involved. In addition there are considerable costs of bookkeeping, collection and general office overhead which enter into this 18 percent annual charge. It thus represents a true interest factor, a risk factor, and administration charges. The consumer may not pay or may be late in paying; and once consumer goods are sold, repossession is expensive, and the resale does not repay the store loss. In order to cover these higher risks, the lender charges higher credit rates.

The risks involved for the borrower are in the matters of ability to repay out of future income and the stability of his income sources. If the borrower works as a schoolteacher, food store manager, or public health officer, his income will probably be stable, his ability to pay will be high, and the risk of his having to default on a loan will be low. On the other hand, if the borrower is a door-to-door salesman or golf pro, his income is apt to be less stable, and this could easily affect his ability to pay and increase the risk involved in his taking out a loan.

This is not to say that the schoolteacher who borrows will have no problems or that the golf pro who borrows will always have trouble paying debts. The point is that there is a correlation between the stability of a person's income and the ease with which he is able to assume credit and complete the repayment procedure. A person's financial position is not enough to insulate him from possible credit problems. The over-use or indiscriminate use of credit can lead to problems whether an individual's income is stable or fluctuates wildly.

It is difficult to pinpoint the exact amount of credit an individual or household can afford. Conservative retailers and lending agencies view 15 to 20 percent of disposable income as the maximum that an individual should borrow, excluding mortgage payments. Usually, the larger the percentage of credit a firm allows an individual to have outstanding, the more that individual is going to have to pay for the additional credit he is seeking. Most bankruptcy cases involve persons who have incurred debt which is up to one-half their monthly incomes. Bankruptcy referees point out that, when an individual or household takes on payments near or in excess of 25 percent of their monthly incomes, they are getting into the dangerous regions of misuse of consumer credit.

With this background on obtaining and maintaining credit worthiness on the part of the borrower, let us look to some of the economic factors which might affect the use of credit and repayment procedures. Generally, American folkways state that the wise use of credit would involve:

1. Borrowing only the amount of money which is needed.
2. Paying off the debt as soon as possible.
3. Never borrowing at excessively high interest rates (over 12 percent).
4. Making a large down payment so that the interest rate will be lower.

These are the type of do's and don'ts that the individual might find if he consulted many of the publications which are available in the area of consumer credit. Unfortunately, these hard and fast rules are the kind of rules which are broken and which often lead the person who follows them to more problems than if he were to ignore them. These rules are part of a carry-over from the Puritan ethic, and they imply that the use of credit, if not completely bad, is very close to the work of the devil.

The economical use of credit would replace these rules with a different set of understandings, which could be utilized by the borrower to determine his credit operations when confronted with various situations. At the top of this set of understandings would be:

1. Know how much credit is going to cost.
   There is nothing inherently good about 5 percent interest and nothing inherently bad about 36 percent interest if the person buying the credit is aware that this is the amount being charged and is willing to pay that amount.

2. Weigh the costs of credit against the other alternative uses for future funds.
   This is the concept of the opportunity costs of a 5 percent loan as against the opportunity costs of a 36 percent loan. If a consumer weighs all the costs and is willing to give up the alternative uses of his future income in order to receive a given commodity at a given interest rate, then he has made a logical decision. He will have to live with the decision until the loan is repaid, whether it be a 5 percent, thirty-year loan or a 36 percent, two-year loan.

3. Study the conditions in the economy before determining how fast to pay off a debt.
   If a person owns a house and has a 4 percent mortgage and the current mortgage rates are 8 percent, he may want to keep his mortgage for as long as possible to take advantage of the low-cost housing which the 4 percent mortgage gives him. On the other hand, if he has a 9 1/2 percent mortgage which he obtained at the peak of an inflationary period and the current mortgage rates are 6 percent, he may want to find ways to accelerate his payment of the expensive mortgage or to refinance his mortgage at a lower rate.

4. Constantly re-evaluate your financial position with regard to cash and credit purchasing and the state of both personal income and the condition of the economy.
   There may be times when it is better to borrow or use installment credit rather than take money out of a stock or some savings plan and miss a dividend or an interest payment. On the other hand, there may be times when it would be better to use money which has already been saved and to pay cash for an item rather than take out a loan. Taking out an 8 percent loan of $1,000 so one can collect 5 percent on a savings account of $1,000 is economically unsound.

THINK IT OVER:

1. What is consumer credit?
2. What are some of the implicit assumptions with which we are dealing when we think of consumer credit?
3. What are the important factors to look for and be aware of when using consumer credit?
4. What factors determine the amount you will be charged for a loan?

CONDITIONS AFFECTING SELECTION OF CONSUMER CREDIT SOURCES

The many varied approaches to the advertising and sale of consumer credit have posed a monstrous problem to the individual or household attempting to shop for consumer credit. The existence of "add-on clauses," "call" features, "balloon" payments, "credit service charges," "insurance fees," and other additional costs have made it difficult for the consumer to find a common denominator for examining costs of credit. The confusion is carried over into other areas after the consumer has finally made his credit purchase. Often he is unaware of repossession laws, garnishment laws and their effect on his present and future credit rating and credit worthiness.

TRUTH-IN-LENDING

In May of 1968, the United States Congress passed and the President signed the Consumer Credit Protection Act which was designed to eliminate some of the above-stated problems. There are four sections which affect the consumer in particular:

1. Consumer Credit Disclosure
2. Extortionate Credit Transactions
3. Restriction on Garnishment
4. National Commission on Consumer Finance

Under the "Credit Disclosure" section, the lender must supply to the borrower, before the loan is agreed on, two items: *the finance charge* and *the annual percentage rate*. The finance charge is the total of all costs which the consumer must pay in order to receive the credit. The annual percentage rate is the relative cost of credit in percentage terms. This method of disclosure allows the individual who is shopping for credit to total the dollar cost of each of the sources he may have investigated and determine the least expensive if the time periods and dollar amounts sought are the same at each source. If the individual knows the percentage rate, he can compare the relative costs of credit even when the dollar amounts and the time periods differ; but he should be aware that he may get a lower percentage rate because he is willing to borrow more money. This will probably cost him more in terms of dollars even though the interest rate may be less.

The area of the Truth-In-Lending Law which deals with "Extortionate Credit" covers the activities of organized crime in which violence or other illegal means are used to force payment of installments on loans. It makes extortionate credit transactions a federal offense.

In the area of wage garnishment the Truth-In-Lending Law attempts to deal with a problem which has plagued the lower class. Wage garnishment allows the lender to go into court and ask for a judgment against a borrower who has not met payments. The judgment usually allows the lender to order the employer to withhold a certain portion of the borrower's paycheck to make the loan payments. This often results in the firing of the employee because the employer does not wish to be bothered with collecting the employee's bad debts. It is often this type of person who gets deeper and deeper into financial problems because the system has prevented him from keeping a job and earning enough to pay his way out of debt. The Truth-In-Lending Law sets specific rules with regard to the garnishment procedure and stiff penalties for violation of the rules. The maximum amount of any individual's weekly disposable income subject to garnishment is limited to whichever is less, 25 percent of such income or the amount by which the weekly disposable income exceeds thirty-one times the federal minimum wage in effect at the time the earnings are payable. It also makes it illegal for a business to fire an employee because he has been garnished for one indebtedness. This section includes provision for allowing the individual who gets himself into a credit problem to bail himself out.

The Act also established The National Commission on Consumer Finance to study conditions in the consumer credit industry and to make recommendations to Congress for future legislation to protect the consumer.

The main objective of the Truth-In-Lending Law is to increase the individual's or household's awareness of the true cost of credit. In order to get the most for their credit dollars, individuals and households will need to use the information provided for under the law. The new information will help the individual or household to shop for credit as carefully as shopping for the items which they buy with the credit.

POSSIBLE CHOICES OF CONSUMER CREDIT

Consumer credit is available in a wide range of forms once a borrower decides to use it. The basic breakdown of consumer credit shows there are regular charge accounts, revolving charge accounts, installment or time-payment plans, cash loans and credit cards.

The regular charge account is often used by persons who despise credit and do not realize that they are using it to make a purchase. Prime examples of this type of account are monthly payments for utilities, for professional services (doctors and dentists) or for other services which are paid for *after* the service has been performed. In effect the purchaser is being extended from ten to thirty days of free credit before the payment is due. In most instances there is no charge for credit extended in this manner.

The revolving charge account is usually set up with the manager of the store where the consumer has an account, and the consumer and manager decide upon a mutually agreeable limit such as $150 or $250. With this account the consumer pays part of what he owes along with a credit charge each month. The payment is a function of the outstanding balance. The buyer has the option of paying the bill in its entirety or of paying only a specified portion. As long as he is below the established limit, he can continue to make purchases on the account.

Installment or time-payment plans are usually used to purchase items which are more expensive than a normal revolving charge will allow. These are items such as refrigerators, color TV's, or other large-cost items. With this type of credit the consumer usually pays a down payment and pays the remainder over a specific period of time with specific payments to include the cost of the product plus the credit charges.

Cash loans provide money when a person needs it. Cash loans fall into two categories: installment loans, which stipulate that the borrower pay back the loan over a stated period of time in payments including a credit charge; or single-payment loans which provide that the borrower pay back the entire amount borrowed and a credit charge on a stated date. These loans are usually secured by one's signature only.

Credit cards are a relatively new phenomenon on the consumer credit scene and are a result of the increased mobility of the general population and of the awareness on the part of retailers that this is a means of increasing sales. In the use of credit cards, the consumer is normally given ten to twenty days after he receives his bill to pay with no credit charges. If he does not pay during that period, he is charged a percentage interest on the unpaid balance. Usually the charge on the unpaid balance is 1 1/2 percent per month, which comes to an annual interest rate of 18 percent. However, there are various methods which the retailer can use in figuring interest charges. Two ways are to use the "previous balance" to figure the interest charge or to use the "adjusted balance." If a customer has a balance at the beginning of the month of $100 (previous balance) and pays $90 back during the month, his "adjusted balance" would be $10. Some stores would use the $10 on which to figure interest charges, but others would use the previous balance of $100. Obviously, the amounts charged by using the two methods would differ substantially.

Just as there is a wide range of forms of consumer credit, there is also a wide variety of businesses to which the consumer can go in order to satisfy his credit needs. The three major sources of consumer credit are commercial banks, credit unions, and consumer-finance companies. Other sources of consumer credit include life insurance companies, retail credit cards, and bank credit cards.

All of the sources provide the consumer with a specific service and charge various rates for the extension of that service. Table 5-1 indicates that there is some duplication of the types of loans offered and that the rates which are charged can vary. It is a good idea for the potential borrower to look at the specific characteristics of his loan needs and to select the source of the loan which most adequately meets his needs.

COMMERCIAL BANKS

Prior to 1936, commercial banks had very little to do with consumer credit. With the general expansion of consumer credit from 1950 to 1970, the commercial banking system saw an opportunity for a profitable return on their deposits through advertising and other means of promotion. The commercial banks hold the largest share of consumer credit (See Graph 5-2 and Table 5-1). The banking industry has a very low loss ratio, possibly because of stricter requirements which the borrower must meet and because the majority of their

TABLE 5-1

THE COSTS OF BORROWING

Type of Credit	Lender	Stated Rate	Approximate Annual Percentage Rate
Auto loans	Banks	$5.50 to $7 per 100 per year	9 to 14
Auto finance (installment)	Finance companies	$5.50 to $7 per 100 for new car	17 to 33
Appliances, T.V.	Retail installment contracts, 1-3 yrs.	$10 to $12 per $100 per year	18 to 24 and up
Home modernization loans	Banks, credit unions, savings associations	$5.50 per $100 per year up to $2,500 $4.25 per $100 per year from $2,500 to $5,000	8½ to 11
Personal loans	Banks	$6 to $8 per $100 per year	12 to 18
Loans (auto, personal)	Credit unions	¾ of 1% to 1% per month	9 to 12
Small loans	Small loan companies	1½% to 3½% per month	18 to 42
Revolving credit (up to set limit)	Department store charge accounts	1½% per month	18

consumer loans are in the areas of home improvements and automobiles. Banks usually use the discount method for their loan rates, whereby the charge for the loan is deducted from the amount of the loan (principal) at the time the loan is granted, and the individual repays the loan in equal monthly payments. Usually it is less expensive to borrow from a bank than it is from other sources, but it may also be more difficult to obtain a loan in the first place. However, banks are becoming a much stronger competitor for the consumer's business.

CREDIT UNIONS

The basis for the operation of a credit union is the concept of the common bond which members share. Membership in the same church, town, business, professional group, or some other characteristic they share in common provides the bond. The credit union is interested more than other lending institutions in the character of the borrower and does its best to help any member in need of credit.

To become a member of the credit union, a person is required to deposit savings in the credit union. These savings are called shares and give him voting power in the operation of the credit union. This voting power is equal for all members whether they save thousands of dollars or just the minimum share value. The saving of one share also allows him to borrow from the credit union.

The credit union provides members with several services which may either not be available through other credit sources or are added to the costs of borrowing. The reason that the credit unions are able to provide these additional services is the fact that they are non-profit operations. While slightly lower interest is paid on savings, the credit unions are also able to provide the borrowing members lower interest rates and more services. Credit unions provide loan protection insurance whereby the loan balance will be paid up by insurance if the borrower is disabled or dies. This service is provided free, while it is usually an added cost of borrowing at banks and other lending agencies.

Credit unions will allow unsecured "signature" loans up to $750 and will allow larger amounts if they are secured either by a co-signer or property. Credit unions will also make loans for very small amounts (as low as five dollars) which other lenders will tend to avoid.

The major drawback of credit unions is that it is sometimes difficult for individuals or households to establish themselves as a part of a specific group which has a credit union. As a result, not all individuals have access to the credit union as an alternative choice in their selection of consumer credit.

CONSUMER FINANCE COMPANIES

Consumer finance companies vary in size from nationally known firms with wide distribution of their offices to state and local loan agencies. On the whole, consumer finance companies lend to people from all income and occupational groups. As a result they tend to have higher charges in order to cover the wider investigative procedures and the riskier backgrounds of their borrowers. Most consumer finance companies use a graduated rate system whereby, as the amount of the loan increases, the rate of interest charged decreases. Under this sytem there might be an interest charge of 3 percent per month on the first $150, 1 1/2 percent per month on the amount of the loan from $150 to $300, and 1 percent per month on amounts over $300.[1] It is difficult to generalize as to the rates charged by consumer finance companies because the maximum rates chargeable are regulated by state law. It is a good policy for the borrower who needs to use a finance company to use either a nationally known firm or a local or state firm with a sound reputation for honesty.

LIFE INSURANCE

The use of a permanent life insurance policy as a source of consumer credit is an easy method of obtaining low-cost credit. Loans are taken out against the cash surrender value of the policy. Repayment of the loan is up to the discretion of the policyholder. He may wish to repay the loan or he may just allow the loan to ride until the policy comes due, either upon death of the policyholder or maturity of the policy, when the amount of the loan and the interest charge is deducted from the amount paid to the beneficiary or to the policyholder. The interest rate is generally low, 4 to 6 percent, and the loan is given without regard to the fiscal or physical condition of the borrower. One problem with this type of loan is that it reduces the insurance feature of the policy by the amount of the loan and interest charges.

BANK CREDIT CARDS

Prior to 1966, bank credit cards were relatively unimportant in terms of their usage, whether measured in dollar volume or distribution of the cards per capita. Since the mid-60's the bank credit card has become a major source of consumer credit. The method for usage of bank credit cards is similar to the usage of oil company and department store credit card plans. The holder of the bank credit card uses his card as an identification form and signs the sales slip authorizing the bank to pay the retailer the amount for which the card holder has made purchases. The card holder then receives a bill from the bank which he will normally have 25 days to pay without a service charge. Some bank credit card systems also allow for the extension of 90-day cash loans of amounts up to $500 with no interest charge if the amount is paid back in that period. Major bank card programs are Bank Americard, Interbank Card Association, Midwest Bank Card, and Master Charge.

[1] These rates are the current maximum in the state of Illinois.

RETAIL CREDIT

Retail credit had its beginnings in the form of informal agreements between the manager of the store and his individual customers. As society became more complex and pay periods stabilized on a weekly or monthly basis, the individual firm developed the 30-day charge account. Today retailers across the country have charge plans of their own or else cooperate in charge plans such as the bank credit programs mentioned above. Most of the retail credit plans carry no service charge if the bill is paid in the twenty days after it is received. If the bill is carried over, there is usually a minimum payment and a 1 1/2 percent per month service charge.

CONCLUSIONS

Consumer credit outlets are providing services. The bank, finance company or credit card issuer allows consumers to use the services of money for a specified period of time. For this service, the consumer is expected to pay a price—the interest charge. Consumers must shop for credit in the same way they should shop for other products. It is important to obtain credit for the lowest possible cost, stated in terms of a true annual interest rate. Once the lowest cost source of credit is established, the consumer must decide if the expected satisfaction or well-being to be gained by obtaining the goods or services today will be greater than the satisfaction that could be obtained by postponing consumption until he has saved the funds to pay for the product or service in cash. The question is one of goods today at a higher cost because of the cost of credit or goods in the future at a lower cost. This is a question of individual choice and desires. The intensity of the desire for goods today determines how large an interest charge the consumer will be willing to pay.

SUGGESTED READING

Personal Economics Readings

AFL-CIO, *Fact Sheet: Consumer Protection.* Industrial Union Department, 815 Sixteenth Street NW, Washington, D.C.

Blair, Lorraine L. *Answers to Your Everyday Money Questions.* Chicago: Henry Regnery Co., 1968.

Boston Federal Reserve Bank. *The Impact of Truth-in-Lending Legislation: The Massachusetts Experience,* Research Report #43, Boston, 1968.

Christ, Carl F. *Cash or Credit.* Baltimore Urban League, Family Life Education Series, 1970.

Channing L. Bete Co. *More for Your Money,* Box 112, Greenfield, Massachusetts, 1970.

———, *The ABC's of Credit—How Your Bank Can Help You Achieve Your Financial Goals,* 1969.

Cole, Robert H. *Consumer and Commercial Credit Management.* 3d ed. Homewood, Ill.: Richard D. Irwin, Inc., 1968.

Commerce Clearing House. *Truth-in-Lending: Law and Explanation.* Chicago, 1968.

Continental Illinois National Bank and Trust Co. of Chicago. *Accepting Credit Responsibility.* Chicago, 1970.

C.U.N.A. International, Inc. *Credit Unions—What are They? How They Operate. How to Start One.* Public Relations Department, Box 431, Madison, Wisconsin.

———, *Managing Your Family's Credit.*

———, *Money Management for Children.*

———, *Money Management for Young Couples.*

———, *Student Loans for Your Higher Education.*

———, *The $30 Million Hole in the Sock: Christmas Savings at Banks.*

———, *Truth-in-Lending: What it Means to You.*

———, *Using Credit Wisely.*

Fetterman, Elsie B. *Licensing and Regulating of Debt Adjustors.* Storrs, Connecticut: University of Connecticut Cooperative Extension Service.

———, *The Wage Garnishment Law.* Storrs, Connecticut: University of Connecticut Cooperative Extension Service.

———, *30 Days to Reality.*

Household Finance Corporation. *Mind Your Money—When You Use Credit.* Money Management Institute, Prudential Plaza, Chicago, Illinois.

Johnson, Robert. *Credit and Credit Cards.* San Francisco: San Francisco Federal Reserve Bank, 1969.

Margolius, Sidney. *Family Money Problems.* Public Affairs Committee, 381 Park Avenue South, New York, New York, 1967.

McCracken, Paul W., et al. *Consumer Installment Credit and Public Policy.* Ann Arbor: University of Michigan Bureau of Business Research, 1965.

Moore, Geoffrey H. and Philip A. Klein. *Quality of Consumer Installment Credit.* New York: National Bureau of Economic Research, 1967.

National Foundation for Consumer Credit. *The Consumer and Truth-in-Lending.* 1411 K Street, Washington, D.C., 1969.

———, *The Emergency Problem—What to Do About It,* 1967.

———, *Using Our Credit Intelligently,* 1970.

National Study Service. *Family Credit Counseling: An Emerging Community Service.* New York: Family Service Association of America, 1968.

Philadelphia Federal Reserve Bank. *Truth-in-Lending: What it Means for Consumer Credit.* Philadelphia, 1969.

Public Affairs Committee. *Guide to Consumer Credit.* New York, 1970.

The Economics
of Housing

CHAPTER *VI*

The largest single expense that a consumer faces in his lifetime is the purchase or rental of shelter for himself and his family. All too often the consumer buys a home on the spur of the moment without considering all the available alternatives or his ability to pay for the purchase. The consumer who is rational in most of his expenditures becomes irrational when it comes time to decide upon the purchase of housing or the signing of a long-term lease. The consumer may "fall in love" with a particular home without considering the true costs involved and so become chained to a home that he cannot afford. He may come to regret buying the home. Such irrational decisions are often assisted by over-eager realtors or developers who deliberately understate the price and payments to make the housing seem more attractive and less costly than it really is. Such misstatements chiefly arise from the realtor's neglect to inform the consumer about the size of the tax bill and the likelihood of tax increases, insurance, assessments and other reserves which must be added to the monthly cost of the housing. These extras must be included if the consumer is to know the total cost of his housing.

As a result of limited information, the consumer may be tempted to buy or rent more expensive housing than he can really afford. This may cause a severe strain on his personal resources. Often such purchases so badly misallocate personal resources that they cause a household to neglect other personal needs such as medical care (braces for children's teeth), savings, and recreation. The sophisticated consumer will attempt to achieve his housing goals without overextending his resources.

When considering the purchase or rental of living space, it is important not to act with undue haste. The sophisticated consumer will take his time when considering housing. Care is required because the decision is of such long-lasting importance; rushing may lead to costly errors. He should be aware of the different kinds of housing and the relative costs, advantages and disadvantages of each type. Attempts should be made in advance to avoid restricting himself to a single kind of home or a particular area or style. In other words he must keep all his options open.

In some cases the sophisticated consumer may find the best solution to his housing need in a mobile home or in a rental. For some, the modern townhouse or even the suburban subdivision split-level model best fits his needs. An aware ness of the different forms of housing helps the consumer improve his ability to obtain the housing he needs at a price he can afford. It should be remembered that from an economic point of view there is no "best" form of housing. All housing involves a series of trade-offs; most homes are a series of compromises. Some homes trade quality off against space. Others stress quality construction in lieu of luxury features. Infinite combinations of trade-offs exist.

FORMS OF HOUSING

CONVENTIONAL HOMES

As the name implies, conventional homes are the most common form of shelter. They range from the nondescript bungelow to the fancy brick styles. The conventional home ranges from 1,000 to 2,000 square feet of floor area and has from two to four bedrooms. It is free-standing upon its own lot, with front and side yards. The conventional home has a garage; it may be attached or free-standing. The conventional home ranges in price, depending upon the area and features, from $15,000 to over $40,000.

Although costs may vary from area to area, costs of the conventional home in 1971 ranged from eighteen to twenty-two dollars per square foot of floor area.

The conventional home fits most people's needs. It provides basic shelter and privacy at a reasonable price. It is long-lasting, retains its resale value and is an excellent hedge against inflation. The conventional home is generally financed with a twenty- to thirty-year mortgage agreement.

Two basic versions of the conventional home are observable: (1) the tract or subdivision home built in large numbers at one time by a developer; (2) the conventional home put upon an ordinary lot (not a tract or subdivision).

When two homes are similar in design the subdivision house has many obvious economies of scale which may give it a cost advantage over the same house built in a non-subdivision setting.

The chief complaint about the subdivision is the "sameness" or lack of variety. It is also the same reason for the low cost of such homes. Steps have been taken in recent years in the more innovative subdivisions to give the owner the feeling of more individuality, chiefly through the use of different facades, slightly different floor plans, winding streets, and the liberal use of color.

Whether the consumer chooses to buy a conventional home in an ordinary neighborhood or opts for basically the same home in a subdivision at a lower price is a matter of taste. Some consumers do not mind giving up their individuality when they can save money; others find subdivisions with their sameness and lack of character horrifying. These people are more than willing to pay extra for a home in a non-subdivision setting. The consumer who is concerned only with price is likely to feel that the subdivision is the best buy. This is an example of the multidimensionality of a product—shelter, location, psychological need, etc.

Both the conventional subdivision home and the home of conventional design not located in a subdivision present few problems when being resold. The conventional home is so common and so numerous in all its diverse styles and sizes that for each basic variation there is a ready market. The resale price of the home is largely determined by forces in the market. Thus, potential second buyers of such homes can easily determine if the house in question is over-or underpriced. The seller knows also the approximate price he can obtain from his conventional home because he has so many ready comparisons. Because the conventional house best fits the needs of the average American family, there are at any one time many people who are in the market for such homes. Therefore, there are many advantages of owning a conventional home.

CUSTOM HOMES

After looking at subdivision and conventional homes of all types, the consumer may yearn for that touch of individuality which only the custom home can provide. The buyer may wish to express his own taste, personality and special needs in the design of his own house.

Perhaps this consumer should build a custom home that is truly different. Working with architect and builder, the consumer can develop a truly unique home. A word of caution is in order for those who would build a custom home. Persons with limited finances often underestimate the cost of their unique homes. Consequently many of the features that are the heart of the uniqueness are cut out of the plans in the interest of economy. Such design changes are costly and may result in so many compromises that the home owner may be dissatisfied with the end result. The consumer considering such a unique design ought to make allowances for cost overruns before construction is started and should make sure that financing can be obtained so the house will be in reality what he really desires.

On a per-square-foot basis, it is well to remember the custom home is likely to cost more than the conventional home. This is true because the home is unique. It is more time consuming and wasteful of materials to construct a one-of-a-kind home than conventional residential or subdivision homes. In short all fixed costs must be covered in the one home while these costs are averaged out over many units in the tract home.

SELLING CUSTOM VS. CONVENTIONAL HOMES

The new custom home and the conventional home (whether or not in a subdivision) are usually priced new on a cost-plus basis. The contractor or developer estimates the costs of construction and overhead and then adds on a percentage for profit. The conventional home may be easier to resell than the custom home. The custom home, because of the uniqueness which appealed to the consumer who constructed it, may eliminate large numbers of potential buyers. The old barn converted into a handsome home or a modernistic A-frame may be found wanting for buyers when the original owners wish to resell them.

Potential second buyers of the custom home may also be discouraged from buying the home because of uncertainty over the price and resale. The conventional home does not have this problem because within an area there are likely to be many similar homes which allow the consumer to compare features and prices. In order to induce the sale of the custom home the owner may have to take a large loss.

The custom home has the advantage of being unique and being tailored to fit the special needs and desires of the owners. Its very uniqueness tends to increase its construction and design costs and may cause it to be difficult to sell.

The problem of pricing can be seen in Figure 6-1. The supply for this home is completely inelastic (vertical supply curve), because it is the only house of its type. The price may be high or low depending upon the demand. There is no approximate or going price to assist the consumer in determining if the price of the home is too high or too low.

If the demand for the home is high (for example, a Frank Lloyd Wright design), the price will be high (D_2). On the other hand, if the demand is not high (for example, a converted barn), the price may be low (D_1). In both cases the cost of the home has little to do with the resale price. The custom home may have cost $100,000 to build; but if no one wants to buy it, the seller may be forced to price it at $50,000 before someone becomes interested in buying it. On the other hand, if the house is featured in *Better Homes and Gardens* magazine, it may be in such high demand that it may be sold for $100,000 (D_2).

FIGURE 6-1

Price Determination of a Custom House

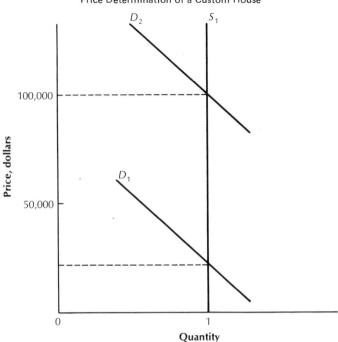

The reason for the sharp swings in price is that the total supply of the house is one; no additional houses are offered for sale. As the demand increases, the price violently swings in response to this change.

The conventional home is numerous in all its styles. The supply curve slopes upward; the greater the price, the more homes that will be offered for sale (see Figure 6-2). The demand for this housing is similar to demand for other products; the lower the price, the greater the quantity demanded. Thus there is a market price for similar homes in a community. For example, in most communities there is a going market price for split-level homes of similar design, style, and features. Should anyone try to sell the home at a price much greater than for similar homes in the community, he would have trouble selling it (Point A). Consumers are able to shop around and compare homes; thus there is some certainty in the buyer's mind as to whether he is paying the market price. If the house is in poorer condition or in much better condition than the average home, the price may be a bit higher or lower. The main point is that there is a definite market for homes of this type. Prices may increase or decrease in response to changing demand and supply, but both the buyer and seller have a good idea at what price the house will and should be sold.

FIGURE 6-2

Price Determination of Conventional Housing

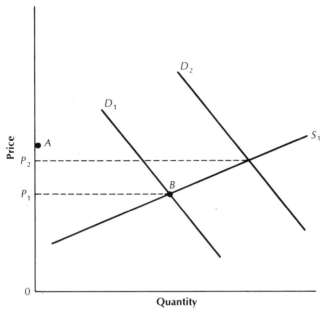

NEW HOUSES VS. OLDER HOUSES

Perhaps the consumer should consider the purchase of an older home as the solution to his housing needs. Unlike the price of the tract home, that of the older home, especially a large one, is highly negotiable. One reason for the negotiable price is that average family size has decreased, and people do not need as much space. Thus fewer buyers are interested in such homes. Older homes may also be out of style, need repairs, or be in declining neighborhoods. The cost per square foot of floor area is much lower in older homes than in new homes. Further, all new house "extras" such as assessments for streets and sidewalks are no longer necessary. Therefore, for some people this form of housing is a good buy, especially if they can do some repair work themselves.

Older homes, on the other hand, because of their age are harder to finance than new homes. Institutions feel that they do not have as much life left as new homes. Older homes are often in need of new plumbing, modern wiring, and insulation, as well as heating plants. Upkeep and maintenance tends to be more costly as well as more frequently needed in older homes.

Offsetting the lower initial cost per square foot of the older home are increased maintenance and modernization expenses. Only the consumer can decide which trade-off to make.

INNOVATIVE PLANNED UNIT DEVELOPMENTS

The ever-increasing cost of conventional homes has fostered the growth of "unconventional" methods of providing housing. Planned unit developments are an example of this trend. They actually combine three trends in American housing. One such trend, caused by high land costs, is toward row houses, which reduce such costs. A second trend is toward cluster planning of developments, wherein large open areas are owned in common. The third trend is the growing market in condominiums, whose owners do not have to do their own snow shoveling and maintenance.

While each of these concepts has been applied in some degree to many developments in the past, the planned unit development incorporates all three. The assumption underlying planned unit developments is that by building town houses (houses with many units in a row) more homes can be built per acre of land. Despite the density of building per acre, more actual open space is provided than in the conventional residential housing developments because open areas are shared.

Economies of large scale construction and denser land usage result in significant cost reductions. Often planned unit developments apply the savings in construction to "extras" such as swimming pools, golf courses, and tennis courts. These can be included in a planned unit development at a cost which is competitive with conventionally designed subdivisions without such facilities.

The developments are supposed to have a feeling of community not unlike that of an old New England village. Homeowners work together to administer the whole complex through an association of owners.

Usually services such as exterior maintenance, snow removal, and yard care are provided for a fee. Yet the owner owns his home and has title to the property. The planned unit development has features of an apartment (no exterior maintenance or yard work for the owner), a house (individual ownership of units), and a country club (pool, golf, and the like).

Single-family homes built in rows in traditional suburban subdivisions may soon be an outdated building concept. It is no longer economically and ecologically practical to build houses arranged in a straight line, perpendicular to the street with fixed setbacks for the front, back and side open spaces. The traditional concept of American housing and the entire residential pattern of living will most likely undergo radical changes.

Changes in home planning, creation of new building systems, and the use of new methods and materials are essential if housing needs are to be met. Land costs, coupled with outdated building codes, are pushing single-family homes out of the reach of a large portion of the potential home-buying market. Over the last fifteen years, the majority of housing units built have been single-family dwellings. A large part of future housing will be multifamily housing—town houses, condominiums and rental apartments.

How does the town house development differ from traditional housing?

FIGURE 6-3

Planned Unit Development

Swimming Pool
Tennis Courts
Club House
Golf

Bicycle Path   Parking for This Cluster

Cluster of Homes

Trees

Main Access Road Goes Around Development not Through Development

Open Area

Units can be designed to provide the maximum green space and interior living area within the price range of the mass market. From five to twelve town houses can be joined together to form irregularly shaped, modular units. The groupings can be clustered around common open areas and parks, with recreational facilities such as swimming pools, tennis courts, playgrounds, and bicycle paths in adjacent open areas. Side streets perpendicular to the main street will provide access to the houses. In addition to minimizing wasted land, the plan can also decrease traffic in front of dwellings.

Examine Figure 6-4 and then consider and figure. Then answer the following questions:

1. At first glance which plan has more units of housing, cluster or grid?
2. Which plan seems to be less crowded?
3. What is the opportunity cost to a buyer of a home built under the cluster system?
4. From a city government standpoint why would you likely be in favor of the cluster system of developments? (Hint: Compare the potential tax base.)

FIGURE 6-4

Cluster Zoning vs. Conventional Development

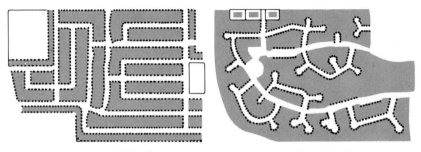

Conventional Development		Cluster Zoning
32	Acres in Streets	24
22,600	Linear Feet of Street	16,055
29	Percent of Site in Street	19
80	Acres in Building Sites	41
500	Dwelling Units	604
0	Acres of Useable Open Space	51

THINK IT OVER:

1. Why are people willing to live in a row or cluster of homes (what economic trade-offs are involved)?
2. What economies are evident by building groups of houses together (as opposed to conventional homes)?
3. If you were a consumer, would you be willing to give up a conventional home for a planned unit development with extras such as a swimming pool or a golf course?

The reader may wish to consider buying into a planned unit development in an area where they are available (large urban areas). The planned unit development appears to be an increasingly attractive alternative to traditional box-like homes. Although appearing somewhat odd to the person who is unfamiliar with them, they are a shelter possibility that should not be rejected without consideration.

MOBILE HOMES: AN ALTERNATIVE FORM OF SHELTER

After considering the alternatives, a person might say that new homes are too expensive to buy; older homes are not modern enough; planned unit developments are too restrictive of personal freedom; and rental units are not desirable because of having a landlord and not being able to count rental payments as an investment.

This person might well find a mobile home suitable to his needs, at least for a few years. If he finds it does meet his needs he can join the ranks of 30 percent of all new homeowners in 1970.

In the $15,000-and-under price range, in which housing needs are the most pressing, mobile homes accounted for over 90 percent of all new home starts in 1970.

Mobile homes have evolved considerably in the past twenty years, from crude trailers to relatively spacious modern housing. The name "mobile home" is really a misnomer; they are not really highly mobile as the name suggests. They are more like houses which can be moved with specialized equipment to a site. Most mobile homes are not moved after they are settled on a lot.

Mobile homes are quite large, with some being up to twelve feet wide and up to seventy feet long. The most common size is the 12' X 60' model.

Mobile home construction techniques differ from techniques used with other forms of houses. They are built on a mass-production basis on an assembly line. From start to finish the assembly takes less than 8 hours.

Therefore skilled craftsmen are not required, and this lowers the wage costs and achieves economies of large-scale production that not even a subdivision can match. Further, because of the method of construction, much waste of material is eliminated, which would be inevitable in conventional homes. Mobile homes do not have to follow local building codes, and innovative techniques and materials can be used which are often not allowed in conventional construction (plastic pipe, for example). Because of efficient use of materials, fabrication techniques, and low-cost labor, the mobile home can be built at a far lower cost on a per-square-foot basis than conventional homes. Although comparison is difficult for many reasons, new homes today cost between eighteen to twenty-two dollars per square foot of interior space while mobile homes cost from four to eight dollars per square foot.

Not taken into consideration in the comparison is the fact that mobile homes generally come completely equipped with new appliances, which are included in the price, and that some even have furniture included. The trend in recent years in conventional homes has been to exclude appliances from the price of homes.

Thus, on a cash-out-of-pocket basis, mobile homes are only about one-third as costly as conventional housing. Of course such comparisons do not include all factors. The mobile home will last from ten to fifteen years, the conventional house about fifty. On the other hand, the mobile home comes with appliances and the conventional home does not. The conventional home price includes the cost of land while mobile homes usually require the monthly rental of space. For these reasons and others, comparisons of cost are difficult but estimates have been made.

For sake of illustration it is instructive to compare costs of mobile and conventional homes over a period of time. When the *New England Economic Review* compared the costs, their figures showed that on a month-by-month basis the mobile home is considerably less expensive for similar living space, even when the land rental (trailer park) is included, than conventional homes.

Examine Table 6-1 and compare the costs for the mobile home to those of the conventional home. The conventional home costs are estimated for two cases, under a thirty-year FHA mortgage and a thirty-year conventional mortgage.

TABLE 6-1

COSTS OF A MOBILE HOME COMPARED
TO A CONVENTIONAL HOME

	$8,000 Mobile Home	*$24,000 House*	
FINANCING TERMS			
type of loan	consumer installment loan	FHA mortgage	conventional mortgage
maturity	7 years	30 years	30 years
interest rate	12%	8½%	8%
down payment	$1,200	$2,400	$6,000
MONTHLY COSTS			
loan repayment and interest	$ 84.74 ⎫ $120.74	$165.32	$132.08
park rent*	36.00 ⎭	—	—
taxes*	9.20	50.00	50.00
maintenance*	3.00	15.00	15.00
heating and utilities*	30.00	50.00	50.00
insurance*	5.00	10.00	10.00
	$167.94	$290.32	$257.08
income tax savings *(20% marginal tax rate)*	−8.79	−42.20	−35.73
net cost	$159.15	$248.12	$221.35

*Estimated.
Source: *New England Economic Review,* May-June 1970, published by the Federal Reserve Bank of Boston.

If the implicit cost of lost interest on invested capital is computed, the differential between the mobile home and the conventional home becomes pronounced. The reader will recall that lost interest on invested capital is the interest which could have been earned on money if left in the bank instead of being invested in a down payment which pays no interest.

The lost interest on invested capital is computed on the basis of 6 percent per year (.5 percent per month).

LOST INTEREST ON INVESTED CAPITAL

	Mobile Home	Conventional Home	
		FHA Loan	*Conv. Loan*
	$1,200	$2,400	$6,000
Interest rate per month	.5%	.5%	.5%
Lost interest on invested capital per month	$ 6.00	$12.00	$30.00

Lost interest on invested capital is an added cost because it is money that would have been earned if it had not been invested in a house; therefore, it should be added into the cost of home or mobile home ownership.

COST COMPARISON FIGURES FROM TABLE 6-1

	Mobile Home	30 Year FHA Mortgage Conventional Home	30 Year Conv. Mort. Conventional Home
Net monthly cost	$159.15	$248.12	$221.35
Plus lost interest	6.00	12.00	30.00
Total monthly cost	$165.15	$260.12	$251.35
Years required to pay off mortgage (loan):	8 years	30 years	30 years

At least for a short period of time the mobile home is less costly to own than a conventional house. The longer the period of comparison, the smaller the difference becomes. One reason is that the mobile home does not last as long as a conventional home. After fifteen years the mobile home is almost worthless (they depreciate like a car), but the conventional home will last at least fifty years and may appreciate in value.

If the conventional home is owned long enough, at least part of the money invested will be recovered when sold. The house, if maintained, is an asset which will appreciate and act as a hedge against inflation. But to calculate the true profit, improvements which have been made should be deducted from the selling price.

As a general rule the owner's equity does not become significant for several years because most of the payment goes into interest, taxes, and insurance. Homes must be owned about five years before the owner can expect to break even when the house is sold. If selling the home requires a broker's services, the homeowner can expect to pay a fee of 6½ percent of the gross selling price. Thus a $20,000 home, if sold, would require a fee of $1,300. The equity of a home purchased and held for five years builds up to about $1,500 during this period of time assuming a six-percent mortgage rate. This house, if owned for five years and then sold, would only yield $200–$1,500 equity minus $1,300 fee. If the house were owned longer, the amount of equity the consumer had built up would increase.

If the mobile home were owned for a five-year period of time. selling it could yield enough money to pay off the balance of the eight-year loan. In other words, the consumer would have broken even on the mobile home while making a $200 profit on the house. However, the monthly out-of-pocket expenses would have been less for a mobile home.

These examples assume no inflation or general appreciation of housing, clearly a questionable assumption in the 1970's. Despite this, it should be clear that conventional houses are expensive to own for short periods of time. The shorter the period, the greater the cost. After five years the built-up equity is usually great enough to pay the selling costs and return some small part of the investment to the seller. The mobile home, on the other hand, becomes increasingly expensive to own for longer than five years because it depreciates to zero value.

In short, if one moves often, from an economic standpoint the mobile home makes more sense than a house. On the other hand if the consumer plans to live in one place for an extended period of time, a house seems to make better sense than a mobile home. Because of frequent moves and the high cost of conventional homes, mobile homes are becoming increasingly popular.

RENTING AS A HOUSING ALTERNATIVE

Up to this point only buying homes or mobile homes has been considered. This has been done because most people aspire to own their own home. It has not been an uncommon attitude, at least in the Midwest and West, for people to feel that renters were people who just did not seem to be able to manage their money. The lack of home ownership was considered proof of this feeling. However, this traditional attitude has been changing in recent years. Many people, through choice or necessity, rent apartments or houses. These rentals range from miserable shacks to luxurious penthouses of great prestige.

Why do people rent? The initial cost of renting compared to buying is very low. Renters have much greater freedom of mobility than home owners. A young person who is likely to be promoted can move with ease. An adjustment of living quarters with changes in income and family size is much easier with rentals. The individual is usually also free from chores connected with home ownership, such as mowing the lawn and painting. Free time can be devoted to other uses such as recreation.

The cost of renting is largely determined by what type of housing the consumer wants. Basic apartments with no frills are, of course, less costly than fancy, high-status addresses such as the John Hancock Building in Chicago. In most areas good quality, low-cost rentals are very hard to find. There is less of a shortage of middle-cost rentals and often a surplus of high-cost rental apartments or houses.

The reason for a surplus in one market and a shortage in another is that fancy apartments are not substantially higher in cost to build than basic apartments. Apartments cost between $10,000 to $20,000 per unit to build, depending upon the region. This figure is for well-built, two-and-three bedroom units. This cost is for the basic structure; the only thing needed to make such an apartment a high-priced luxury rental is to add wall-to-wall carpets, fancy appliances, cable television and more landscaping. Compared to the basic cost of the structure, such extras do not add a great deal to the cost. Accordingly, landlords attempt to build for the middle- and luxury-rental market to obtain the greatest rents without a commensurate increase in building costs. The reason for the shortage of sound, low-priced apartments is that they do not provide as large a return on investments. Recent federal legislation has allowed for changes in depreciation rules in an attempt to increase the supply of low-income housing.

METHODS OF RENTING

The month-to-month basis is the simplest method of renting an apartment. Every thirty days the rent is paid in advance; this automatically renews the tenant's right to live in the apartment for the month. The landlord or the tenant may terminate the month-to-month relationship on thirty day's notice in writing. The tenant can be asked to leave or have the rent raised if given a proper thirty-day notice.

The main advantage of the month-to-month form of renting is that the tenant can move as soon as he wishes, providing that he has given thirty day's notice. Thus if a consumer is renting while looking for a better apartment or a home to buy, he can move as soon as he finds what he wants. On the other hand, the landlord can ask him to move on short notice. Many a month-to-month renter has found that suddenly his rent is raised or that he must find new quarters on short notice. The month-to-month basis provides both landlord and tenant great flexibility, but both parties have greater uncertainty.

The other common rental arrangement is a lease. A lease is simply a binding contract between two parties, the landlord and tenant. It specifies the terms, rights, and obligations of both parties. The lease has a specified length of life, usually one year. If either party violates the terms of the agreement, the offending party may be taken into the courts to enforce the provisions of the lease.

RIGHTS AND RESPONSIBILITIES OF LANDLORD AND TENANT

The tenant is responsible for paying the rent on time and as specified. The tenant is also responsible for keeping the apartment in good order and is responsible for any major damage except normal wear and tear. The tenant has the right to peace and freedom from harrassment by the landlord. The landlord does not have the right to come into the apartment whenever he desires; he must arrange this in advance with the tenant. The tenant also must be given proper notice if he is to be evicted or is to have his rent increased.

The main advantage of the lease to both landlord and tenant is that each party can make their plans for specific lengths of time. If the lease is a one-year agreement, the landlord does not have to worry about vacancies for the period of the lease. By the same token, the tenant does not have to worry about having to move on short notice or about having his rent suddenly increased.

Most leases are drawn up using standard printed forms. However, the lease, being a contract between two parties, can be amended or altered to fit the specific needs of both parties. The tenant would be wise to take the lease to his attorney for advice and possible alterations before signing it. Once the lease has been signed it is too late to alter it.

Leases containing the following provisions are the greatest source of tenant abuse by landlords:

1. *Waiver of Tort Liability.* This is simply a provision in some leases which means that the tenant gives up his right in advance to sue the landlord if he suffers damages or injury caused by the landlord's negligence.
2. *Confession of Judgment.* This provision means that the landlord's attorney has the right to go into court and can admit or plead guilty for the tenant in the event the landlord feels he has damaged his property or in some other way has violated the terms of the lease. In effect, the tenant admits guilt before he commits any act.

Provisions of this nature should be removed before the lease agreement is signed. The consumer ought to consult with an attorney before signing a lease to insure that such provisions are not included.

DETERMINATION OF RENT

Basic market forces of supply and demand determine rent. Consider this case. Most of the apartments in town are rented, and landlords desire to preserve a normal rate of return. If taxes are increased, the landlords will be in a position to pass most of their increases on to the tenants. The reason landlords can do this is that, in the absence of a large number of empty rental units, costs in an area will tend to increase for all landlords. When all landlords attempt to preserve their profit, all rents will increase and tenants will have little choice but to pay the increase. (See Figure 6-5)

Impact of taxes on rentals where demand for apartments is great may be described as follows:

1. Rentals in an area have a rent of R_1 resulting from $S_1 D_1$ equilibrium point A.
2. The landlords' costs increase from A to B amount because of the tax increase.
3. A new supply curve exists (landlords will now supply the housing only at a higher price).

FIGURE 6-5

Impact of Tax Increase on Rent in an Area of High Occupancy Rates

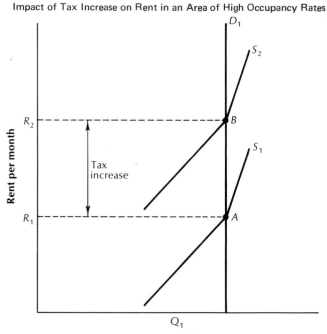

Quantity of apartments rented

4. Because of the interaction of S_2 and D_1, equilibrium level B price R_2 will now be charged.
5. The increased cost due to the tax increase (A to B) has now fully shifted to the consumer in the form of higher rent.

Note that demand in the short run is assumed to be inelastic. If demand for housing is assumed to be elastic, then a portion of the tax increase must be absorbed by landlords in the short run.

If there is a severe imbalance between supply and demand for apartments in an area, the results may be different. Assume that you are the owner of a West Coast apartment house. Because of high unemployment in the area around the aerospace industries, apartment vacancies are about 35 percent. Because of the large number of vacancies, landlords will be competing for tenants. If any landlord tries to increase his rent, his tenants will likely move into easily obtainable vacant rental units in the area. Thus the landlord is restrained from increasing his rents even if his costs increase. Suppose that the city increases the property tax by quite a large amount. Can the landlord pass this increase along to his tenants? (See Figure 6-6.)

FIGURE 6-6

Impact of Tax Increase on Rent in an Area of Low Occupancy Rates

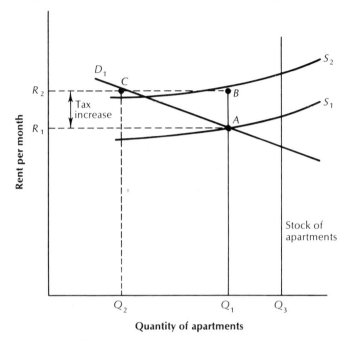

Quantity of apartments

1. This is an area with a high vacancy rate; accordingly the demand for any particular apartment house may be assumed to be highly price elastic.
2. The stock of apartments in the short run is fixed at Q_3.
3. The price of the apartments $D_1 S_1$ equilibrium level A results in rent R_1.
4. If increased taxes increase the cost of renting to point B, the landlord would like to cover at least this cost with an equal increase in rent.
5. However, if the landlord attempts to raise the rent to R_2 to cover the increased costs, he will rent fewer apartments (Q_2) than before.
6. Rather than have his tenants leave, at least in the short run, he will continue to rent at price R_1, and absorb the increased cost due to the tax himself.

The graph thus shows that the landlord will not be able to pass the increased tax along to his tenants. To do so will cause him to lose more money (because the tenants will move) than if he simply absorbs the increased cost himself. In such cases the landlord will continue to rent, even if it means losses because he knows that to increase the rent will result in greater losses.

Should the landlord have to rent at a loss for too long a time, however, he will be forced to sell the building or go bankrupt. He can absorb losses in the short run but not for extended periods of time. If bankruptcies become common, the supply of apartments available for rent is reduced, which will tend to increase rents since the supply of apartments has declined but the demand remains constant. In the long run oversupply and exceptionally low rents will become corrected. (See Figure 6-7.)

1. The price of rentals is high (P_1). The rental price is determined by the interaction of $S_1 D_1$ equilibrium point A.
2. Because of unemployment, the number of people wishing to rent declines. (They move out of the area.) There are fewer people wishing to rent at each price; thus the new demand curve (D_2).
3. Because of the interaction of supply (S_1) and demand (D_2), the price of rent declines to P_2 (equilibrium point B).
4. Assuming the break-even cost of rentals to the landlord is at point D, it can be seen that the new equilibrium rent is *below* the cost of the apartments to the landlord. The landlord is now losing money.
5. After a period of time, many landlords are unable to continue to absorb losses (renting below cost) and will abandon their property or go bank-

FIGURE 6-7

Market Adjustment to a Decline in Housing Demand

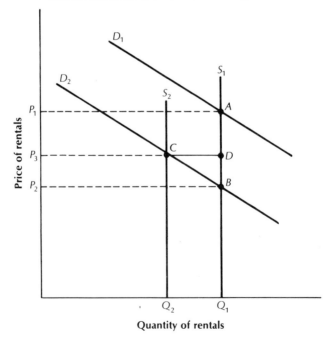

FIGURE 6-8

Increase in Demand for Housing

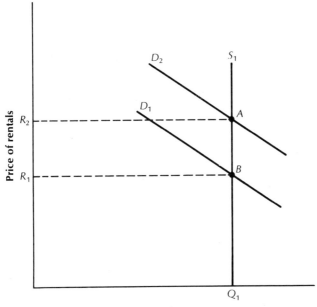

Quantity of apartments

rupt. Therefore, the supply of apartments shrinks. A new supply curve is established (S_2).

6. Because there are fewer apartments being offered for rent with demand unchanged (D_2), the rent increases to P_3, equilibrium point C. The rents and quantity of apartments will stabilize at this level.

Another condition will prevail if there is a severe shortage of apartments relative to the number of people who desire them. (See Figure 6-8.) Such a condition may come about when a new industry opens up in a town or when students are allowed to move off-campus. Many people will move to the town to take advantage of the new jobs. The existing supply of rental units will not increase rapidly, and with a high demand for apartments, renters will bid up rental rates even if costs remain stable. The rents will continue to increase until the number of people willing to pay high rents is balanced with the existing supply of apartments. Those unable to pay high rents will have to move from the town or take apartments of lower quality than they would have previously been willing to rent. As the rents are driven up, profits for landlords increase. As the profits increase, more people will be willing to build new apartments as well as to convert existing residential structures into apartments. Gradually the supply of apartments increases, thus choking off further rent increases.

FIGURE 6-9

Market Adjustment to Increase in Supply of Housing

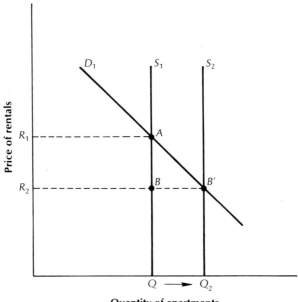

Quantity of apartments

Should construction continue, the area might even become *oversupplied* with housing; this would cause rents to decline and profits to fall. As profits begin to fall construction will cease, thus serving to stabilize the rent. (See Figure 6-8.)

1. Rents in town are at R_1 (D_1S_1 equilibrium B).
2. New industry moves to town, attracting many new workers to the city. People are now willing to pay more for an apartment. This results in a new demand curve (D_2).
3. With the interaction between S_1 and D_2, a new level of rents becomes established at R_2.

The rental market tends to go through cycles of high rents (shortage of apartments), followed by a building boom of apartments, followed by excessive vacancies (excess supply) and stable or declining rents, with little new construction. (See Figure 6-9).

The following then occurs:

1. With a shortage of apartments in the community, the price of rentals are in excess of the landlords' costs (cost is at B while profit can be seen between points B and A).

2. Since profits are being made, more apartments will be built. The supply expands and there are more apartments available at all prices (S_2).
3. Given the same level of demand, the price falls (rent R_2). If costs remain at the same level as before B, profits will disappear.
4. With no profits no more apartments will be built, and the rent will stabilize.

The periods of excess demand and supply may be of relatively long duration. If excess demand develops, it requires several years to build sufficient dwelling units. During that period rents will be above the normal level. On the other hand, excess supply may persist for an even longer period since the housing units may have a useful life of fifty years or more.

BUYING A HOUSE

Suppose a consumer wishes to buy a home or a condominium unit. How does he go about this task? Naturally the first step is to locate a home to buy. Such a task generally includes many hours of "house-hunting." The consumer should consider various factors such as price, quality, extra features, and subjective items such as styling, landscaping, and location. Once the buyer has shopped for a home for a time, he will develop a "feel" for the market. He will have a good idea of what he wants, the going price for various types of homes, and what he can afford.

Once the choice is narrowed down to a particular home, the actual buying procedure can be initiated. In order to insure peace of mind many homeowners, before going further, will hire an appraisal firm or perhaps a realtor from a firm not connected with the proposed transaction. Such an outside appraiser is an expert and can give the consumer valuable advice concerning the market price of the home and any possible defects in the structure. Such an appraisal is not costly and can help the consumer avoid costly errors. Further such advice will do much to ease the consumer's nagging doubts as to whether he is getting a good deal or not. Many buyers will find the service worth the cost. Armed with the appraiser's advice as to the condition and value of the house, the consumer can begin to negotiate for the house in earnest.

NEW HOUSING DEVELOPMENT

If the house is in a new development, the price is not usually negotiable. The results of an appraisal should help a buyer determine if the developer is asking a reasonable price. If he is not, the buyer has two options: (1) he can pay too much but get the house he wants, or (2) he can look elsewhere for a more reasonable price on a similar house.

USED HOMES

The task of buying is not as easy with a used home. While most houses generally have an established market price determined by supply and demand factors, the asking price is usually well above that level. The seller, in determining the asking price, will generally set the initial price above that which he knows is the typical for such a house in that area. He does this for two reasons. First, he hopes that someone will be foolish enough, or will want the house badly enough, to pay a premium for his house and increase his profit. Second, if such a naive buyer is not found, the seller knows that he can make price adjustments when confronted by a serious buyer. This makes the buyer feel that he is getting a good buy because the price has been lowered.

A buyer generally knows that a previously owned home has a negotiable price, and he will offer to the seller a price that is below the existing market. He has two reasons for this. First, he hopes that the seller is anxious for a quick sale and will accept the lower-than-market offer, thus saving him money. Second, the buyer has a strong bargaining position; he can gradually improve his offers. Such negotiations take nerve and are much like a poker game. Both buyer and seller are attempting to get the best possible price. Such a process may take several weeks with offers and rejections and counter-offers being made by both parties. With each offer or counter-offer the terms are adjusted. The end result of this "horse-trading" is the settlement on a price which the seller may consider too low and the buyer may consider too high. Usually the price settled upon is close to the market price for similar homes in the area. A person who must sell quickly or buy quickly will not usually get the best price.

How is the "horse-trading" done? This is accomplished with a formal written offer to buy. The potential buyer expresses interest in the home to a realtor if the home has been listed with a realtor. The realtor writes down the particulars of the offer the buyer is making (terms, price, down payment, and special conditions which the buyer stipulates). This document is signed by the potential buyer and is accompanied with a small deposit, usually 1 percent of the purchase price. This is called an earnest money deposit, and it is a sign of good faith to show that the offer to buy is serious.

Should the seller accept the offer but the prospective buyer does not make good on it, the buyer forfeits the deposit or earnest money. The earnest money keeps "Sunday" shoppers from bothering the seller with insincere offers which they do not intend to honor. Should a purchase offer be rejected by the seller, the prospective buyer is entitled to a refund of his deposit. When the seller decides to sell, he signs this document, indicating that he has accepted the formal offer. The transaction is then processed.

CLOSING THE TRANSACTION

Closing the "deal" involves a process whereby the title is transferred, money is passed from the buyer to the seller, city property records are changed, and settlement of property taxes and insurance premiums is made. Normally the closing is done by an impartial third party, representing neither seller nor buyer. Thus equal and fair treatment of both parties is insured. An important aspect of "closing" is the issuance of a title insurance policy. A title insurance company is employed to examine the records to insure that the title (the document representing ownership) is valid and that there are no outstanding claims against the title. Such a claim against the title might be caused for many reasons, such as the nonpayment of taxes or the use of the property as collateral against unpaid debts. If there were a lien against the property, the buyer would be responsible for someone else's debts.

If the title insurance company is satisfied that the title is "clear" and that it is free of any legal defects, the company will issue the buyer (via the closing agent) a title insurance policy. If the title to the property is ever questioned in court, the insurance will protect the investment to the limit of the policy. The closing agent transfers all records and legal documents to the buyer. The seller is given the proceeds, and the title is turned over to the buyer. The buyer now has purchased the property.

Many buyers forget that the "closing" process is not included in the price of the house. Thus the agent who is closing the "deal" must be paid, as well as the title insurance company. For example, a closing fee of $500 is not uncommon on a $20,000 house. The fee is due the day the deal is closed. Usually the closing costs are split between the buyer and seller, each paying 50 percent. The buyer should be sure he has the money to pay for these fees. Many consumers scrape together all the money they can for a down payment, not knowing that additional fees must be paid. When confronted with the demand for these fees, they must go to a finance company or friends and relatives to borrow money before they can take possession of the home. The wise consumer sets aside a little extra money for such expenses. Generally the realtor does not mention these fees because he is afraid that the extra expense might cause him to lose a potential sale.

By the same token, if the consumer is going to sell his house, he should remember that selling is not free. Realtors charge from 5 to 6 percent of the selling price of the home as their fee. Thus, a 6 percent commission which must be paid the agent on a $30,000 home is $1,800. The agent justifies these fees on the grounds that he has high costs, such as advertising and office help. Some consumers attempt to sell their own homes to save the broker's fee for themselves. Most people find that they do not have the knowledge, salesmanship, or contacts to successfully sell them. Ultimately, most people employ a broker to sell their homes. The fee is, however, tax deductible.

FINANCING A HOME

To finance the purchase of a home a consumer has three options. They are:

1. To obtain a new mortgage
2. To take over an existing mortgage
3. To buy on a contract

For most people, paying cash is out of the question. More realistically the consumer will have to arrange some form of long-term financing. The consumer who is buying a home can arrange for a mortgage from a bank, savings and loan, or insurance company.

Obtaining a mortgage is similar to obtaining long-term financing as practiced by corporations. The consumer, through financial institutions, is borrowing funds from savers. The interest rate that the consumer must pay is largely determined by the state of the economy and the demand for loans. When government and business are borrowing heavily, there may be a shortage of loanable funds. The consumer will have to pay a high interest rate to obtain the funds. In a sense the consumer is competing with all other borrowers. If money is "tight," the consumer may not be able to obtain the funds at all. A bank will not likely lend funds to the consumer for twenty-five years at 8 percent if it can lend the funds to General Motors at 12 percent. Thus the financial markets will have some bearing on the consumer's ability to finance a home. This is one reason why the construction and sale of new homes usually drops when the rest of the economy is booming. During such a period demands for money from business are great. During a recession there is a smaller amount of corporation borrowing; as a result home mortgages are easier to obtain.

Aside from conditions in the money markets, a lending institution will consider the consumer's credit rating, income, and perhaps his health and job. The institution wants to be assured of repayment. If the consumer is considered a good risk and money is available, he will get the mortgage.

The most common forms of mortgages are the twenty-, twenty-five-, and thirty-year types. The shorter the term, generally the lower the interest rate which the consumer will be charged. With a short mortgage, however, payments are large. On the other hand, the longer the payment period the larger the total dollar amount which will be paid over the life of the loan.

TABLE 6-2

MONTHLY PAYMENTS AND TOTAL INTEREST COST TO BUY A $20,000 HOME, BY SIZE OF DOWNPAYMENT, RATE OF INTEREST, AND LENGTH OF MORTGAGE TERM

Down payment	Amount borrowed	Monthly Payments				Total Interest			
		15 yrs.	20 yrs.	25 yrs.	30 yrs.	15 yrs.	20 yrs.	25 yrs.	30 yrs.
Dol.	Dol.	Dol.	Dol.	Dol.	Dol.	Dol.	Dol.	Dol.	Dol.
					7½ percent interest				
0	20,000	186	161	148	140	13,340	18,650	24,330	30,190
500	19,500	181	157	144	136	13,010	18,180	23,720	29,430
1,000	19,000	176	153	140	133	12,670	17,710	23,120	28,680
2,000	18,000	167	145	133	126	12,010	16,780	21,900	27,170
3,000	17,000	158	137	126	119	11,340	15,850	20,680	25,660
4,000	16,000	148	129	118	112	10,670	14,920	19,470	24,150
5,000	15,000	139	121	111	105	10,000	13,980	18,250	22,640
6,000	14,000	130	113	103	98	9,340	13,050	17,030	21,130
8,000	12,000	111	97	89	84	8,000	11,190	14,600	18,110
10,000	10,000	93	81	74	70	6,670	9,320	12,170	15,090
					8 percent interest				
0	20,000	191	167	154	147	14,390	20,110	26,280	32,780
500	19,500	186	163	151	143	14,030	19,610	25,630	31,960
1,000	19,000	182	159	147	139	13,670	19,110	24,970	31,140
2,000	18,000	172	151	139	132	12,950	18,100	23,650	29,500
3,000	17,000	163	142	131	125	12,230	17,090	22,340	27,860
4,000	16,000	153	134	124	117	11,520	16,090	21,030	26,220
5,000	15,000	143	126	116	110	10,800	15,080	19,710	24,580
6,000	14,000	134	117	108	103	10,080	14,080	18,400	22,940
8,000	12,000	115	100	93	88	8,640	12,070	15,770	19,670
10,000	10,000	96	84	77	73	7,200	10,060	13,140	16,390
					8½ percent interest				
0	20,000	197	174	161	154	15,440	21,640	28,200	35,340
500	19,500	192	169	157	150	15,050	21,100	27,500	34,460
1,000	19,000	187	165	153	146	14,670	20,560	26,790	33,570
2,000	18,000	177	156	145	138	13,900	19,480	25,380	31,810
3,000	17,000	167	148	137	131	13,120	18,400	23,970	30,040
4,000	16,000	158	139	129	123	12,350	17,310	22,560	28,270
5,000	15,000	148	130	121	115	11,580	16,230	21,150	26,500
6,000	14,000	138	122	113	108	10,810	15,150	19,740	24,740
8,000	12,000	118	104	97	92	9,260	12,990	16,920	21,200
10,000	10,000	98	87	81	77	7,720	10,820	14,100	17,670
					9 percent interest				
0	20,000	203	180	168	161	16,490	23,160	30,220	37,820
500	19,500	198	176	164	157	16,070	22,580	29,460	36,880
1,000	19,000	193	171	160	153	15,660	22,000	28,710	35,930
2,000	18,000	183	162	151	145	14,840	20,850	27,200	34,040
3,000	17,000	173	153	143	137	14,010	19,690	25,690	32,150
4,000	16,000	162	144	134	129	13,190	18,530	24,180	30,260
5,000	15,000	152	135	126	121	12,360	17,370	22,670	28,370
6,000	14,000	142	126	118	113	11,540	16,210	21,150	26,480
8,000	12,000	122	108	101	97	9,890	13,900	18,130	22,690
10,000	10,000	102	90	84	80	8,240	11,580	15,110	18,910
					9½ percent interest				
0	20,000	209	187	175	168	17,560	24,660	32,370	40,490
500	19,500	204	182	170	164	17,120	24,040	31,560	39,480
1,000	19,000	199	177	166	160	16,680	23,430	30,750	38,470
2,000	18,000	188	168	157	151	15,800	22,190	29,130	36,440
3,000	17,000	178	159	149	143	14,920	20,960	27,510	34,420
4,000	16,000	167	149	140	135	14,050	19,730	25,890	32,390
5,000	15,000	157	140	131	126	13,170	18,500	24,270	30,370
6,000	14,000	146	131	122	118	12,290	17,260	22,660	28,340
8,000	12,000	125	112	105	101	10,540	14,800	19,420	24,300
10,000	10,000	104	93	87	84	8,780	12,330	16,180	20,250

Source: *Family Economics Review, 1969*, U.S. Department of Agriculture, September, p. 15.

The total amount of money paid will increase dramatically as the repayment period is extended. For example, at an interest rate of 7 percent a $20,000 house will require a total payment of $33,340 over the life of a fifteen-year mortgage. If the mortgage for the same house were a thirty-year 7 percent loan, the total amount of money required over the life of the loan is $50,190. A tabulation of monthly payments and interest charges is included for your future use.

A home buyer must decide between alternative sources of mortgage credit. The most common sources are savings and loan associations, mortgage companies, and commercial banks. The savings and loan and mortgage companies specialize in providing housing credit for both single-family and multiple-family units. Federal regulations limit the extent of commercial bank participation in this market as the result of a concern for bank liquidity. As a general rule, banks cannot loan as high a percentage of the market price of the house as savings and loans and must also loan for a shorter period of time—usually twenty years.

The Veteran's Administration and the Federal Housing Administration are vehicles for implementing our national policy of home ownership. Their role is of major importance in assuring the availability of loan funds for low-income or high-credit risk families. The availability of funds is assured in two major ways: (1) by insuring the private lender against loss of principal should the borrower default and (2) by standing ready to be a lender of last resort if funds are unavailable in the market. These services are provided for a fee of 1 percent per year of the outstanding mortgage. That is, a borrower pays a premium of 1 percent more than the going mortgage rate in order to assure that he can borrow the funds. This fee also assures the lender of no loss of principal.

THINK IT OVER:

1. Many people give such advise as "put as much down on a house as you can," and "pay off your house as soon as possible." What is the advantage of a short repayment period compared to a long mortgage? What is the advantage of a large down payment?
2. What are the disadvantages of each of the preceding suggestions (prepayment, short-mortgage period, large down payment)?
3. Many economists suggest that it might be a wise consumer who takes as long as possible to pay off the mortgage and who makes no prepayments and obtains a mortgage with as small a down payment as possible. Why might an economist take this position?
4. If you are living in a period of inflation, should you pay a loan off as soon as possible or take as long as possible to pay?

Assumption of Existing Mortgage.   Another option open to the consumer considering financing a home is assuming an existing mortgage. This can be done only if there is an existing mortgage on the property he wishes to buy.

Suppose the buyer wants to buy a $25,000 home which is only four years old. The balance of the mortgage is $21,000. To assume the mortgage, assuming the lender approves, the buyer simply assumes the liability for the mortgage and takes over the payments. The seller will agree to this if the down payment is large enough to cover the "spread" between the amount he owes and the selling price. To assume the mortgage in this example would require that the buyer make a $4,000 cash down payment to the seller directly.

There are several advantages to this procedure. Since the house has an existing mortgage, which in this example is four years old, the interest rate may be lower than the current rate. Second, the consumer's credit worthiness is not closely examined by the lending institution. People unable to obtain a mortgage on their own because of income, health, or credit rating can thus obtain one indirectly.

The chief drawback of assuming a mortgage is that it requires a larger cash down payment than a new mortgage. The older the home the greater the down payment, since the mortgage balance becomes smaller as more payments are made.

Financing a Home on a Contract. Suppose the buyer wishes to buy a pre-owned home but for some reason cannot get a mortgage. This buyer is also blocked from assuming an existing mortgage because he does not have the large cash down payment required. Must the consumer give up the idea of owning a home?

There is one last alternative method of financing a home which may be open to this consumer. He may wish to consider the purchase of a home on a contract. In a contract sale, the seller loans the buyer the money to purchase the home. He loans the buyer the money, not in cash, but by accepting a low down payment, a payment not great enough to cover the "spread" between his mortgage balance and the selling price. In exchange for the loan the consumer agrees to make payments directly to the seller, including interest, taxes, and insurance. Ordinarily the interest the seller will charge the consumer is higher than the current rate. If the going mortgage interest rate on a 30-year mortgage is 6 percent, the contract seller may require the buyer to pay between 8 and 10 percent.

Most contract sellers are not crooks but are rather compensating themselves for assuming a high degree of risk, as evidenced by the financial institution's unwillingness to grant a mortgage to the contract buyer. Further the seller is compensating himself for not obtaining the proceeds of the sale in cash but rather in collecting it over a period of years. The seller's money is "tied up" and he must be compensated for this. The seller is in a position to make a high-risk loan, and unless compensated for the risk, he will not be willing to sell on a contract.

After several years the contract is fulfilled, and the seller has obtained his money. The buyer has two options. He may now be able to obtain a mortgage from a bank, or he may take over the seller's mortgage payments by assuming his mortgage. In effect the contract sale is usually used to finance the down payment; once that amount is paid, the conventional mortgage is used.

Such a form of real estate sale is similar to a privately placed loan that corporations often obtain. The lender and the borrower bypass normal financial institutions. Such a privately placed loan may be advantageous to both parties. The lender may obtain a higher interest rate than the current bank rate, and the borrower who is unable to meet the strict loan requirements of lending institutions can obtain financing. Financing is possible for those who could not otherwise obtain it, and both parties gain from the relationship. The contract is a method in which people who are unable to obtain financing any other way can buy a home.

The reader should note however that there are dangers for the contract buyer. The dangers lie in the use of standard provisions contained in some contracts. Some of these are:

1. If one payment is missed or even if it is one day late, the seller can legally demand immediate payment in full of the entire contract. The buyer, unable to meet this requirement, can lose the property and his money.
2. Confession of Judgment. Most contracts require that the buyer agree to a confession of judgment. This simply means that the buyer admits guilt in advance. Thus the seller's attorney can plead guilty in court for the buyer (even against his will), should any of the provisions of the contract be violated.
3. Title Of Property. The house is not the buyer's property. It remains the seller's property until the contact is paid in full. The buyer does not have the rights of ownership, but he does have the responsibilities—for taxes, insurance, etc.

If a buyer is considering buying on a contract he would be well advised to hire a lawyer. An attorney can point out the dangers and pitfalls in a contract. Since a contract is drawn up between two parties, he can delete obnoxious and dangerous portions before the contract goes into force. One should not depend upon the seller or his attorney to draw up a contract. The seller is interested in protecting his rights, not the buyer's. The buyer must protect his own rights. Hiring an attorney after a contract is signed is of little use. A consumer who trusts the seller in such matters is asking for trouble. If the buyer has a competent attorney, a contract, although less desirable than other methods of financing a home, is still useful.

TRENDS IN HOUSING

Why is housing so expensive compared to other more complex items such as cars?

A number of factors are responsible for this fact. Except for mobile homes, housing is not built on an assembly-line basis. Rather, housing is still produced on a piece-meal basis by hand. Capital invested in equipment is low compared with industry, and the building laws and codes tend to fragment the market. Thus few economies of large-scale production are realized. Productivity has risen only slowly in the building industry, while wages have increased rapidly, reflected in rapidly rising costs of building. It would be interesting to speculate on the cost of cars if they were built on the same basis as houses. If they were built on this basis there would be hundreds of producers each making a few cars per year by hand. All cars would be produced using parts made from raw materials by hand. Each car would require highly skilled craftsmen working slowly and carefully. Clearly, if cars were built using the same method of production as housing, they would be many times more expensive than they are now.

Why not build houses in factories like cars? To some degree this is now being attempted, but there are problems involved with these homes. Houses are very bulky and hard to transport to a desired location. Accordingly, factories must be near the building sites, causing the potential market to be small. Such a restriction on the market prevents a large enough factory from being built which could achieve truly impressive economies of scale. A new approach is not building entire homes but modules, thus easing the transportation problems. However, much work needs to be done in the area before the concept is proven.

Probably more important than the physical problems of building homes in a factory are the problems with building codes. Each community has its own building standards and inspection requirements. Most codes are rooted in the concept of "established practice;" that is, materials and methods are approved which have been found to be acceptable in the past. In many communities, for example, costly copper pipe is required in the plumbing of a house, while modern, superior plastic pipe—which is less costly, longer lasting, and cheaper to assemble—is prohibited.

Many labor-saving materials and methods are prohibited not because they are unsatisfactory, but simply because they are not established practice.

A better, but untried technique in the building industry, would provide for codes that only specify performance. That is, no material specifications would be made; only general performance codes, such as that a roof must support "xx" number of pounds of snow would be required. Or rather than specifying copper pipe, a code could read that the plumbing must withstand some pressure, temperature, and stress level and have some specified life. Such codes would be based only upon performance, rather than tradition. These performance specifications have worked well in shipbuilding, aircraft, and other areas. Figure 6-10 shows how airplanes would be built today if they had to pass "established practice" codes instead of performance codes.

The existing codes prevent labor-saving materials and methods. Much of the inspiration for these codes has come from the small contractor and craft unions who fear technological displacement. The crafts, by limiting the number of workers in any field (plumbers, electricians, etc.), have been able to drive wages above productivity increases. The result of this has been increased prices of construction.

FIGURE 6-10

If Aircraft Building Codes Were Based on "Established Practice" As Are
Housing Codes, Modern Aircraft Would Look Like the One Below.

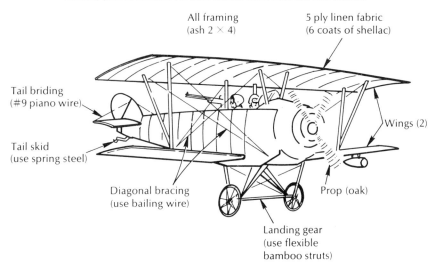

All framing
(ash 2 × 4)

5 ply linen fabric
(6 coats of shellac)

Tail briding
(#9 piano wire)

Wings (2)

Tail skid
(use spring steel)

Diagonal bracing
(use bailing wire)

Prop (oak)

Landing gear
(use flexible
bamboo struts)

Another factor causing a rise in the cost of construction besides increases in labor and materials has been the inflation of land prices in the large urban areas caused by the trend of movement from the rural to the large urban areas. The supply of land in the urban areas remains fixed, while the demand for that land increases. When the price of land increases, the cost of the housing built on that land also increases.

In response to the rapid increase of land prices, the last ten years has witnessed the beginning of what may be a trend towards land-saving housing such as mobile homes (chiefly in the West), planned unit developments, and apartments.

The rapid increase in housing costs, caused by many factors, has stimulated the search for less expensive alternative forms of housing. Pressures are rising for revision of building codes to allow the use of modern materials and factory-built homes. As costs continue to increase, radical changes may occur. Some futurists predict that people will live in geodesic domes, urban communes, and new towns. No doubt the pressure for new types of housing and new methods of building will increase as conventional housing becomes more expensive.

RENTING VS. BUYING A HOME

Advertisements in the real estate section of newspapers proclaim, "Why throw your money away on rent—buy a home" or "Rent money is spent money!" It is an article of faith that one always makes money in buying a home, and that money spent on renting is thrown away. Is this always true?

No such hard and fast rule is economically true. Often renting will be found much less expensive than buying a home when all costs are considered. In other situations the home is a good investment and much less expensive than a rental. In the decision process one must consider all the relevant facts and costs. In some cases the decision would dictate the purchase of a home, while in others it would suggest renting. The decision maker must consider at least the following factors. Others may be necessary in particular cases.

Renting		*Buying*	
Monthly Rental	$ _____	Monthly payment	$ _____
		Insurance	
		Taxes	
		Repairs	
		Gross monthly cost	_____
		−Value of increased equity	
		−Value of income tax deduction for interest and taxes	_____
Monthly Rental Cost	$ _____	Net monthly cost	$ _____

Assume you are buying a modest home for $20,000. The interest rate on the home is 6 percent, and the down payment is about $3,000. The total payment, including principal, taxes, and insurance will be $105 per month (excluding maintenance, which authorities estimate will cost about $15 per month if your time is considered "free.")

The monthly cost for shelter with this home is $165 per month. However, lost interest on your invested capital must be considered. Assuming that you could earn 6 percent in a saving and loan, the lost interest each month (.5% interest × $3,000 down payment) is fifteen dollars per month. The total cost of your home including implicit and explicit costs is $180.

This house is a modest, 1,000-square-foot, two-bedroom home. To rent a similar home or apartment would, at this time, range from $180 to $210 a month. To compare costs we will assume that you could rent a similar home for $190.

The consumer, when comparing, would say that the house is ten dollars cheaper per month. In out-of-pocket expenses this is correct, but such comparisons are not valid unless you plan to own the home until it is paid for. Most Americans do not live for long periods at the same address. As promotions occur or family size increases, the typical young couple moves up to bigger, more luxurious, modern homes. How would you fare on a comparison basis if you moved from this home in five years?

The equity you will have built up is surprisingly small. Only $104 per month of your implicit and explicit monthly costs ($180) are actually applied to your home principal and interest payments. Only $17 is used to pay off the loan (increase your equity) while $87 applies to interest. By payment number sixty (fifth year) $23 is being applied to the loan while the interest expenses have dropped to $81.05. After five years of making payments the outstanding balance of the loan has dropped from $17,382 to $16,185. (FHA Amortization Schedule). In other words, the equity has increased by $1,197.

The amount of money that you have in the home, $180 per month over five years, is $13,800 including your down payment.

Assuming the house has appreciated in value to $21,000 in the five-year period of time and you decide to sell it, you will gross $21,000 minus the balance of the loan, which is $16,185, to give a profit of $4,815.

Selling requires a real estate broker whose fee is usually 6½ percent of the gross sales price. In this case it would be $21,000 × 6½ percent = $1,365 selling commission. The net proceeds will be $4,815 − 1,365 selling fee = $3,450. Because the investment was $3,000 (down payment), your "profit" was only $450. The total housing expense for the period was $180 per month for 60 months or $10,800. The total expenses must be reduced by the profit realized when the house was sold, which is $10,800 - $450 = $10,350. Thus the true housing costs for the period were $10,350 or $172 per month.

The difference between buying the house and renting amounted to $18 per month. If income tax deductions are included, the difference becomes $34 per month.* Of course, this is an estimate. The house may have appreciated more in value than this example demonstrates, but it may also have declined in value. Further, in this example, maintenance expenses are understated compared to what most people probably pay. By the same token, no provision was made in the estimate for taxes on the home, which usually increase over the years.

Thus over a five-year period the home owner is a little ahead of the apartment dweller, but the savings are not of the magnitude that many people associate with home ownership. The slight economic advantage of ownership has a cost. In exchange for the slight savings the owner will have his potential mobility reduced. In addition, considerable time must be invested in household maintenance, at which the homeowner "works" for free. The renter pays a little more but does not have to do the usual maintenance.

---

*Note: The home owner can deduct a portion of his interest payments from his income taxes. A person in the 20 percent bracket would save $17 a month with this deduction. This can be seen by taking the monthly interest payment ($870 x 20% = $17 tax deduction). In effect such tax breaks serve as a subsidy to the home owner.

If the homeowner had sold the home before the five-year period had ended, as many people do, the house would have been more expensive than the apartment. Should the homeowner have kept the home for longer than the five-year period, his gain would have been greater. As a rule of thumb, it is not economical to buy a home for a short period of time—less than five years. On the other hand, renting becomes increasingly costly compared to home ownership if you are going to rent for more than five years.

Some people are only happy owning their own home and would not be happy renting even for a short period of time. If the consumer buys a home in which he intends to live for only two years, he should recognize that it is more expensive than renting. This would be like a luxury which the owner felt was worth the cost. It should not, however, be considered an investment.

On the other hand, many people hate the work and lack of freedom that comes with home ownership. These people should realize that to live in an apartment for longer than five years is costing them more money than necessary. Thus, the apartment can also be viewed as a luxury.

HOME OWNERSHIP IN RETIREMENT

Many people consider that housing is free once the final mortgage payment is made. Often elderly people share this belief and struggle to maintain their homes on small retirement budgets. Does this make economic sense? Assume that an elderly couple owns a home free and clear. Its value is about $30,000. What is the true cost of living in this home? If the couple sold the house they could put $30,000 in the bank. (This ignores any tax liability.) They could earn 6 percent on their savings per year, or .5 percent per month. The $30,000 in the bank at this rate of interest would earn $150 interest per month. The local property tax on this home would be in many areas from $600 to $800 per year. Using the $600 figure, tax would be $50 a month. Maintenance, at a bare minimum, would average $15 per month. Thus the house, even when owned free and clear, would cost the owner (including implicit and explicit cost) at least $225 a month. The computation was as follows:

Lost interest on invested capital	$150
Taxes per month	50
Comprehensive home insurance	10
Maintenance	15
Total Cost Per Month	$225

The house is not free at all. Even where no money is owed on a mortgage the costs are still considerable. Many elderly people do not realize this and struggle to maintain a home on a small budget.

Perhaps such a couple ought to consider selling the home and putting the proceeds in a bank. If this were done, the interest earned on the proceeds plus the savings of not having home ownership expenses would pay for an apartment for the rest of their lives and not require them to spend their capital. Such an apartment might require less work and effort and might be more suitable to the elderly couple's abilities.

THINK IT OVER:

1. Many cities reduce taxes on homes that the elderly own. Many of these homes are large and expensive units acquired when children were living at home. Why might an economist say that such a reduction in taxes represents a misallocation of the nation's resources and worsens the housing shortage?
2. How can people say that a house owned free and clear can still be expensive?
3. How might property tax increases reduce the housing shortage?
4. If property were taxed on a progressive rate (geared to income and family size) would this tend to redistribute housing away from those who don't need it to those who do?
5. Should the elderly be subsidized with tax breaks on their homes? What are the effects of such tax reductions?

At this point it may strike the reader that no matter what form of housing one has, the cost of shelter is high. The costs of home ownership are not too much less than renting, even in the long run. Inexpensive mobile homes in the long run are as expensive as conventional homes. Thus for similar housing there is no big cost difference between renting, owning conventional housing, or living in mobile homes. If a marked cost differential existed, in the long run the economist would view the market system as tending to force people into the form of housing that was less costly. In response to such a shift, other forms of housing would become less common and would diminish in numbers. Some suggest that such forces may be at work at the lower end of the housing market with the increasing popularity of planned unit developments, mobile homes, and rentals. In this market (less than $20,000) conventional homes accounted for less than 10 percent of all housing starts in 1970. The point is that people still desire conventional homes, but the forces in the market are shifting them into other forms of housing. When the differential in cost is small, people tend to buy what they like; when the cost differential becomes great, they tend to buy what they can afford.

THINK IT OVER:

1. Do you think that the government should subsidize one form of housing over another?

2. Is ownership of conventional homes a national governmental policy? Should it be?

3. Should the government simply rely on housing provided by the market, or should housing be subsidized?

4. If housing were to be subsidized to a large extent, in what area should the government reduce its expenditures so that tax increases will not be necessary—defense, education, health, etc.?.

SUGGESTED READING

Personal Economics Readings

Beyer, Glenn H. *Housing and Society.* New York: MacMillan Co., 1965.

Brown, Robert Kevin. *Real Estate Economics.* Boston: Houghton Mifflin, Inc., 1965.

Kuchler, Frances W. H. *Landlord and Tenant.* New York: Oceana Publications, 1960.

McMichael, Stanley L. and Paul T. O'Keefe. *How to Finance Real Estate.* Englewood Cliffs, N.J.: Prentice-Hall, Inc., 1968.

Moger, Byron. *How to Buy a House.* New York: L. Stuart, Inc., 1969.

Ratcliff, Richard. *Real Estate Analysis.* New York: McGraw-Hill Book Company, 1961.

Ring, Alfred A. *Real Estate Principles and Practices.* Englewood Cliffs, N.J.: Prentice-Hall, Inc., 1967.

Rose, Jerome G. *The Legal Advisor on Home Ownership.* Boston: Little, Brown, and Co., 1967.

Watkins, A. M. *How to Avoid the Biggest Home Buying Traps.* New York: Meredith Press, 1968.

Income Distribution
and Some
Proposed Solutions
to Inequalities

CHAPTER VII

DEFINITION OF INCOME

In our market economy, income takes the form of wages and salaries, interest, rents and profits. The sum of these components in any one year equals national income. Each person in the economy is concerned with receiving a share of the national income. Whether his share will be large or small depends in large measure on the goods or services he has to offer for sale in the market in relation to the demand for these goods and services. If his services are in demand, then a larger income can be expected than if they are not in demand.

A market distribution of income raises some interesting questions regarding equity and justice. Should the income of some persons be large when that of others is small? Has the share of income accruing to wages changed over time?

To answer these questions, it is necessary to understand how the income of each of us is determined. An examination of Table 7-1 and Figure 7-1 will provide insights into the current distribution of income to wages, rents, interest and profits and into the trend in functional shares since 1929. Looking at Figure 7-1, it appears that the share of national income going to wages and salaries has increased. Over the same period the portion accruing to business, professional and farm income has declined. This reflects a structural change in the economy, in that there has been a tendency for self-employment to decline and for wage and salary employment to increase in relative terms; but the *total* share of

TABLE 7-1

CURRENT DISTRIBUTION OF INCOME TO WAGES, RENTS, INTEREST, AND PROFITS

Types of Income	1970 Amount of Income (Billions of Dollars)	1970 Percent of Total National Income
Compensation of employees	$599.8	74.9
Proprietors' income	67.6	8.4
Rental income of persons	22.7	2.8
Corporate profits	77.2	9.7
Net interest	33.5	4.2
Total national income	$800.8	100.0

Source: *Statistical Abstract of the United States, 1971*, p. 309.

FIGURE 7-1

Functional Distribution of National
Income in the United States, 1929-1971

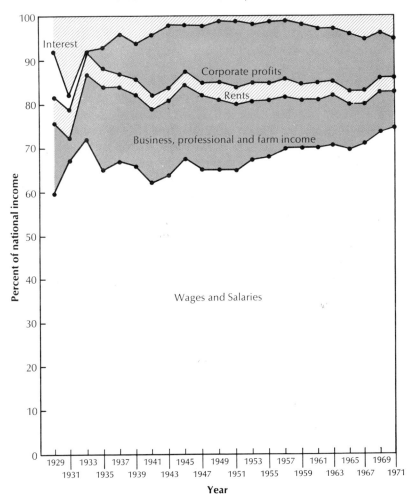

Source: Calculated from *Economic Report of the President*, 1972, p. 209.

national income accruing to labor has not markedly changed in the period 1929 to present. This analysis describes only the allocation of income to the five basic groups earning income in the economy and does not describe shares going to individuals.

The sum of $599.8 billion (See Table 7-1) for wages and salaries in 1970 indicates the predominance of this category when aggregate income is divided functionally. The other components of income—rent, profit and interest—are received by individuals in return for the use of land, managerial ability, and money capital. These sources are significantly smaller than the wages and salaries component. Thus, any scheme of income redistribution must be established in terms of either earned income or transfer of income from the workers. This income is still based on aggregates and fails to provide the needed information as to how the income accrues to individual households.

PER CAPITA INCOME

Another method of evaluating aggregate income is on a per capita basis. This is aggregate income divided by population. Table 7-2 indicates the per capita income by states and regional areas in 1970. The states in which there has traditionally been an emphasis on agriculture tend to have the lowest per capita incomes, and the states which have experienced the greatest amount of indus- trialization tend to have the highest per capita incomes. Connecticut, New York, and Alaska share the top three spots by rank. Alabama, Arkansas, and Mississippi rank numbers forty-eight, forty-nine, and fifty respectively.

These per capita divisions of the national income do not provide a view of the relative distribution of income received by a particular income group. If income distributions are plotted, there are a certain number of people in the high income bracket, a certain number of people in the low income bracket and a vast number in the middle bracket (see Figure 7-2). Using this graph, we are able to see the pyramidal nature of personal incomes in the United States.

Figure 7-2 shows one method of presenting the actual distribution of income, but economists have found that the Lorenz curve shown in Figure 7-3 is more useful as a device for viewing changes of income distribution over a period of time. Curves I, II, and III represent three different time periods, and the 45° line represents a condition of all incomes being equal. Population is represented in percentages on the horizontal axis and the percent of income received is measured on the vertical axis. If 5 percent of the people receive 5 percent of the income, 10 percent receive 10 percent, 20 percent receive 20 percent and so on, then all incomes would be equal, and the line would bisect the box. Curve III shows an extreme inequality in income shares, wherein 85 percent of the people receive only 5 percent of the income, and the remaining 15 percent of the people receive 95 percent of the nation's income. Curve II shows more equal distribution of incomes. Curve II is plotted from income data for 1969 in the

TABLE 7-2

PER CAPITA PERSONAL INCOME AND RANK ORDER BY STATES, 1970

Regions of the United States	Per Capita Income	Rank	Regions of the United States	Per Capita Income	Rank
United States	$3,910	—	South Atlantic (continued)		
New England	4,235	—	West Virginia	$2,929	46
Maine	3,243	36	North Carolina	3,188	39
New Hampshire	3,608	26	South Carolina	2,908	47
Vermont	3,491	31	Georgia	3,277	34
Massachusetts	4,294	9	Florida	3,584	28
Rhode Island	3,920	15			
Connecticut	4,807	1	East South Cent.	2,908	—
			Kentucky	3,060	42
Middle Atlantic	4,461	—	Tennessee	3,051	43
New York	4,797	2	Alabama	2,828	48
New Jersey	4,539	5	Mississippi	2,561	50
Pennsylvania	3,893	16			
			West South Cent.	3,321	—
East North Cent.	4,088	—	Arkansas	2,742	49
Ohio	3,083	14	Louisiana	3,065	41
Indiana	3,773	19	Oklahoma	3,269	35
Illinois	4,516	7	Texas	3,515	30
Michigan	4,043	12			
Wisconsin	3,722	21	Mountain	3,507	—
			Montana	3,381	33
West North Cent.	3,677	—	Idaho	3,206	38
Minnesota	3,793	18	Wyoming	3,420	32
Iowa	3,714	22	Colorado	3,751	20
Missouri	3,659	25	New Mexico	3,044	44
North Dakota	2,937	45	Arizona	3,542	29
South Dakota	3,182	40	Utah	3,210	37
Nebraska	3,700	23	Nevada	4,544	4
Kansas	3,804	17			
			Pacific	4,351	—
South Atlantic	3,523	—	Washington	3,993	13
Delaware	4,233	11	Oregon	3,700	23
Maryland	4,247	10	California	4,469	8
Dist. of Col.	5,519	—	Alaska	4,676	3
Virginia	3,586	27	Hawaii	4,530	6

Source: *Statistical Abstract of the United States, 1971*, p. 314.

FIGURE 7-2

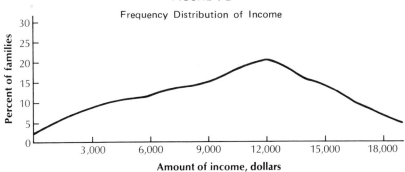

Frequency Distribution of Income

Amount of income, dollars

Source: Calculated from *Statistical Abstract of the United States, 1971*, p. 317.

FIGURE 7-3

Lorenz Curve

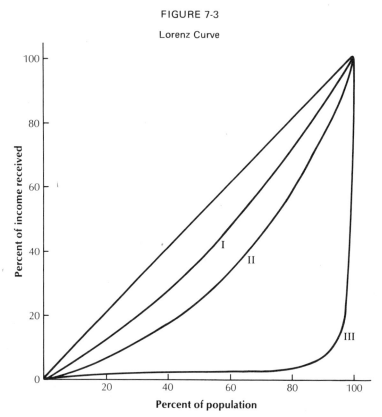

Percent of population

Source: Hypothetical data and *Statistical Abstract of the United States, 1971*, p. 317.

United States. Curve I would represent a movement very close to the equality of income shares as might exist in Sweden.

Table 7-3 illustrates the fact that the relative shares received by various fifths of income earners in the United States have stayed fairly constant over the twenty-year period from 1947 to 1967. There has been a very slight shift in the percent of income received by the highest 20 percent of the people to the three middle groups, but the relative share going to the lowest 20 percent has remained almost constant. This reflects the limited skills offered by wage earners of the lowest income group. However, the dollar gains in annual earnings on a family basis since World War II have been substantial.

If one looked at only these dollar amounts, he could assume that there had been a major improvement in the economic conditions of the non-white American. The percentage distribution of income shares gives perspective as to the changes within a time period and helps one decide whether or not they are meaningful improvements.

TABLE 7-3

PERCENT OF AGGREGATE INCOME RECEIVED BY EACH FIFTH AND TOP 5 PERCENT OF FAMILIES AND UNRELATED INDIVIDUALS: 1947 TO 1969

Item and Income Rank	1947	1950	1955	1960	1965	1967	1968	1969
Families	100.0	100.0	100.0	100.0	100.0	100.0	100.0	100.0
Lowest fifth	5.0	4.5	4.8	4.9	5.3	5.4	5.7	5.6
Second fifth	11.8	12.0	12.2	12.0	12.2	12.2	12.4	12.3
Middle fifth	17.0	17.4	17.7	17.6	17.6	17.5	17.7	17.6
Fourth fifth	23.1	23.5	23.7	23.6	23.7	23.7	23.7	23.4
Highest fifth	43.0	42.6	41.6	42.0	41.3	41.2	40.6	41.0
Top 5 percent	17.2	17.0	16.8	16.8	15.8	15.3	14.0	14.7
Unrelated Individuals	100.0	100.0	100.0	100.0	100.0	100.0	100.0	100.0
Lowest fifth	1.0	2.3	2.5	2.6	2.6	3.0	3.2	3.4
Second fifth	5.8	7.0	7.3	7.1	7.6	7.5	7.8	7.7
Middle fifth	11.9	13.8	13.4	13.6	13.5	13.3	13.8	13.7
Fourth fifth	21.4	26.5	25.0	25.7	25.1	24.4	24.4	24.3
Highest fifth	59.1	50.4	51.9	50.9	51.2	51.8	50.8	50.9
Top 5 percent	33.3	19.3	21.7	20.0	20.2	22.0	20.4	21.0

Source: *U.S. Statistical Abstract of the United States, 1971*, p. 317.

TABLE 7-4

MONEY FAMILY INCOME IN 1969 DOLLARS

Race of Family Head	1947	1966	Percent of Increase
White	$3,157	$9,794	310
Non-White	1,640	6,190	384

Source: *Statistical Abstract of the United States 1971,*.p. 316.

TABLE 7-5

PERCENT DISTRIBUTION OF FAMILY MONEY INCOME 1950-1969 IN 1969 DOLLARS

Year	Percent Earning Less Than $3,000	Percent Earning More Than $10,000
1950	21.6	12.1
1955	17.2	18.6
1960	16.3	26.8
1965	11.2	37.1
1969	8.1	48.6

Source: *Statistical Abstract of the United States, 1971*, p. 317.

TABLE 7-6

FAMILY INCOME EARNED IN SELECTED YEARS
IN CURRENT DOLLARS

Family Units Income Rank	1960	1965	1969
Lowest 20% earned less than	$2,640	$ 3,000	$ 3,900
Highest 20% earned more than	8,593	11,200	14,460
Ratio	3.25	3.73	3.74

Source: *Statistical Abstract of the United States, 1971,* p. 317.

Although the earnings of full-time employed males has risen in absolute terms, there has been no improvement in the distribution of income. The disparity between the lowest and highest fifth of the labor force has grown in dollar terms, but there has been little change in the portion of income received. This can be seen by comparing the rise in the portion of families earning more than $10,000 and the decline in the portion earning less than $3,000. However, the ratio of mean family income of the highest to the lowest fifth has actually risen. This greater degree of income inequality in 1969 occurred because the incomes of the lowest fifth grew relatively slower than the incomes of the highest fifth.

The distribution of income and the relative position of Americans in that distribution can be viewed in still another way when the *wealth position* is taken into consideration. This is done by evaluating the cash money balance held by the population. (See Table 7-7) In 1963 22 percent of the family units held no cash balances; only 10 percent of the units held more than $10,000 in 1969.

TABLE 7-7

FAMILY UNITS—PERCENT DISTRIBUTION
BY LIQUID ASSET HOLDINGS: 1963 TO 1969

Asset Size-Class	1963	1965	1968	1969
All family units	100	100	100	100
Own no assets	22	20	19	19
Own assets	78	80	81	81
$1-$199	15	17	15	14
$200-$499	14	11	12	12
$500-$1,999	21	21	24	22
$2,000-$4,999	14	14	13	15
$5,000-$9,999	8	9	8	8
$10,000 and over	6	8	9	10
Median holdings	$490	$575	$660	$730

Source: *Statistical Abstract of the United States, 1970,* p. 320.

Studies indicate that the top 1 percent of adults in the United States held more than 28 percent of the nation's wealth in 1958. Trends in national surveys conducted by the Federal Reserve Board indicate that there has been no appreciable change in the shares of wealth held by various groups in the United States.

The wide variance in the percentage of total liquid assets held by various spending units indicates the problem posed by the unequal distribution of income and job opportunities in the United States. The ability of an individual or spending unit to hold liquid assets reflects his general income status and also his basic position on the standard-of-living scale. While the number of spending units which hold zero assets has declined from 1963 to 1969, it should be remembered that this was a time of rapid economic expansion. Although there

TABLE 7-8

HOUSEHOLDS OWNING CARS AND APPLIANCES—PERCENT DISTRIBUTION,
BY INCOME LEVEL: 1960 AND 1970

| | Cars | | Television | | | | Refrig-erator | | Air |
| | One or more | Two or more | Black and white | Color | Washing machine | Clothes dryer | or freezer | Dish-washer | condi-tioner |
Income Level									
1960									
All households	75.0	16.4	86.7		74.5	17.4	86.1	4.9	12.8
Annual income:									
Under $1,000	24.8	1.8	49.1		48.1	1.4	70.2	0.3	2.7
$1,000-$1,999	42.9	3.1	71.4		58.6	3.4	77.6	0.6	4.6
$2,000-$2,999	61.3	6.4	80.1		67.6	5.9	82.5	1.2	6.2
$3,000-$3,999	75.7	9.0	88.3		73.3	9.6	84.9	1.5	9.3
$4,000-$4,999	82.3	12.3	92.9		77.3	14.9	86.3	2.0	9.0
$5,000-$5,999	90.2	17.9	94.5		82.8	20.5	90.7	2.5	12.2
$6,000-$7,499	93.3	21.6	97.0		85.6	26.8	92.3	4.0	17.3
$7,500-$9,999	95.1	31.4	96.3		85.9	30.9	92.6	7.6	20.3
$10,000-$14,999	95.4	42.7	97.0		84.9	38.6	92.0	18.3	27.5
$15,000 and over	94.2	58.8	98.2		86.5	50.3	93.7	43.4	42.2
1970									
All households	79.6	29.3	77.4	37.8	69.9	40.8	83.3	17.3	20.5
Annual income:									
Under $3,000	42.5	4.5	77.3	13.1	50.0	11.8	75.5	3.0	4.3
$3,000-$3,999	64.1	9.7	78.9	23.0	60.7	19.6	77.7	3.8	12.9
$4,000-$4,999	75.7	17.9	78.1	25.2	62.8	26.1	80.0	5.6	14.7
$5,000-$5,999	83.2	17.8	78.9	27.6	62.9	29.0	78.1	6.4	18.9
$6,000-$7,499	88.9	25.3	76.4	38.9	70.5	37.3	83.0	10.2	21.6
$7,500-$9,999	91.6	34.7	75.6	45.5	76.3	49.7	85.5	15.0	28.5
$10,000-$14,999	95.9	48.4	76.9	53.3	82.9	62.9	90.0	29.3	33.7
$15,000-$24,999	96.6	62.2	78.4	61.8	86.2	73.1	91.5	49.8 }	44.9
$25,000 and over	95.3	66.6	79.2	73.4	88.1	81.8	92.0	71.0 }	

Source: *Statistical Abstract of the United States, 1971*, p. 321.

has been some shifting in the amount of assets held by various groups, the studies continue to indicate that a relatively small portion of society holds the vast amount of the nation's total wealth.

Similar conclusions can be drawn by looking at the household ownership of cars and appliances as compared with incomes. Notice, in Table 7-8, that the ownership of appliances falls off rapidly when the income of the household falls to the level of $3,000 to $3,900, the current federal poverty standard for a family of four. Since appliances and cars are another measure of relative well-being, the break in the amount of assets of this type held indicates the relative difference in the wealth position, income position, and general well-being of individuals in the United States.

There are several conclusions that can be drawn from Table 7-8 with respect to the general welfare of the country. It is also possible to draw conclusions with regard to the impact of the American free enterprise system on individuals in the system regardless of their income levels. The fact that 55 percent of the people with incomes under $3,000 do not own cars has a great impact on the ability of these individuals to seek out employment. These persons are hampered in their job search because of the lack of sufficient mass transportation from the central city areas where they live to the potential jobs in the suburban areas.

It is of interest to note that there is a high percentage of television ownership, 77.5 percent, in this low-income group. This would tend to suggest the impact mass advertising campaigns can have on persons in the lower income strain. The existence of television aerials in the poorer areas of communities is perplexing to individuals who do not understand the impact which advertising and entertainment have on the status needs of individuals in the American economic system.

THEORY OF INCOME DISTRIBUTION

The theoretical basis for the study of income distribution is the productivity of factors and price of the factors. In order to develop a theory of income distribution, one must first consider the theory of production. The theory of production determines the number and kind of productive resources used and the value of each factor.

The basic microeconomic concepts of supply and demand, diminishing returns, and marginalism are useful in studying the allocation of productive resources. The term "marginal" means "the amount gained or lost by the addition or subtraction of one unit of a factor." With this in mind, we find that if the total revenue goes from $100 to $125 with an increase of sales from ten to eleven, then the marginal revenue produced by the eleventh unit is $25. In the theory of production we deal with the concept of marginal productivity of factors. If a factory is operated with 100 employees and a fixed amount of land and buildings, and the number of employees is increased from 100 to 101, we would find the marginal product of the 101st by measuring the increase in output. If the production of 100 workers was 1,000 units and the production of 101 workers was 1,015 units, then the marginal product of the 101st worker would be 15 units. This concept allows us to determine the value of a factor in terms of its marginal product.

DERIVED FACTOR DEMAND

In the development of productivity theory, one should ask the question "why does a firm demand a given factor of production?" On the consumer side, we know from personal experience that we demand goods and services for the satisfaction they provide. What are the conditions which determine the demand for a machine, a worker, a building, or other productive factors? The answer to this question is closely related to the consumer. The demand for a productive factor is a *derived demand.* Factor demand is dependent on the consumer demand for a given product. The producer will demand factors of production only if he is assured either of current or future consumer demand for the output of that factor. The demand for the productive factor is "derived" from the demand for the output.

Using the example of hiring a 101st worker, it is possible to show the way the return to the 101st worker is determined. In this example, the increase in output credited to the addition of the 101st worker was 15 units. As the owner of the firm, which factors would you consider in determining whether to add the additional worker? We have already mentioned the consumer demand for the good or service produced, the comparative cost of other factors of production, and finally the value of the marginal product of the 101st worker. As the owner, you would pay this worker his marginal revenue product, the additional contribution to total revenue, and no more. Since the worker would not be demanded at a wage greater than his marginal product, the worker would receive the amount equal to the marginal revenue he produced. This concept holds for the other types of productive factors: land, capital, and management.

THINK IT OVER:

1. Would the redistribution of income in the United States so that everyone would receive the same income improve the well-being of persons?
2. What changes in the present distribution of incomes would you propose in order to benefit all of the members of the labor force?
3. Which of the measures of relative well-being seems to do the best job of reflecting the real world well-being?

4. What types of considerations would you want to make when selecting an occupation? Relate this to derived demand.
5. Would you prefer a job in a labor-intensive industry or a capital-intensive industry? Why?

CHARACTERISTICS OF VARIOUS INCOME GROUPS

The best source of information on the characteristics of various income groups is the Bureau of Labor Statistics, which takes monthly, quarterly, and yearly labor force participation surveys. The Bureau defines anyone who is employed or actively seeking employment from the age of sixteen as part of the labor force. Anyone who falls into this category is counted as a part of the total labor force and is included in the employment and unemployment estimates. Table 7-9 contains the statistics representing the size of the labor force in two different years, 1961 and 1971, and the breakdown between the number of civilian workers who have jobs and the unemployed. The total labor force has grown

TABLE 7-9

COMPOSITION OF THE CIVILIAN LABOR FORCE AND UNEMPLOYMENT,
BY SEX AND AGE, 1961 AND 1971
[Numbers in thousands]

	Civilian labor force		Unemployment		
Sex and age	Number	Percent distribution	Number	Percent distribution	Rate
1961					
Total, 16 years and over	70,460	100.0	4,714	100.0	6.7
Men, 20 years and over	43,860	62.2	2,518	53.4	5.7
20 to 24 years	4,253	6.0	458	9.7	10.8
25 years and over	39,605	56.2	2,061	43.7	5.2
Women, 20 years and over	21,664	30.7	1,368	29.0	6.3
20 to 24 years	2,697	3.8	265	5.6	9.8
25 years and over	18,967	26.9	1,103	23.4	5.8
Both sexes, 16 to 19 years	4,936	7.0	828	17.6	16.8
Married men	36,259	51.5	1,676	35.5	4.6
1971					
Total, 16 years and over	84,113	100.0	4,993	100.0	5.9
Men, 20 years and over	47,861	56.9	2,086	41.8	4.4
20 to 24 years	6,194	7.4	635	12.7	10.3
25 years and over	41,666	49.5	1,451	29.1	3.5
Women, 20 years and over	28,799	34.2	1,650	33.0	5.7
20 to 24 years	5,071	6.0	486	9.7	9.6
25 years and over	23,728	28.2	1,164	23.3	4.9
Both sexes, 16 to 19 years	7,453	8.9	1,257	25.2	16.9
Married men	39,183	46.6	1,251	25.1	3.2

Source: *Manpower Report to the President, 1972*, p. 41.

from 70,460,000 to 84,113,000, a growth of over 14 million in the ten-year period.

Table 7-9 also allows us to see the impact of unemployment on various groups. Note that the unemployment for persons age sixteen to nineteen is three times that of the labor force as a whole. It is of interest to note that the labor force includes a larger portion of persons sixteen to nineteen years of age and more women. This indicates that the population is growing and that the potential of women is being better utilized.

This table shows only the characteristics of various employment groups with regard to rates of employment or unemployment. To further delineate the characteristics of the various employment groups, it is helpful to look at the technological change of the labor force requirement; the impact of age, sex, and unemployment on the labor force; and the effect of racial discrimination on the labor force participation rates.

TECHNICAL CHANGE AND LABOR FORCE REQUIREMENTS

There are nine major categories of employment, wage, and productivity statistics produced by the Bureau of Labor Statistics. They include agriculture; mining; contract construction; manufacturing; transportation and public utilities; trade; finance, insurance, and real estate; service; and government. Tables 7-10 and 7-11 show the employment trends in the United States. Table 7-10 includes the statistics for these industries in 1968 and Table 7-11 represents the statistics for 1930. At first glance, it can be noted that there has been a major shift into the service-producing area. Some areas of employment have lost employees between 1930 and 1968; for example, agriculture has decreased from 10,750,000 to 3,817,000 employees and mining has dropped from 1,150,000 in 1930 to 610,000 in 1968. While manufacturing gained approximately 90 percent and construction has more than doubled the number of people employed, it is

TABLE 7-10

**TOTAL NATIONAL EMPLOYMENT BY
INDUSTRY, 1968**

Goods-Producing Industries		Service-Producing Industries	
(In thousands)			
Agriculture	3,817	Transportation and	
		public utilities	4,313
Mining	610	Trade	14,081
		Finance, insurance	
Construction	3,267	and real estate	3,383
		Service	10,592
Manufacturing	19,768	Government	11,846
	27,462		44,215

Source: *Manpower Report of the President, 1971,* p. 297.

TABLE 7-11

TOTAL NATIONAL EMPLOYMENT BY
INDUSTRY, 1930

Goods-Producing Industries		Service-Producing Industries	
(In thousands)			
Agriculture	10,750	Transportation and	
		public utilities	4,850
Mining	1,150	Trade	6,030
		Finance, insurance	
Construction	3,030	and real estate	1,420
		Service	3,084
Manufacturing	10,490	Government	3,149
	25,420		18,533

Source: *Historical Statistics of the United States, 1961*, pp. 73 and 76.

indicative of a major movement from producing goods to producing services when we note that the government sector has increased by more than 300 percent in the thirty-eight year period from 1930 to 1968. The vast majority of the 300 percent increase comes on the state and local levels as a result of demands for increased police and fire protection and for health and educational services. The goods and services sectors are double what they were in 1930, but there has been a shift from almost 60 percent goods in 1930 to a position in which almost 60 percent of all employment in 1968 was in the service-producing area.

When all nine major industrial areas are viewed in terms of employment projections, the direction in which the composition of the labor force is moving becomes obvious. In Table 7-12, the goods-producing area as a total will probably increase by 12 percent in the ten years from 1970 to 1980 while the service-producing sector of the economy will experience an increase of 22 percent over the same time period. The impact of these projections becoming reality will be felt most severely by unskilled workers and workers in job areas which require the least amount of formal education.

The shift in employment opportunities from the goods-producing area is the result of both technological and economical factors. It seems a condition of technology that those jobs which are most easily mechanized are jobs which deal with things rather than people. As a result of this factor, the miner is replaced by a power digger, the farm hand by a mechanized loading and baling device, and the assembly line worker with a machine that can do his job better and more accurately. Technology is not the only reason for the shift. Businessmen do not buy new machines unless there is an economic advantage.

In recent years there has been a spiraling of labor costs to the point that the managers of large corporations have found they can cut costs by employing machinery to perform tasks which were previously performed by manual laborers. An example is the development of packaging and package-moving equipment which has eliminated the physical handling of packages by employees. This has, in the process, eliminated some occupations.

TABLE 7-12

TOTAL NATIONAL EMPLOYMENT BY INDUSTRY, ACTUAL 1970
AND PROJECTED 1980

Industry Division	Employment in Thousands		Change 1970-80	
	1970	1980	Thousands	Percent
Goods-producing total	28,402	31,835	3,433	12
Agriculture	3,462	3,000	462	−13
Mining	637	560	− 77	−12
Manufacturing	19,735	22,175	2,440	12
Construction	4,568	6,100	1,532	34
Service-producing total	61,356	74,985	13,629	22
Transportation and public utilities	5,065	5,465	400	8
Trade	16,030	18,180	2,150	13
Finance, insurance and real estate	3,862	4,405	543	14
Service	20,739	29,435	8,696	41
Government	15,660	17,500	1,840	11

Source: *Tomorrow's Manpower Needs*, U. S. Department of Labor, Bureau of Labor Statistics, Bulletin 1737, pp. 14-16.

In Table 7-13 the projected rates for types of employment hold a bleak view of the future for those members of the labor force who have few years of formal education. The percent of common laborers in the labor force will drop by 1 percent, and the number of farm workers will fall by 17 percent. These two categories, along with blue collar workers, will fare less well than many other occupation types. The average projected increase over the ten-year period is 19 percent, and people with skills in the categories with rates less than 19 percent will find it increasingly difficult to find and hold employment.

These statistics do not necessarily give the complete data. There are a significant number of people (1½ million in 1966) who are not counted as being in the labor force, but who do want work if they could get jobs. Using the definition that the labor force is people who are employed or who are actively seeking employment, the data excludes persons who have voluntarily withdrawn from the labor force since they are not looking for work. When these persons were asked why they were not seeking jobs, they gave various reasons. (See Table 7-14.)

The failure to include these people in the labor force statistics may or may not have the effect of increasing the amount of unemployment and the number of jobs needed to fully employ the labor force. For the economic policymaker the fact that they do exist indicates potential problems for policy prescriptions. From the sociological view, these people are not leading full lives. It is worthwhile to note that while the major percentage of the group gave "attending school" as a reason for not working, there were several other important reasons which affected many of the workers. Physical disability took a high percentage

TABLE 7-13

EMPLOYMENT BY MAJOR OCCUPATIONAL GROUP
ACTUAL 1970 AND PROJECTED 1980

Occupational Group	Employment in Thousands		Change 1970-80	
	1970	1980	Thousands	Percent
Total	70,473	84,005	13,532	19
White collar total	37,998	48,045	10,047	26
Professional and technical	11,140	15,500	4,360	39
Proprietary and managerial	8,289	9,500	1,211	15
Clerical	13,715	17,285	3,570	26
Sales	4,854	5,760	906	19
Blue Collar total	27,791	31,380	3,589	13
Craftsmen	10,158	12,240	2,082	20
Operatives	13,909	15,440	1,531	11
Laborers	3,724	3,700	−24	− 1
Service	1,558	1,980	422	27
Farm	3,126	2,600	−526	−17

Source: *Tomorrow's Manpower Needs*, U. S. Department of Labor, Bureau of Labor Statistics, Bulletin 1737, pp. 18-20.

of both men and women. Family responsibilities and child care problems affected 44.1 percent of the women. These two areas, combined with those who believed it would be impossible to find work, make up 43.5 percent of the males and 61.3 percent of the females who did not seek employment but would work if they could obtain employment. Policy planners continue to seek ways of accounting for this group of people who are willing to work but are not recorded in the normal employment figures because they are not actively seeking jobs.

TABLE 7-14

REASONS FOR UNEMPLOYMENT

	Men	Women
Believe it would be impossible to find work[1]	16.2%	13.4%
Ill health, physical disability	29.3%	16.4%
In school	43.0%	14.7%
Family responsibilities	—	29.6%
Inability to arrange child care	—	11.9%
Miscellaneous personal reasons[2]	8.8%	7.9%
Expect to be working shortly	2.7%	6.2%

[1] Includes—employers think they are too old or young; couldn't find or did not believe any job (or suitable job) was available; lacks skill, experience, education, or training; no transportation; racial discrimination; language difficulties; and, pay too low.
[2] Includes—old age; entering or leaving armed forces; death in family; planning to go back to school; and, no need to work at present time.
Note: Percentages may not total to 100 percent due to rounding.

Source: *Manpower Report of the President*, 1968, p. 23.

UNEMPLOYMENT, UNDEREMPLOYMENT, AND OLD AGE

The lowest fifth of our nation's income groups is usually the group which suffers most in terms of unemployment. Economists, politicians, sociologists, and others have attempted to determine the reasons for excessive unemployment within this group and to propose possible solutions to the problem of their unemployment. In order to be classified as unemployed an individual has to be actively seeking employment but unable to find it.

When considering the impact of unemployment, the length of unemployment, age, racial composition, and sex of the unemployed group must be considered. Unemployment which lasts four to fifteen weeks will have a much more serious consequence on men in the age group of twenty-five to forty-four than on men in the age bracket of sixteen to twenty-four or sixty-five-plus years due to the high probability that men in the twenty-five to forty-four age group will have families to support.

The type of unemployment has a great deal to do with the impact it will have on society. There are a large number of persons who change jobs during the year, and they often experience some unemployment in the process of the job change. This is transitional unemployment and is not as important or critical to the economy as unemployment of a more permanent nature.

The youngest and oldest members of the labor force seem to suffer most when the economy is experiencing levels of unemployment at greater than 2 to 4 percent. The youngest are first to be layed off because of their lack of experience, and the oldest are often less educated and have more difficulty competing in the job market once they are unemployed.

Economists do not agree on the percent which can be considered full employment, and the figure floats between 2 and 5 percent. This is clearly a question of policy and definition. The real concern with unemployment comes when we experience a rise in the percentage of people who are unemployed above the "fully employed" minimum level.

Another concept which is one of great concern to economic planners is the amount of "underemployment" in the economy. The concept of underemployment is particularly important in the determination of the potential of the economic system. There are two types of underemployment:

1. Part-time workers who are seeking full-time jobs. This is the easiest to measure because underemployment can be thought of as part-time employment.
2. Workers who have jobs below their educational and/or skill level.

Rarely is anyone used to 100 percent of his educational and/or skill levels; but the closer we can come to the 100 percent usage level of our human resources, the higher the level of productivity and economic growth. Examples of underemployment with respect to education or skill level would be college graduates who work on an assembly line performing menial tasks because of a shortage of jobs in fields for which they are trained. This happened in 1970 and 1971 in Seattle, Washington, as a result of cutbacks in air defense spending. Many of the engineers with the Boeing Corporation were released from their jobs. The saturation of the Seattle labor market with engineers forced people with these skills to take whatever jobs they could get: taxi driver, gardener, painter, etc. A similar situation took place in Southern California when, as a result of the mild recession of 1969-70, people throughout the country spent less on entertainment. As a result of the reduction of spending for entertainment, there was a cutback in the demand for actors; and the actors in Southern California were forced to take whatever jobs they could get—as dishwashers, car salesmen, manual laborers.

The greatest portion of workers in the United States form a stable core experiencing full-time work the year around. In 1968 seven out of every ten persons in the labor force were employed for the entire year. The most stable of this group was the married male, who is most likely to experience participation in the labor force for the entire year with no unemployment.

The remaining three out of ten persons pose a rather large problem for policy planners. In 1968, 91.5 million persons looked for work and, of that number, 11.3 million (12.4 percent) experienced unemployment of varying durations during the year.

For our purpose, we will consider an unemployment level of 4 percent or less to be full employment and unemployment of less than 4 weeks duration to be transitional in nature. When the unemployment rate goes above 4 percent it affects different areas of the country in different ways. When the unemployment rate for the United States was over 5 percent in 1960, the unemployment rate for the areas of the country which are considered to be industrial was significantly higher than the rate for the nation; i.e., Michigan 6.9 percent; Pennsylvania 6.2 percent; California and the Pacific region 7 percent. In areas of the country where the major form of employment was the production of consumer durable goods or raw materials for production of these goods, the unemployment rates were higher than the national average. Again we have a situation where the problem of an "acceptable" unemployment rate may mean one thing as a national average and quite another thing to a particular region or urban area. Just as these national unemployment rates have greater or lesser impact on the various geographical areas, they also have a varying impact on groups within the labor force.

RACIAL AND ETHNIC DISCRIMINATION

The actions of the black urban populations of the mid-1960's brought to light not only their own plight but also the plight of other minority groups. Americans of Mexican, Puerto Rican, and Indian descent have suffered many of the same problems which are faced by the black American. Each of these ethnic groups suffers a higher-than-average unemployment rate and lower-than-average educational achievement. They are often forced by these economic consequences to live in older areas of our major cities or by government restrictions on remote reservations. In the 1950's and early 1960's, the building of major expressways in our larger cities allowed the members of society who were employed to "forget" these less fortunate members. The actions of Watts, Detroit, Newark, and Chicago brought the plight of these groups of the labor force to the forefront of policy planners' attention.

FIGURE 7-4

Negro Workers Moved into Better Jobs Between 1961 and 1969

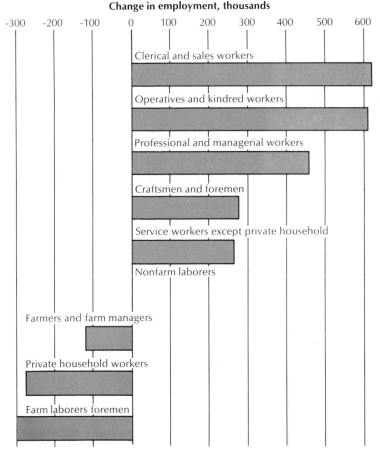

Note: Includes small numbers of members of other races.

Source: *Manpower Report to the President,* 1970, p. 91.

From 1961 to 1969, there was some movement in the type of employment which is open to racial minorities. The shift has been greatest in relatively unskilled jobs, and black Americans continue to experience difficulty in obtaining employment in management-type positions.

In the early 1960's, most breakthroughs were in "show case" positions, for which a store or company would hire black workers to meet a quota and to avoid confrontation with more militant black groups in the store's or company's community. After the initial arm twisting by the black militants, the firms discovered that they would not lose business as the result of having black employees and in some cases would have a better company image if they did not discriminate. While the rate of growth of job opportunities for blacks in the 1970's has been higher in some fields than that for white workers in the same fields, it is important to remember these are rates of growth and can be deceiving. If a particular firm has no black employees and hires two workers a year, the rate of growth is infinite. On the other hand, if a firm has twenty white workers and hires ten more workers, this is only a growth rate of 50 percent. Meaningful movements in the breakdown of racial barriers to employment have begun to take place but still have a long way to go before equal opportunities for jobs can be realized by all persons seeking employment.

Table 7-15a shows that there was a decline in the unemployment rate of non-whites by almost half between 1965 and 1967; this was at a time when there was a general reduction of all unemployment. The unemployment rate of non-white Americans remained almost double the rate of unemployed white Americans in the labor force, fluctuating with the business cycle—declining in the period 1965-1969 but rising again in the period of economic slowdown, 1970-71. This is an indication of the extreme difficulty of bringing and keeping non-whites into the production process.

The unemployment rates of non-white teenagers in the age group sixteen to nineteen showed little or no drop. In Table 7-15b the rate of unemployment for non-white teenagers in 1968 was more than six times that of non-white adults as

TABLE 7-15A

UNEMPLOYMENT RATES FOR WHITE AND NON-WHITE
MALE WORKERS OVER 20: 1965-71

| Year | Unemployment Rate (Percent) | |
	White	Non-White
1965	2.9	6.0
1966	2.2	4.9
1967	2.1	4.3
1968	2.0	3.9
1969	1.9	3.7
1970	3.2	5.6
1971	4.0	7.2

Source: *Manpower Report to the President, 1972*, p. 163.

TABLE 7-15B

UNEMPLOYMENT FOR NON-WHITE TEENAGERS AND MALE AND
FEMALE NON-WHITE ADULTS

Year	Non-White Teenagers (16-19) (Percent)	Non-White Adults Male (Percent)	Female (Percent)
1968	25.0	3.9	6.3
1969	24.0	3.7	5.8
1970	29.1	5.6	6.9
1971	31.7	7.2	8.7

Source: *Manpower Report to the President, 1972*, p. 163.

FIGURE 7-5

Negro Young Adults are Better Educated Than Older Negroes.

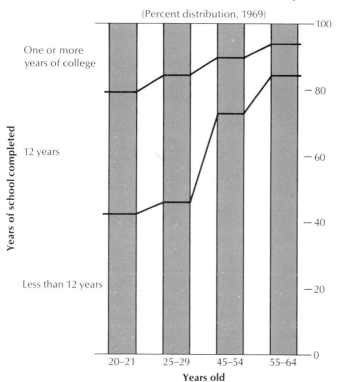

(Percent distribution, 1969)

Source: *Manpower Report to the President, 1968*, p. 93.

compared with a rate variation of two-to-one for white youth vs. white adults. This is despite the fact that there has been a marked increase in the number of this group who complete twelve or more years of formal schooling (Figure 7-5).

Over 55 percent of the black Americans in the age group of twenty to twenty-one years have completed twelve or more years of formal education. As we will see when we discuss poverty in America, the level of education for blacks in the age group of sixteen to nineteen reflects an increasing level of formal education. Despite their increased educational levels, minority groups have continued to experience the excessive levels of unemployment depicted in Table 7-15. Some of this must also be attributed to the general discrimination which the younger worker faces.

THE YOUNG WORKERS AGE SIXTEEN TO TWENTY-ONE

The problems confronting high school graduates and dropouts in obtaining employment have not been conquered by the existence of a boom in the economy. In the 1968-1969 boom periods, when there was full employment with an unemployment rate below 4 percent, the decline experienced in the unemployment rate of young persons in the labor force was not what might have been expected. Most of the problems the young face occur precisely because they are young. Employers often view age, lack of experience, and lack of maturity as key reasons for not employing them. High school graduates and dropouts both suffer from this problem. Viewing unemployment rates as a group, one finds that both white and non-white dropouts experience about twice as much unemployment as the high school graduate.

One of the economic factors currently disputed by professional economists is the impact of minimum wage laws on the unemployment rates of the graduate or the dropout. With the passage of more and broader minimum wage legislation, this dispute becomes a very important consideration for persons involved in employment programs.

In the ten years 1960-1970, there was a large increase in the number of students in the labor force. This was a result of three major factors:

1. The increase in the number of persons in the sixteen to twenty-one age group.
2. The proportion of persons in the age group who remained in school to finish their high school or college work.
3. The proportion of students who worked.

Students seemed to work for reasons other than those related to family income levels. Reasons given by working students covered a broad range; i.e., tuition, expenses, car ownership, work experience, and basic necessities for education.

In the period from 1959 to 1969, there was a major shift in the type of employment and the share of the labor force experienced by students. With the reduction of the percentage of workers employed in agriculture because of technological developments, there was a drop in the portion of student workers in the agricultural area by 10 percent. Student workers showed an increase of 7 percent over the same period of time in service-related employment. There was also a shift for female students from service occupations (household work) to white collar jobs (clerks, secretaries, etc.).

> While the school calendar governs much of the students' movement into and out of the labor force, out-of-school youth typically switch jobs as opportunity allows when working conditions, pay, or other factors make another job more desirable. In the absence of the structured school-to-work patterns found in many European countries,[1] finding "permanent" employment in the United States becomes a process that may take several years rather than a single act of choice. This type of labor market produces relatively high rates of unemployment.[2]
> When jobs become scarce, the greatest difficulty in finding work may be expected to occur among the young, less qualified workers. . . . many young students encountered difficulty securing summertime employment. Some of them may not be able to continue with their college studies (or may have to work during the school year) if they do not earn enough during the summer, especially if Federal Government loan funds or bank loans at reasonable rates are not readily available. The rate of demobilization of the Armed Forces will also affect the labor market for young workers as young men re-enter civilian life.[3]

SEX DISCRIMINATION AND EMPLOYMENT

The excess demand for laborers experienced in the late 1960's played an important role in the increased number of married women who participated in the labor force. As shortages developed in various occupational categories, jobs which had previously been for "men only" began to open up for women. The excess demand for laborers holds the key to the reduction of the amount of sexual discrimination which takes place in the labor market. Other factors, however, have effected a reduction in the amount of sexual discrimination in the labor force. Some of these are:

1. The educational level of women as a group has increased proportionately with increases in the general educational level of the labor force. Thus the bargaining power of women in the labor market has increased.
2. There has been a reduction of the birthrates in the twenty to thirty age group and a desire by young married couples to put off child rearing until they have attained some other goal, i.e., Europe, building a house, saving $5,000, finishing undergraduate or graduate school, etc.
3. The increased participation by women in the labor force has brought

[1] Anne M. Young, "Employment of School Age Youth," *Monthly Labor Review*, Vol. 93, No. 9, September 1970, p. 9.
[2] *Ibid.*, p. 9.
[3] *Ibid.*, p. 11.

forth many proposals. There was a movement in the Congress of the United States to remove from the law books legal restrictions on the number of hours women can work and the types of jobs they can perform.

4. Another proposal is for the development of professional child day-care centers for the children of working parents. The concept of the day-care center is currently being experimented with by various levels of government, private agencies, and private enterprise.

The expansion of various groups in the labor force—youth, blacks, women, and elderly—has provided a challenge to government and economic policy planners. In the 1960's it became apparent to policy makers that more and better jobs were needed. With this demand came the concept of manpower development programs.

> Manpower policy as it has evolved in the sixties is aimed primarily at improving job opportunities and earnings for the American people—by assisting men and women to become more *employable* and *productive* through education and training and improving the processes by which workers and jobs are matched in the manpower market.[4]
>
> If conditions are favorable at the *macro* level of the economic system. . .and if things go well at the *micro-organizational* level. . .then the stage is set for programs that operate at the *micro-individual* level. The successful meshing of the macro and micro organizational and micro-individual policies from the view point of the system as a whole will provide *full employment* with high *productivity*.[5]

THINK IT OVER:

1. What are the basic causes for the shift from the goods-producing sector to the service-producing sector?

2. What characteristics make a person more apt to be the first to be layed off and the last to be hired?

3. Is there a better definition of the labor force than the one we have used?

4. What factors are responsible for unemployment and underemployment in the U.S.? How do economic theories assess these factors?

5. What kinds of policies should economic planners follow in their efforts to reduce underemployment in the economy?

6. What are the economic factors which lead to lower employment levels for non-white groups in the labor force?

7. What considerations should employers take into account in filling a job vacancy? Are these economic, social, or political considerations?

8. What factors contribute to lower employment levels and higher unemployment levels among younger workers? Are these economic or socio-political factors?

[4]Robert L. Darcey, "Helping Youth to Bridge the Gap from School to Work Through Manpower and Economic Education" (Paper, University of Washington, August 1970).

[5]*Ibid.*

POVERTY IN AN AFFLUENT SOCIETY

It is a paradox to many that it is possible for the richest nation in the world to have 12 percent of its population living in poverty. In 1970 the United States spent $14.2 billion on welfare and reached only 13.5 million Americans. This 13.5 million represents only half of the estimated number of persons who are needy and eligible for welfare payments. The 1970 federal poverty level standard is an income of $3,999 for a family of four and $1,500 for a single person. However, poverty is relative. In comparing the living standards of the ghetto black with those of people in foreign countries, one finds that poverty means very different things in different cultures. A ghetto family of six in the U.S. with an income of $2,000 is in dire need judged by American standards, but not by the standards of Hong Kong or Rio de Janeiro ghetto dwellers whose yearly incomes may be $500 or less. Thus we realize that cultural differences determine the level of subsistence.

In order to appreciate the meaning of the $3,999 federal poverty level figure, it is useful to consider how much income is necessary to support an "average" standard of living.

The Bureau of Labor Statistics publishes monthly and yearly estimates of the annual costs of the city worker's family budget. The costs are based on a family of four with a husband age thirty-eight, wife age thirty-six, son age thirteen, and daughter age eight with a "moderate" standard of living. A "moderate" standard of living is that of a family owning a five-to-ten-year old house with a twenty-five-year mortgage, a two-year old car, and a black-and-white television. The family is able to go out to eat once a month. Throughout the entire urban United States the budget costs were $9,191 in 1966. Comparing such figures with the federal standard for a poverty level, we can see the desperate position in which the poverty-stricken find themselves. If a family requires over $9,000 to have a moderate standard of living in an urban area, then the family of four in the ghetto with an income at the upper end of the poverty scale is earning only 40 percent of what it needs to reach that standard.

THEORETICAL PROBLEMS OF POVERTY MEASUREMENT

Some people have suggested that the solution to our poverty problem would be to raise the incomes of the lowest fifth of the labor force, the rationale being that this would eliminate the poor by raising their incomes. Unfortunately, using this solution, we would always have a lowest fifth, and hence the poor would always be with us in terms of their relative position. Two theoretical-graphical depictions of income distribution which are used to measure poverty are the Lorenz curve analysis and the Distribution of Family Incomes.

The Lorenz curve in Figure 7-6 has three lines, A, B, and C, representing

FIGURE 7-6

Lorenz Curve

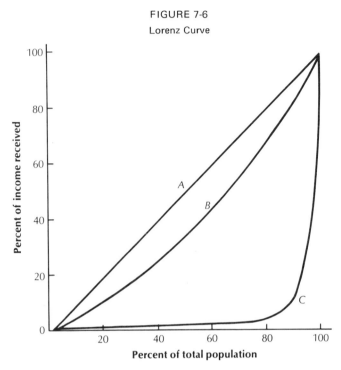

Percent of total population

complete equality of income distribution, relatively equal income distribution, and relatively unequal distribution of income, respectively. With the Lorenz curve approach to poverty measurement, poverty is reduced when the lowest fifth of the income earners receive an increased share of the total income. Using the Lorenz criterion, there has been little or no change in poverty in the United States in that the share of income accruing to the lowest one-fifth of the population has changed very little in the last thirty years. With the Lorenz curve approach, eliminating poverty is a matter of more equally distributing income, as with line A.

The Distribution of Family Incomes for the years 1950-1969 as shown in Figure 7-7 is a means of measuring the improvement of real purchasing power accruing to families. The income scale measures in logarithms the real family income, and the vertical scale indicates the percentage of families with incomes below a certain level. For example, 32 percent of the families received incomes below $3,000 in 1950, while only 8 percent of the families received a real income below $3,000 in 1969. The more equal the income distribution, the more vertical will be the curve. An equal distribution of income would be a vertical line rising from the income of that year.

One of the major benefits of applying this technique is that income levels can be measured in the dollars of a particular base year. All of the poverty levels are expressed in terms of 1969 dollars, eliminating the problem of purchasing power differences in poverty standards over time.

Victor Fuchs has suggested an alternative method of measuring poverty calculated from distribution of family incomes as shown in Figure 7-7. The Fuchs point analysis of income allows a poverty point to be determined at a particular point in time, to be used as a guide to poverty and manpower policy planners. At the same time, it allows shifts of the relative poverty point.[6] The Fuchs analysis is concerned only with the lower half of income distribution;

FIGURE 7-7

Family Income Distribution, 1950-1969

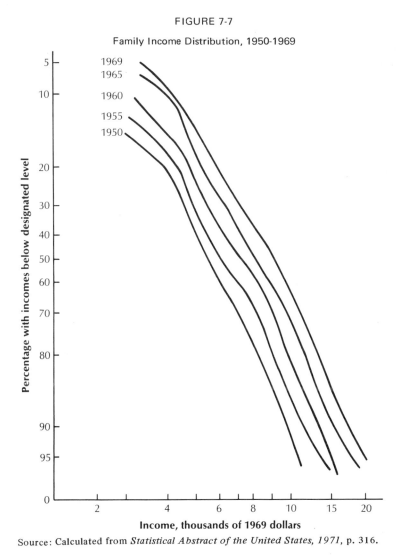

Income, thousands of 1969 dollars

Source: Calculated from *Statistical Abstract of the United States, 1971*, p. 316.

[6]Victor R. Fuchs, "Toward a Theory of Poverty," *The Concept of Poverty*, (Task Force on Economic Growth and Opportunity, Chamber of Commerce of the United States, Washington, D.C., 1965), pp. 69-92.

this relates poverty to the position of the median income earner. Fuchs' studies indicate that in the United States about one-fifth of all families have income levels less than half the median income. The Fuchs criterion establishes a floating poverty level at 50 percent of the median income.

To illustrate the manipulation of the Fuchs point and its use, we look, for example, at the percentage of persons with incomes of $7,000. If we study the four time periods, we can see that in 1950 over 70 percent of the people in the United States had income levels of less than $7,000. In 1955 the percentage of persons having incomes of less than the $7,000 figure had dropped below 60 percent. By 1965, 50 percent earned less than $7,000; and by 1969 this number had been reduced to less than 30 percent. It is of interest to note the sharp reduction in the percentage of persons earning less than $3,000 from 1960 to 1965 during years of rapid economic growth.

The problem of determining the level of income at which a person is in poverty and the level at which he is not is a very difficult one, and there seems to be no easy solution. The Lorenz curve analysis gives a good graphical picture of the amount of inequality. Fuchs' analysis provides a tool to compare the constant dollars to a poverty criterion over a period of time and also provides a floating poverty level which can serve as a guide to manpower and poverty program policy makers.

SOME CAUSES OF POVERTY

AGE, SEX, RACE, NATIONAL ORIGIN

Why is there such a high incidence of unemployment in groups of black, Puerto Rican, and Mexican Americans? Unemployment statistics give us some measure of the conditions of these minority groups. Unemployment figures neglect a major problem of minority groups, that many minority workers are employed at full-time jobs with levels of income below the national poverty standards. This is the concept of sub-employment, which attempts to bring in the "quality" of employment as reflected in the income which the employment produces. In terms of their numbers, the sub-employed pose a much greater problem to manpower planners than do the unemployed.

The 1968 *Manpower Report to the President* designated three groups of labor market barriers facing minority workers:

1. Social-psychological barriers
2. Barriers in attaining access to work
3. Institutional barriers

No group in society is homogeneous, and hence any discussion of the social-psychological barriers will of necessity require some generalization. The first category involves differing levels of aspiration and the effect of this attribute on motivation for employment. Most studies indicate that, while there is less demonstrated need for achievement by the sub-employed, this is not necessarily a barrier to fuller employment.

In the areas of access and institutional barriers, there are personal, environmental, and institutional sub-barriers. In the case of many black, Puerto Rican, and Mexican Americans there is a lack of basic mastery of the English language which is required in most occupations. This factor, combined with other educational deficiencies, provides a large barrier to employment. Added to this problem is the fact that police and debt records are often reasons for rejection from job selection. Besides these personal factors, the minority laborer is often confronted with the fact that his personal, environmental, and cultural background includes a certain style of dress or a certain hairdo which is acceptable to his peers but cause for rejection in the employment office. The minority members of the labor force are often rejected from employment in an interviewer's mind before they have begun an interview. Other considerations include lack of adequate child-care facilities and the lack of access to the job market. As mentioned earlier, most of the unemployed and sub-employed are residents of urban areas. The absence of day-care centers forces poor urban mothers to leave children unattended or to remain at home to care for the children. In addition to the lack of day-care centers is the fact that the amount of money that a welfare mother earns is deducted from her welfare allotment, and it becomes economically impractical for the welfare mother to seek employment.

To examine this problem further, let us consider the case of the following welfare mother. Mrs. X is thirty-two years old, divorced, and the mother of three children, ages five, three, and one. She receives a welfare check of $250 per month. Mrs. X never finished high school and has no particular skill which she could sell in the labor market. The only work she has been able to find is in the local canning factory as a box packer. Her hourly wage at this factory is the federal minimum of $2 an hour. For a forty-hour work week, she will receive $80 or $320 per month. But she will have this amount, $320, deducted from her normal welfare payment and will receive nothing from welfare. Note that she is still $70 ahead because she works, but consider the cost of seeking and locating work. Child care is usually 75 cents to $1 an hour in non-professional day care centers. This is generally on a per-child basis, but we will assume Mrs. X pays the minimum of $1 per hour, or $40 a week. She then pays $160 a month which must be deducted from her $320 income. By going to work, Mrs. X earns a pre-tax income of $160. By staying home on welfare she can collect $250 and be with her children.

The problems of access to the job market are related directly to the location of the urban poor or, for that matter, the rural poor. As cities have decayed in the last twenty years, business firms have moved to the suburbs in an effort to escape the higher city taxes. The few jobs available close to the homes of the unemployed or sub-employed drastically limit the size of the job market within which they can conduct their job search.

Along with this reduced job market is the problem that minorities are often the "last to be hired, first to be fired." As a result of the factors mentioned above involving lack of education, prejudice on the part of employers, and distance from the job source, the sub-employed and unemployed are at the bottom of the job ladder. When there is a slowdown in economic activity, these workers are the first to be laid off and in most cases the last to be rehired. They are also the first to be put out of work by automation because of their lack of formal education and the menial nature of the jobs they are performing.

LACK OF EDUCATION

Educational success and job success seem to have a very close correlation. Of those people who should have completed or did complete high school in June of 1969, those who had not completed it were less likely to be in the labor force and more likely to be unemployed. The dropout was apt to suffer twice the amount of unemployment as his counterpart who completed high school. The dropout is often in the position of having not only his lack of education against him in the labor market, but also the state employment laws with regard to age, the businessman's attitude that the dropout is too immature, and the dropout's own lack of experience. The dropout is also apt to come from a family earning less than $3,000 a year and is apt to be discouraged easily from looking for employment. This last fact would tend to demonstrate that the poverty environment is self-generating or perpetuating.

Lack of formal educational experience is a major factor in the inability of an individual to gain and hold employment. Because of the large number of persons with more years of education, amount of education is often used as a sorting device even though a job may require little or no formal education.

MARKET IMPERFECTIONS

Economists often make the assumption that the participants in the job market have perfect knowledge of all the happenings in the market and that they also have a fairly large degree of mobility. Unfortunately, this is not the case in the labor market; as a result, market imperfections are a major cause of unemployment and sub-employment. The inability of the job seeker to locate acceptable openings determines the length of his unemployment. Even after he finds employment opportunities, he may have difficulty getting transportation to where they are located.

If a worker is an unemployed tool and die operator in Newark, New Jersey, and is out of work because there is a surplus of tool and die workers there, where does he find a job equal to his skill? At the same time he is unemployed in Newark, there may be a shortage of tool and die men in several other areas of the U.S. or even in the New York metropolitan area. Because of a lack of knowledge and lack of mobility, however, he may be trapped in the unemployment, sub-employment, and/or welfare lines of Newark.

MASS UNEMPLOYMENT

The stories of Lawrence Brooks and Jerry Fuller provide us with some insights into the effects of massive amounts of unemployment in the economy such as were experienced in 1961 and 1970.

Brooks and Fuller do not exactly fill the conventional image of people who need welfare. *Time* magazine points out that many Americans imagine the typical welfare family to be a black family who moved from the deep South to get better welfare benefits. The wife is a baby maker, the man in the family is capable of working but won't, and the ten kids can't wait to grow up so they can be on welfare and enjoy life too. These images of welfare probably developed from the Puritan heritage, in which work, thrift, and godliness were opposed to laziness, squandering, and sin. As a result it has been difficult to develop a sound commitment to the development of manpower and poverty programs which will begin to meet the challenge of the problem.

JERRY FULLER, white, 38, former $14,000-a-year electrical engineer who helped build the command module for the 1969 moon landing, is not sure he can hang on to the house in Granada Hills, Calif., where he lives with his wife Pat and three young daughters. "Welfare just doesn't pay enough to make the mortgage payments, buy food, pay doctor bills," he says. After he was laid off in April, 1970, by the North American Rockwell Corporation, he spent seven months seeking another engineering job. He still sends out resumes. But he has been able to find only a low-paying, night shift clerical job, not enough to cover the cost of medical care for one of his daughters. Welfare was his only recourse, and he turned to it reluctantly.

It was not easy. He usually votes Republican, considers himself a conservative. But welfare, from which he receives $108 a month, was the only way. He says: "I was born at the time of the Depression, but I never knew anything about it. You really do develop compassion toward people in a situation like this. Maybe you don't really understand how poor people feel and why they can't pull themselves out unless you have been there yourself." His wife adds: "I can drop down to a certain level because it is always with the knowledge that I am going to go back up again. But what do people look forward to if they don't believe they are going to rise out of it?"

LAWRENCE BROOKS, white, 41, is the very antithesis of the stereotyped welfare client: a Maine lobsterman by trade in summer, logger in winter and breadwinner for his wife and three young boys all year round. Until this year they lived in a wood and tarpaper shack. Now they are in an installment-bought trailer, and to Brooks it is palatial: "I never had living so good. We got central heating."

Winter in Milbridge on the coast is harsh with or without central heating, but Brooks chops down trees in a torn Army jacket too thin for the sub-zero cold. "Most years I can tide us over till summer," he says. "I can get a deer out in the woods. That'll keep a family fed for a while. This one's a mean winter, though."

Pride is giving way to hunger for many this year in Milbridge; the welfare rolls are steadily climbing, and long lines form for free food. The demand for Brooks' logs fell, his wife became ill and the bills simply could not be paid. Brooks and his wife decided that they had to seek help, and he went to the welfare office. "We got some papers in the mail," he recalls, "and it bothered me so bad I got my wife to fill 'em out." He still hopes a thaw, in both the frozen woods and the demand for logs, will let him regain his pride and independence. In the meantime there is only welfare.[7]

The image of the welfare recipient is far from correct. Over half of all welfare recipients (58 percent) are white. The remaining 42 percent who are nonwhite form a disproportionately large number from the minorities, considering the proportion of society made up of minorities and the general labor force. When massive unemployment hits the economy, many Americans who used to look disdainfully on the welfare rolls find that they are forced to live on welfare. As Mrs. Fuller described the situation, "I can drop down to a certain level because it is always with the knowledge that I am going to go back up again. But what do people look forward to if they don't believe that they are going to rise out of it?"

PROPOSALS TO REDUCE INEQUITIES IN INCOME DISTRIBUTION

Measures to alleviate structural and technological unemployment were the goals of much of the planning in the federal government during the 1960's. The Area Redevelopment Act was directed toward giving aid to depressed areas by providing an economic base for industrial development. The Trade Expansion Act was designed to reduce trade barriers by the reduction of tariffs. It was hoped that this would increase employment in the types of industries which export from the United States. In 1962 the Congress of the United States

[7]Reprinted with permission from *Time*, weekly news magazine, February 8, 1971.

enacted the Manpower Development and Training Act (MDTA) with the goal of providing training which would qualify the unemployed and underemployed for jobs, reemployment, and full-employment. An outgrowth of the MDTA was the development of on-the-job training programs as opposed to separate formal training situations. In these programs the learning of new trades took place in the factory or on the construction site rather than in the formal classroom. In 1968, President Johnson called for the establishment of a program called Job Opportunities in the Business Sector. (JOBS) The JOBS program differs from the other programs in that it is directed at specific targets of persistent high unemployment problems. JOBS serves only the disadvantaged and is targeted at the fifty largest urban areas in the United States. With the JOBS program the businessman helps develop the program, supportive programs, and course structures. Other programs of the 1960's which were directed at alleviating the unemployment problems of groups in the labor force included: The Office of Economic Opportunity, The Volunteers in Service to America (VISTA), Vocational Opportunity Centers, and other specific acts directed at specific regions; i.e., Appalachian Regional Development Act.

One of the important factors in the development of Manpower policies has been the effort not only to eliminate unemployment but to assure that the share of the national prosperity which the lower portions of society receive improves over time. Programs in this area center around the Fair Labor Standards Act of 1938 (FLSA) and various amendments to that act. Amendments to the FLSA have attempted to raise the minimum wage and hence the income which accrues to the lower portion of the labor force. The objective of raising the hourly minimum wage is to improve the position of the laborer on the lower end of the labor force and to raise him above some pre-defined poverty level.

The major problem with the FLSA approach of setting a minimum wage is graphically depicted in Figure 7-8. Prior to the existence of the minimum wage, the wage level for street sweepers might have been 75 cents an hour and the employment level, 100 workers. With the imposition of a minimum wage of $1.60 per hour, there would be a reduction in the number of workers demanded. The wage increased to $1.60 an hour for those who were still employed, but the employment rate dropped from 100 workers to 66, while the number of workers willing to work at $1.60 an hour increased to 133. The minimum wage is to the advantage of the workers who are still employed, but it may cause greater employment problems for the economy as businessmen either have less street sweeping done or attempt to find a less expensive method of doing the job, i.e. power street sweepers which can do the job of ten men and can be operated by one.

The concept of society's taking on the responsibility of income maintenance is basically foreign to the American experience. In the past, it was felt that the individual would be able to attain needed income through hard work and clean living. In the case of invalids and individuals who were mentally incapacitated, the family or church-related social services would take care of them.

FIGURE 7-8

Effect of Rising Minimum Wage on Employment

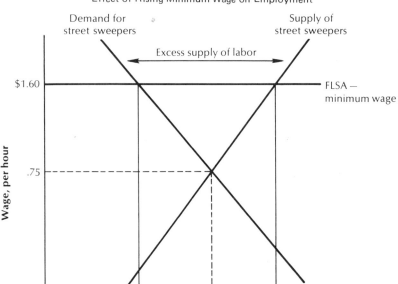

As American society became more complex, the ability of these traditional institutions to meet the needs of the disadvantaged decreased. The passage of Social Security and the development of various types of insurance programs were designed to help meet the needs of the disadvantaged.

GUARANTEED ANNUAL WAGE

Some members of the labor force were able to develop their own protection systems through retirement and pension funds. Unions, through their collective bargaining process, were able to develop programs for income maintenance for the worker who was currently employed and a member of their union. The Guaranteed Annual Wage (GAW) is a system whereby the company guarantees the wage of the worker and then coordinates the production of goods or services to provide stable employment for a stable supply of labor. This system is usually financed by holding back the employees' overtime pay until periods of lessened business activity, thereby guaranteeing the employees a certain number of work weeks.

SUPPLEMENTARY UNEMPLOYMENT BENEFITS

Another proposal for maintenance of the income of workers who are already employed is Supplementary Unemployment Benefits (SUB). This program was negotiated into the labor contract of the United Auto Workers in the mid-1950's. With the SUB program, the company is required to contribute to a fund a stipulated amount of money for each worker per hour. The fund serves as a reserve fund, and when the worker is unemployed, he receives payments from the SUB fund in addition to his regular unemployment compensation. Both the GAW and the SUB programs have provisions which limit the financial liability of the firm.

While the GAW and SUB are a start toward the solution of the income maintenance problem, they are not a cure-all. What about those workers who are not covered by the programs? The portion of workers covered is less than 10 percent. What about the individual who has not worked at the plant long enough to be covered? Most importantly, what about the unemployed, aged, and disabled?

The fact that the GAW and SUB plans have helped those covered by the programs cannot be denied. The problem remains, though, that these programs have been very limited in their impact on the hard-core unemployment and poverty problems in the United States.

The awareness that the economic system, even at full employment, does not provide the basic necessities of life to large numbers of persons has led to a rethinking of the standard American work ethic. The notion that someone should be guaranteed a minimum income, regardless of whether or not he or she works, has been repugnant to many Americans. This repugnancy has been greatest with those groups of people who hold the view that all the virtues associated with work—clean living, thrift, and frugality—are inherent in the godly person. The impetus for some income support level has come from politicians, economists, sociologists, and even businessmen who see the guaranteed level of income as a vehicle capable of solving many of the socio-economic problems of the American economic system. The proposals have had various targets, ranging from work incentive programs to guaranteed minimum incomes with no strings attached.

As a result of investigations into the whole area of poverty, economists have developed various proposals which embody the concept of a Guaranteed Annual Income (GAI). Milton Friedman, Robert Theobold, Edward Schwartz, James Tobin, Robert Lampman, and Daniel Moynihan have been the major contributors of GAI proposals. These proposals have been based on economic, social, humanitarian, and perhaps even political motives.

Friedman Plan. Professor Friedman's plan is based on the utilization of the market mechanism to aid the poor. The idea is that the market mechanism should not be disturbed in the process of aiding the poor. Friedman's proposal for a guaranteed annual income is based on the negative income tax. The lowest level of income of any person would be $1,000. If a family had a pre-tax income of zero dollars they would file their income tax and they would receive from the federal government an income tax payment of $1,500. As a family's income increased from zero, the amount of their negative income tax payment would decrease. Based on a four-person family with the normal deductions of $625 per person, Friedman adds $500 for other exemptions and arrives at his breakeven point of $3,000. A family that earned $3,000 would have a tax rate of zero and a negative tax payment of zero. A family that received an income of less than $3,000 would receive only 50 percent of the difference. The idea of this partial payment is to provide an incentive for the person to work. If he received the full difference, he might not seek employment; but with the 50 percent payment of the differential, he could increase his income by working.

An example is helpful. If a family earned $1,000, the gap between its income and the established breakeven point of $3,000 would be $2,000. The income of the family after the negative income tax payment would be $2,000 ($1,000 plus 50 percent of the gap of $2,000). If the same family sought other work and raised its pre-tax income to $2,000, its income after the negative tax payment would be $2,500.

Since the negative income tax plan which Freidman has proposed utilizes the existing income tax structure for collection and payment, the costs of the program would be relatively small. In conjunction with this proposal Friedman would see the existing welfare programs dropped, the reduction in welfare costs in this area to offset, and even exceed, the cost of the negative income tax plan.

Theobold Plan. A variation of the negative income tax plan proposed by Friedman utilizes a higher base of pay. Theobold's plan calls for a minimum income of $3,200 for a family of four. Theobold sets the level of $3,200 on the basis of $1,000 per adult and $600 per child. This proposal differs from the Friedman approach in that it pays the recipient 100 percent of the difference between his actual income and the $3,200 level. In order to build an incentive into his program he gives a bonus of 10 percent of the individual's privately earned income.

Under the Theobold plan a family which received zero level of income would be paid $3,200. If a family earned an income of $1,500, it would receive $1,700 in the form of a negative income tax which would bring its earnings up to the basic economic security level of $3,200. In addition to the $1,700, the family would receive an incentive bonus equal to 10 percent of the private income it had earned. In this case the family would receive an additional $150. This would bring its total income to $3,350. Using 1960 for his data, Theobold estimated that 20 million people would be covered by his BES proposal. It is his hope that by the development of self-sufficiency other welfare programs can be phased out and the BES level raised to reflect a "moderate" standard of living.

The basis for a moderate level would be the City Worker's Family Budget as compiled by the Bureau of Labor Statistics.

Tobin Plan. Tobin proposes that the head of the family be given an allowance of $400 for each member of the family. This would give a family which received zero income a base income of $1,600. To act as an incentive to work, the family would be allowed to retain two-thirds of any additional income which it earned. Using this formula a family which earned $600 would retain $400 and use $200 to pay back on the base subsidy of $1,600. The total income of the family earning $600 would be $2,000.

Schwartz Plan. Schwartz's proposal involves the extension of our present tax structure. According to his proposal, the poor would fill out forms stating their expected income. The federal government would establish a minimum guaranteed income, and if an individual felt that his income might fall below this minimum, he would file a claim for a federal security benefit. (FSB) The individual would then receive his negative income tax payment, and at the end of the year payments and underpayments would be adjusted.

The FSB and the guaranteed minimum income would be adjusted as to geographical location, the age of the recipients, and the recipient's financial holdings. The Schwartz plan does not have a work incentive program built into it; but if this were necessary for the sake of public acceptance, Schwartz would structure the scale of FSB payments in such a way that the families would benefit more by working than by receiving only the FSB payments.

Lampman Plan. Lampman worked with the Office of Economic Opportunity to devise a proposal which would take into consideration the following goals: improving tax equity, narrowing the poverty income gap, and replacing the present welfare program with a method to aid the poor. Because the poor suffer a greater burden from consumption taxes (sales, food, excise) and because they seldom pay income taxes and therefore do not benefit from the various deductions and exemptions, Lampman proposes two basic plans. The first of these would allow the poor to claim 14 percent of their unused exemptions and deductions *from* the government in the form of a negative tax payment. The second proposal is based on a guaranteed income with various poverty levels and various degrees of Guaranteed Annual Incomes.

Moynihan Plan. Daniel Moynihan served the administration of President Richard M. Nixon from 1968-1970 and convinced the Nixon Administration that the proper course it should follow is a proposal which is called the Family Assistance Plan (FAP). The idea of the FAP proposal is to change the system from one which helps only those who are completely dependent to a system which will move people from dependency to self-sufficiency. President Nixon stated: "We'll place a floor under the income of every family with children. The assistance will not be based on dependency; we will help all families who are below a certain income level."

CONCLUSION

The foregoing shows that, in the market for labor, supply and demand play the predominant role in determining the wage rate and the annual income of the worker. For a large number of persons, however, the market does not and cannot function. In some cases there is no demand for their labor services. In other cases, the worker has few or no services to offer to the market. In both cases there is general agreement that it is the role of government to prevent undue hardship either through employment or income-support programs.

THINK IT OVER:

1. What are the economic factors which permit an affluent society to exist with such a high percentage of poverty?
2. What are the considerations involved in the development of a poverty level?
3. If the Irish, Italian, and Jewish Americans were all able to achieve relative economic affluence, why can't the Mexican, black, and Indian American do the same thing?
4. What factors prevent the individual in the labor force from improving his educational level on a part-time basis and thus "pull himself up by the boot straps?"
5. Should the government pay some members of the labor force not to work? What would be the economic reasoning for your answer?
6. Why shouldn't we allow the free enterprise system to solve the poverty problem with the market system and collective bargaining rather than with federal or state welfare programs?
7. What is the advantage of GAI proposals over the union GAW and SUB programs?
8. What is the economic justification for GAI proposals?

SUGGESTED READING

Economics Readings

Hailstones, Thomas J., Bernard L. Martin and Frank V. Mastrianna. *Contemporary Economic Problems and Issues.* Chicago: South-Western Publishing Co., 1969. (Chapters 4 and 7)

McConnell, Campbell R. *Economics.* 5th ed. New York: McGraw-Hill Book Company, 1972. (pp. 556-578, 658-673)

Samuelson, Paul A. *Economics.* 8th ed. New York: McGraw-Hill Book Company, 1970. (pp. 106-122, 513-522, 762-794)

Silk, Leonard. *Readings in Contemporary Economics.* New York: McGraw-Hill Book Company, 1970. (pp. 107-138, 215, 301)

Personal Economics Readings

AFL-CIO. *Toward Eliminating Poverty.* Industrial Union Department, 815 Sixteenth Street, N.W., Washington, D.C.

Caplovitz, David. *The Poor Pay More.* New York: Free Press of Glencoe, 1963.

Darcy, Robert L. *Helping Youth to Bridge the Gap from School to Work Through Manpower and Economic Education.* Paper, University of Washington, August, 1970.

Delehanty, John A., ed. *Manpower Problems and Policies.* Scranton, Pa.: International Textbook Co., 1969. (pp. 89, 150, 172)

Federal Reserve Bank of Philadelphia. *The New Poverty.*

————. *Unemployment in Prosperity.*

Gordon, Marget S. *Poverty in America.* San Francisco: Chandler Publishing Co., 1965.

Manpower Report to the President 1970, 1971, 1972. Washington, D.C.: U. S. Government Printing Office.

Will, Robert E. and Harold G. Vatter. *Poverty in Affluence.* New York: Harcourt, Brace and Jovanovich, Inc., 1965.

Wolfbein, Seymore L. *Occupational Information.* New York: Random House, 1968. (Chapter 1)

The Dynamics
of Occupations
and of
Occupational Choice

CHAPTER *VIII*

THE DYNAMICS OF OCCUPATIONS AND OF OCCUPATIONAL CHOICE

"Two men working side by side may be performing the same simple task, yet for one the activity is merely a job and for the other it is a step in a career ladder. The first worker feels 'used', unvalued, disposable; the second worker feels involved, valued, committed."[1]

As one looks at the various opportunities available to people entering the labor force, it is important to consider the quality of the job opportunity. One of the most important first steps in improving the quality of the job is looking at the job as a career rather than as a dead-end means of making a living. The sooner this concept is adopted on a broad basis, the more apt we are to be able to reduce discouragement, the greatest problem associated with the marginal worker in the labor force.

In recent years there has been a shift in the concern and direction of manpower policy. Policy makers are no longer interested only in the quantitative aspects of employment. Now the emphasis in manpower programs has shifted to the qualitative aspects. What characteristics of employment are adverse to the development of one's self-image? Does the work fall smoothly into the life pat-

---

[1] Sidney A. Fine, "Guidelines for the Development of New Careers," (Staff Paper, Kalamazoo, Michigan, W.E. Upjohn Institute for Employment Research, September, 1967).

terns of the worker or is it an unpleasant burden which he must bear? These kinds of concerns require close investigation into the work, not the sterile work environment but the larger area of the impact which the work has on an employee.

There are many methods which can be used to ascertain trends in this area. Surveys of employees' attitudes toward their jobs appear to be the most logical and dependable approach at the present time. Questionnaires dealing with the desire of workers to have a job change, their degree of satisfaction with their current employment, and their reasons for liking a particular type of employment all provide researchers with insight into the qualitative aspects of manpower employment programs.

Table 8-1 provides some insight into the value people place on certain factors with regard to their employment. After studying such data, manpower planners are able to make suggestions for the improvement of the quality of the job. It is significant that workers who are considered to have "good" jobs rate the intrinsic factors considerably higher than the group of workers (clerical and unskilled) who fall into what might be considered dead-end jobs. It would appear that when the job a person is performing requires little initiative he rates the use of his own resources lower than the person who sees his job as a career with possibilities for advancement or personal enrichment.

TABLE 8-1

IMPORTANCE OF DIFFERENT JOB FACTORS TO EMPLOYED ADULTS

Occupation	Number	Percent specifying intrinsic factors			Percent specifying extrinsic factors		
		Interesting work	Use of skill, talent	Feeling of satisfaction	Pay	Security	Co-workers
Total white-collar	400	65	57	58	62	23	35
Professional and managerial	217	68	64	68	59	16	25
Clerical and sales	183	62	48	46	66	31	46
Total blue-collar	233	55	42	42	73	42	46
Skilled	98	61	51	46	70	33	40
Semiskilled and unskilled	135	50	35	39	74	49	52

Source: *Manpower Report to the President, 1968*, page 51.

OCCUPATIONS CURRENTLY EXPANDING IN THE LABOR FORCE

The education explosion spanning the years from 1950 to 1985 will have a profound impact on the nature of the labor force and the types of occupations available to persons in the United States. In the space of 35 years, the labor force will have increased by nearly 80 percent, but the number of college graduates will have tripled. The effects of the increased educational level will have the greatest impact on those people who are currently in the labor force and those who are entering the labor force with less education than the average.

By the year 1985, the median educational achievement will be 12.6 years, and the level for blacks will be 12.3 years. Compare this with 1965, when the median for the nation was 12.2 years for white workers and 9.9 years for non-white workers.

These increasing levels of educational achievement will pose a problem for the manpower planners of the future. While the labor force ages twenty-five and over will be growing at a rate of 1.6 percent, the level of high school graduates will increase at a rate of 3.7 percent. The implications of this growth will be felt in the desired expansion of employment opportunities allowing meaningful work experiences for individuals with higher educational levels.

The projected educational levels present two major problems: (1) The measurement does not consider the quality of the educational experience. (2) There is a tendency to understate the value of informal training. The emphasis on formal instruction tends to overstate the qualifications of those workers who attend institutions of inferior quality. The man who "passed" all of the courses on an attendance basis and received his diploma may not be as qualified as an individual who completed only grade school but who has had years of on-the-job experience. Yet, the person with the diploma will tend to get the job simply because he has a diploma.

These shifts in educational levels of the general labor force will cause problems for those individuals who do not have a formal education. The education explosion will result in increased employer expectations of the necessary educational level. The common laborer will need a high school diploma to get a job sweeping floors. The store clerk may need post-high school work in order to compete in the labor market. The result of this situation is that in a period of slack economic activity, the job applicant without formal educational experience may not be given equal opportunity. The high school or college diploma becomes a means of sorting workers from an over-supplied labor market.

Figure 8-1 gives us a view of educational experience during three different time periods: average of 1964-66; projected to 1975; and projected to 1985. As the bar chart indicates, the more recent entrants to the labor force, those in the twenty-five to thirty-four years of age group, will exert great pressure on the older workers with less formal education.

Employment opportunities are changing from a goods-producing orientation to a service-producing orientation (refer to Tables 8-3 and 8-4 for statistical support). In 1950 little more than one-third of the jobs occupied fell into the white collar classification. In 1960, 43 percent of all jobs were categorized as

FIGURE 8-1

Percent of Persons in Population and Civilian Labor Force with 4 Years
of High School or More, by Age and Sex, Selected Years.

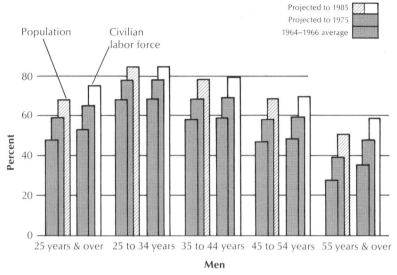

The projected increase in the proportion of high school graduates among adult men
points to a more educationally uniform population and labor force by 1985.

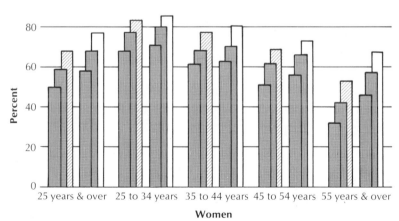

Increased educational homogeneity is also foreseen among adult women
in the population and labor force by 1985.

Source: Denis F. Johnston, "Education of Adult Workers: Projections to 1985," *Monthly Labor Review*, August, 1970, p. 49.

TABLE 8-2

MEDIAN MONEY INCOME OF PERSONS BY SEX AND OCCUPATION: 1947 TO 1969

Sex and Occupation	1947	1950	1955	1960	1965	1968	1969
Male employed civilians	$2,406	$2,831	$3,797	$4,822	$5,907	$7,080	$7,659
Professional, technical, and kindred workers	3,972	4,073	5,429	6,692	8,313	9,960	11,062
Self-employed	5,472	6,188	8,338	9,545	13,423	16,356	17,886
Salaried	3,705	3,880	5,269	6,564	7,987	9,715	10,730
Farmers and farm managers	1,456	1,496	1,283	1,941	2,985	3,734	3,887
Managers, officials, proprietors, except farm	3,354	3,814	5,228	6,519	8,143	9,765	10,822
Self-employed	3,084	3,263	4,532	5,036	6,442	7,365	7,787
Salaried	3,673	4,431	5,712	7,591	8,991	10,717	11,762
Clerical and kindred workers	2,654	3,103	3,950	5,011	5,772	7,034	7,458
Salesworkers	2,687	3,137	4,472	4,990	6,033	7,367	7,876
Craftsmen, foremen, and kindred workers	2,746	3,293	4,423	5,582	6,592	7,705	8,344
Operatives and kindred workers	2,373	2,790	3,695	4,477	5,395	6,209	6,741
Service workers, except private household	2,096	2,303	3,036	3,412	4,161	4,820	5,041
Farm laborers and foremen	846	854	1,039	1,103	1,411	2,073	2,124
Laborers, except farm and mine	1,707	1,909	2,599	2,868	3,405	4,165	4,464
Unemployed	858	848	1,680	2,739	2,358	3,200	3,823
In Armed Forces or not in labor force			967	1,198	1,432	1,853	1,965
Female employed civilians	1,372	1,559	1,926	2,348	2,771	3,380	3,598
Professional, technical and kindred workers	1,889	2,175	2,994	3,870	4,732	5,598	6,054
Self-employed	(B)	(B)	(B)	1,397	2,705	1,803	2,294
Salaried	1,919	2,238	3,043	4,020	4,863	5,733	6,158
Farmers and farm managers	(B)	(B)	(B)	(B)	(B)	(B)	1,919
Managers, officials, proprietors, except farm	1,858	1,674	2,375	2,948	3,495	4,616	5,346
Self-employed	1,639	1,129	1,438	1,532	2,257	2,902	3,177
Salaried	2,025	2,297	3,253	3,728	4,090	5,192	5,836
Clerical and kindred workers	1,728	2,074	2,667	3,122	3,525	4,002	4,271
Salesworkers	1,118	1,109	1,300	1,505	2,063	2,248	2,222
Craftsmen, foremen, and kindred workers	(B)	(B)	(B)	3,125	3,529	4,145	4,457
Operatives and kindred workers	1,406	1,661	2,110	2,489	2,832	3,506	3,700
Private household workers	428	427	610	614	728	806	800
Service workers, except private household	913	913	1,246	1,636	1,764	2,226	2,321
Farm laborers and foremen	(B)	(B)	(B)	412	713	795	839
Laborers, except farm and mine	(B)	(B)	(B)	(B)	(B)	2,984	2,957
Unemployed	517	488	778	1,138	1,161	1,374	1,686
In Armed Forces or not in labor force			575	654	811	1,046	1,094

B Not shown; base too small.

Source: *Statistical Abstract of the United States, 1971*, p. 320.

white collar; and in 1971 over 50 percent were white collar. The greatest increases in job opportunities are anticipated in state and local government, construction, and service industries which tend to be non-mechanized operations. Geographically the Mountain states and the Pacific coast states will have the fastest increase in job opportunities, and New England and the Middle Atlantic states will experience comparatively slower rates of job increase. *Time* Magazine listed the following as "promising occupations" in an article of February 15, 1971.

Computer Programmer
Physician
Dietitian
Salesman
Medical Technician
Optometrist
Dentist
Repairman
Geologist
System Analyst
Craftsman
Psychologist
Financial Expert
Social Scientist
Oceanographer[2]

FINANCIAL REWARDS AND UNEMPLOYMENT ASSOCIATED WITH VARIOUS OCCUPATIONS

The financial return of various occupations is of great concern to the individual who is attempting to plan for the future. Table 8-2 provides information as to the median incomes of various occupations in the United States from 1947 to 1969. The income levels described are in dollar figures and do not reflect changes in the cost of living. Once again, the jobs which provide some degree of challenge and opportunity for individual growth and development are also the jobs which generally return the highest financial remuneration. The chart provides a view of the changes in income that have taken place in various jobs over a 22-year period.

Figures 8-2 and 8-3 provide other insights into the incomes associated with various occupations. Once again the types of jobs which provide the *least* opportunity for personal growth are those which have the highest rates of unemployment. These jobs are the first to be cut in slack economic periods.

[2]Reprinted with permission from *Time*, a weekly news magazine.

FIGURE 8-2

Unemployment Rates by Occupation 1958 to Date
Seasonally Adjusted

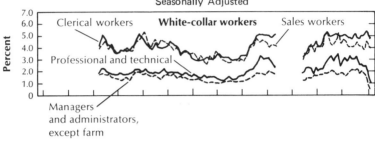

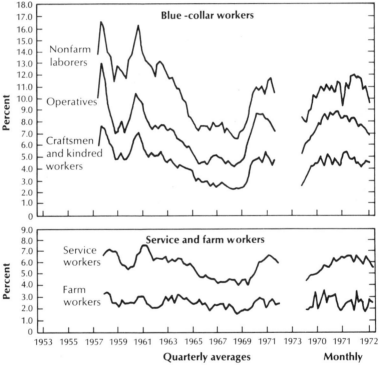

Source: *Employment and Earnings*, U.S. Department of Labor, Bureau of Labor Statistics,
Vol. 19, No. 1, July, 1972.

Workers in the services or semi-professional and professional fields suffer far less
unemployment than the typical non-farm laborer. The occupation which requires
the least skill is apt to produce the greatest percentage of full-time employees
who earn less than $3,000.

In attempting to determine the characteristics of occupations with great financial reward, certain pictures come to mind. People who put out oil well fires receive $2,000 an hour, professional athletes receive contracts for over $100,000, plumbers get paid $8 an hour for their services, medical doctors receive $10 for a ten-minute office call, and car hops make less than $1.75 per hour in most drive-in restaurants. What do these occupations have in common? Are there some characteristics which determine who will be the most financially rewarded?

First and foremost in our consideration of these questions is the type of demand for these occupations. Most high-paying jobs face either a high demand for the good or service provided or else a low supply of persons willing and able to perform the production of the good or service. In the case of the athlete there is usually a great deal of demand for the personality, and he is able to receive a relatively high wage. With the plumber and the doctor as with the athlete, there

FIGURE 8-3

Proportion of Men with Low Earnings Has Dropped at All Occupational Levels.

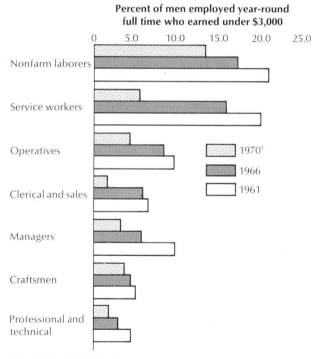

Percent of men employed year-round full time who earned under $3,000

Note: Nonfarm occupations only.
[1]Below 1970 poverty level definition.

Source: *Current Population Reports, Consumer Income,* December 1970, U. S. Department of Commerce, Bureau of the Census, p. 57.

is a high demand for their services and a limited supply; as a result they are well paid. Car hops have a problem. While there is a demand for their services, there is an excess number of persons who can perform the service. As a result of the large supply, the car hop receives a lower wage than the other occupations in the example. The oil well fighter has the advantage of providing a service that is demanded and that has a short supply of people willing to perform the service because of the personal danger.

If an occupation requires some degree of skill and/or formal education and is demanded by large numbers of the buying public, then that type of occupation will tend to be high paying. Some examples of occupations which meet all of the criteria are: television entertainers, computer programmers, nuclear physicists, chemists, and others.

HIGH DEMAND OCCUPATIONS IN THE FUTURE

The trends that have been discussed with regard to technological change and its impact on the labor force would indicate certain movements in the labor force with regard to the kinds of job opportunities which will exist in the future.

TABLE 8-3

U.S. EMPLOYMENT BY OCCUPATION, 1964 AND PROJECTED 1975

Occupational Group	Actual 1964 Employment		Projected 1975 Employment		Percent Change, 1964-75
	Number (Thousands)	Percent	Number (Thousands)	Percent	Percent
White-collar workers:	31,125*	43.9%	42,800	48.3%	+ 38%
Professional & technical	8,550	12.2	13,200	14.9	+ 54
Managers, officials, & owners	7,452	10.2	9,200	10.4	+ 23
Clerical workers	10,667	15.2	14,600	16.5	+ 37
Sales workers	4,456	6.3	5,800	6.5	+ 30
Blue-collar workers:	25,534	36.4	29,900	33.7	+ 17
Craftsmen & foremen	8,986	12.8	11,400	12.8	+ 27
Operatives	12,924	18.4	14,800	16.7	+ 15
Nonfarm laborers	3,624	5.2	3,700	4.2	+ 3
Service workers	9,256	13.2	12,500	14.1	+ 35
Farm workers	4,444	6.3	3,500	3.9	− 21
TOTAL, All Groups	70,359	100.0%	88,700	100.0%	+ 26

Note: Percentages do not add to 100 because of rounding.
*To be read as 31,125,000 (31 million, 125 thousand)
Source: *America's Industrial and Occupational Manpower Requirements, 1964-75*, U. S. Department of Labor, Bureau of Labor Statistics, January 1, 1966, p. 128.

Increased educational levels and the automation of menial tasks will cause a shift to occupations which are in the nature of performing a service. In Table 8-3 growth in the period from 1964 to 1975 is centered in the professional and technical fields with this area increasing its number of workers by 54 percent. Clerical and service worker employment will increase by greater than 30 percent. A reduction of job opportunities is expected to occur in the unskilled areas, with farming experiencing a loss of 21 percent and non-farm laborers experiencing only a small gain of 3 percent. The total gain over the eleven-year period will be an increase of greater than 25 percent. Any occupation group which experiences a growth rate of less than 25 percent is apt to be a declining or dead-end job.

It should be noted that economic, political, and social conditions can have a great impact on the occupational outlook. In the period of time since 1966, the environmental revolution has occurred. The cut-back in military spending resulted in layoffs that made the aerospace engineer and aerospace skilled worker occupations look less enticing. For this reason the *Occupational Outlook Handbook* of the U. S. Department of Labor is revised yearly with information for the person seeking a career with opportunity for future growth.

Projected labor force demand for the period ending with 1980 indicates a strong need for workers in the professional and technical areas. A 50 percent increase in employment of professional workers will be forthcoming as a result of plans to put more effort into the country's socio-economic progress. Urban renewal, mass transportation, and improved environmental quality are some

FIGURE 8-4

Extent of Education and Training Necessary in Job Categories

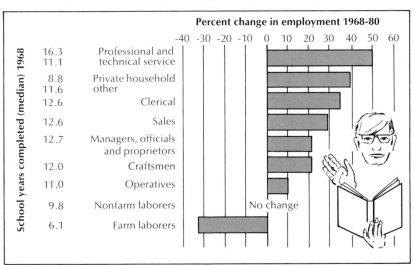

Source: *Occupational Outlook Handbook, 1970-71*, U.S. Department of Labor, Bureau of Labor Statistics. p. 16.

of the more pressing issues. The areas of social and medical services should see outstanding growth. Service, clerical and sales groups will continue to expand, but at a rate slower than the professional sector. Craftsmen and machine operators will have a slow growth rate, at less than 2 percent per year. Perhaps most importantly, the demand for laborers and farm workers will actually decline. Thus there is the need to plan for careers which have a future. This cannot be left to chance. Demand considerations and the expected supply of entrants must be carefully evaluated. One must search for a high demand area which has only a modest expected growth in job applicants. This process requires a careful search of the available data sources for accurate forecasts of these variables. It is of interest to note that there is a direct relationship between expected demand for workers and the level of educational attainment (see Figure 8-4). Members of the professional category have completed 16.3 years of schooling, whereas those in the labor group have only completed nine years. The conclusion is that the level of formal schooling is a basic factor in determining job classifications available to the worker.

INCOME, OCCUPATIONS, AND EDUCATION

The correlation between level of education and the amount of income, in most cases, is a very direct relationship. In Table 8-4 we are able to study the percent distribution of families by income, educational level, and race of the head of the family.

First, it should be noted that the percentage of people with low incomes is highest with that group of persons who had less than eight years of schooling. Over 40 percent of the persons with less than eight years of schooling earned less than $5,000. In the group of people with four or more years of college only 5 percent earned less than $5,000. At the opposite end of the income scale, the same data can be related. Almost 80 percent of those who complete four or more years of college earned incomes of over $10,000 while less than 22 percent of the group with less than eight years of education earned $10,000 or more.

Further evidence of the impact of education on income level can be seen by considering the expected life-time earnings of individuals with various educational backgrounds. Table 8-5 indicates expected life-time earnings and correlates them with the level of formal education attained by the prospective worker. In this table, incomes are measured on the percentage of income of high school graduates.

It should be noted that there are levels with greater differences between them than other levels. For example, the difference between the high school graduate and the person with one to three years of college is only 19 percent, but the difference between the high school graduate and the college graduate is

TABLE 8-4

MONEY INCOME – PERCENT DISTRIBUTION OF FAMILIES, BY INCOME LEVEL, BY YEARS OF SCHOOL COMPLETED AND RACE OF HEAD: 1961 AND 1969

Race of Head and Year of school Completed	Number of families (1,000)	Number Under $3,000	$3,000-$4,999	$5,000-$6,999	$7,000-$9,999	$10,000-$14,999	$15,000 and over	Median income
1961								
White families	39,630	18.3	18.8	22.7	22.4	12.6	5.4	$ 6,100
Elementary school	13,525	32.9	24.2	19.3	15.0	6.7	1.9	4,419
High school	17,645	12.3	19.2	27.3	25.6	12.1	3.4	6,344
1-3 years	7,103	15.2	20.1	27.4	24.2	10.5	2.6	6,036
4 years	10,542	10.4	18.5	27.2	26.6	13.2	3.9	6,548
College	8,460	6.9	9.3	18.4	27.3	22.8	15.3	8,560
1-3 years	3,773	9.9	11.9	21.4	28.4	17.8	10.5	7,586
4 years or more	4,687	4.3	7.2	16.2	26.4	26.9	19.0	9,503
Negro and other familes	4,190	45.7	24 7	14.4	9.3	4.8	1.3	3,340
Elementary school	2,416	57.4	24.2	10.7	5.1	2.0	0.7	2,593
High school	1,414	33.7	27.8	18.3	11.8	6.3	2.0	4,115
1-3 years	804	39.6	28.9	17.7	6.8	4.9	2.1	3,711
4 years	610	26.0	26.5	19.3	18.2	8.1	1.9	4,773
College	360	16.7	14.3	23.1	26.5	17.0	2.3	6,593
1-3 years	201	23.6	16.8	24.1	22.8	11.4	1.3	(B)
4 years or more	159	7.8	11.3	21.8	31.3	24.3	3.4	(B)
1969								
White families	42,967	7.7	9.3	11.1	21.4	28.8	21.9	10,089
Elementary school	10,852	17.4	18.6	15.6	21.4	18.6	8.3	6,769
Less than 8 years	5,207	23.1	20.0	16.2	19.1	15.1	6.5	5,799
8 years	5,645	12.3	17.2	15.1	23.5	22.0	9.8	7,651
High school	20,984	5.3	7.3	11.6	24.5	32.4	19.1	10,181
1-3 years	7,026	7.6	9.8	13.3	24.4	29.4	15.7	9,342
4 years	13,958	4.2	6.0	10.6	24.4	34.1	20.7	10,563
College	11,131	2.9	3.6	5.6	15.8	31.7	40.5	13,426
1-3 years	4,914	3.8	4.6	7.5	19.4	33.8	30.8	11,949
4 years or more	6,216	2.3	2.7	4.1	12.9	30.0	48.1	14,685
Negro and other families	4,746	19.5	18.9	17.3	19.7	15.9	9.0	6,340
Elementary school	1,988	29.1	23.5	17.8	16.0	9.9	3.7	4,754
Less than 8 years	1,485	32.1	24.6	16.9	14.5	8.5	3.5	4,351
8 years	503	20.3	20.1	20.6	20.5	14.2	4.4	5,927
High school	2,178	14.6	16.8	18.6	22.7	19.3	8.1	7,002
1-3 years	1,078	19.6	20.2	17.9	22.0	14.8	5.6	6,217
4 years	1,101	9.9	13.6	19.2	23.2	23.7	10.6	7,875
College	580	4.3	11.0	10.0	21.0	23.7	30.0	10,555
1-3 years	306	6.3	14.3	13.5	25.7	23.0	17.0	9,194
4 years or more	274	2.1	7.4	5.9	15.6	24.5	44.4	13,682

Source: *Statistical Abstract of the United States, 1971,* p. 319.

TABLE 8-5

ESTIMATED LIFETIME EARNINGS, BY YEARS OF SCHOOL COMPLETED*

Year of School Completed	Lifetime Earnings*	Earnings as % of H. S. Graduates
Less than 8 years	$143,000	58%
8 years	184,000	75
1 to 3 years of high school	212,000	86
4 years of high school	247,000	100
1 to 3 years of college	293,000	119
4 years of college	385,000	156
5 or more years of college	455,000	185

*Total earnings between ages 18 and 64; data for males only. Estimates are based on actual earnings in 1959, with projections for the future based on continuing growth of the economy.

Source: Herman P. Miller, Bureau of the Census, *Income Distribution in the United States, 1966,* p. 270.

TABLE 8-6

LIFETIME EARNINGS BY OCCUPATION AND YEARS OF SCHOOLING

Occupation	1 to 3 years of high school	4 years of high school	1 to 3 yrs. of college	4 yrs. of college
Accountants & Auditors	$272,000	$286,000	$292,000	$361,000
Carpenters	193,000	209,000	207,000	229,000
Clerical Workers	203,000	218,000	225,000	258,000
Electrical & Electronic Technicians	263,000	270,000	263,000	–
Farm Laborers & Foremen	97,000	117,000	138,000	167,000
Laborers (nonfarm)	157,000	173,000	174,000	192,000
Plumbers & Pipe Fitters	242,000	252,000	258,000	–
Policemen & Detectives	217,000	230,000	246,000	286,000
Sales Workers	232,000	276,000	306,000	287,000

Note: Estimates are for males only.
Source: *Income Distribution in the United States*, Bureau of the Census, pp. 269-296.

56 percent. The break between the person with only eight years of education and the person who is a high school dropout is only 11 percent, but the difference between the high school graduate and the eight-year man is 25 percent.

There is a direct correlation between income and the educational background of the income earner. However, there are situations in which the increase in income may not be worth the cost involved in obtaining more education. In Table 8-6 are the life-time earnings of nine specific occupational types. In this breakdown it is evident that it is better to have completed high school and started work than go on to partial completion of college. This difference is due largely to the lost income which the person who only partially completes college never received and the fact that an unfinished degree does not allow a person to enter some professions or jobs. In some of the job categories—for example, plumbers, pipe fitters, and sales workers—the additional education will probably cost more than the expected gain in life-time earnings.

SUGGESTED READINGS

Personal Economics Readings

Becker, Gary S. *Human Capital.* New York: National Bureau of Economic Research, 1964.

Burt, Samuel M. and Herbert Striner. *Toward Greater Industry and Government Involvement in Manpower Development.* Kalamazoo: W. E. Upjohn Institute for Employment Research, September, 1968.

Committee on Unemployment Insurance Objectives. *Unemployment and Income Security Goals for the 1970's.* Kalamazoo: W. E. Upjohn Institute for Employment Research, 1969.

Darcy, Robert L. and Phillip E. Powell. *Manpower and Economic Education.* New York: Joint Council on Economic Education, 1970.

Fine, Sidney A. *Guidelines for the Design of New Careers.* Kalamazoo: W. E. Upjohn Institute for Employment Research, September, 1967.

——. *Guidelines for the Employment of the Culturally Disadvantaged.* Kalamazoo: W. E. Upjohn Institute for Employment Research, June, 1969.

Gaines, Tilford. *Prices and Pay.* New York: Economic Report of the Manufacturers Hanover Trust, January, 1971.

Galenson, Walter. *A Primer on Employment and Wages.* 2nd ed. New York: Random House, 1970.

Haber, William and M. G. Murray. *Unemployment Insurance in the American Economy.* Homewood, Ill.: Richard D. Irwin, Inc., 1966.

Hyghe, Howard, "Employment of High School Graduates and Dropouts," special Labor Force report #121, *Monthly Labor Review,* August, 1970.

Johnston, Denis F., "Education of Adult Workers: Projections to 1985," *Monthly Labor Review,* August, 1970.

LernBae, Eric and Rolf Meyersohn. *Mass Leisure.* New York: Free Press, 1958.

Levitan, Sar A. *Federal Manpower Policies and Programs to Combat Unemployment.* Kalamazoo: W. E. Upjohn Institute for Employment Research, February, 1964.

National Manpower Council. *Woman Power.* New York: Columbia University Press, 1970.

——. *Work in the Lives of Married Women,* 1958.

New England Business Review, "Does Retraining Pay?" Boston: Federal Reserve Bank of Boston, July, 1966.

——. "The Case of the Displaced Worker." Boston: Federal Reserve Bank of Boston, December, 1965.

Perrella, Vera C. "Employment of High School Graduates and Dropouts," *Monthly Labor Review,* #2657, 1970.

Rosenberg, Jerry M. *Automation, Manpower, and Education.* New York: Random House, 1966.

Schwab, Paul M., "Unemployment by Region and in Largest States," *Monthly Labor Review,* 1969.

Sheppard, Harold L. *Effects of Family Planning on Poverty in the United States.* Kalamazoo: W. E. Upjohn Institute for Employment Research, December, 1968.

Striner, Herbert E. *1984 and Beyond: The World of Work.* Kalamazoo: W. E. Upjohn Institute for Employment Research, October, 1967.

Transfer Payments, Insurance, and Investments as Sources of Family Income

CHAPTER *IX*

TRANSFER PAYMENTS, INSURANCE, AND INVESTMENTS
AS SOURCES OF FAMILY INCOME

The source of income of most people during most of their adult lifetime is wages or salaries. In the preceding section a rather detailed discussion presented the trends in occupational demand over the past several years and attempted to provide insight into the occupations which would be demanding increasing numbers of workers. For most persons the major economic decision is a decision to enter a particular vocation that will allow them to earn a satisfactory level of income over their lifetime. Obviously the purpose of earning this income is to obtain purchasing power to buy desired goods and services. Even though the working portion of our lifetime is the most important, there are times and situations when individuals are not gainfully employed.

We all, at some point in our lifetimes, must face the prospect of retirement and withdrawal from the work force. At this period in our lives, we hope and expect to be able to continue consuming goods and services in quantities and combinations somewhat similar to the quantities and combinations consumed during the working, productive years. Thus it becomes crucial that individuals plan during their working years for retirement and in so doing either save, invest, or build up pension fund credits so as to be able to continue making expenditures at a time when income from wages and salaries approaches zero.

A second factor facing nearly all individuals is the possibility of being unemployed for short periods of time. In a growing dynamic economy, there will be changes in the demand for labor. There was recently a shift from the aerospace industry. As a result of this change in the demand for aerospace goods, many employees in that industry found that their services were no longer needed and that they were faced with termination. This unemployment situation varied from temporary unemployment to extremely long-run unemployment situations in which individuals found that it would be impossible for them to return to their previous jobs and that they had to find gainful employment in other areas. Here again the individual is faced with a problem of a limitation on current income from wages and salary sources. However, the obligations and desires of the individual and his family do not cease. There are still rental or mortgage payments to be met; food must be purchased; and certain quantities of income must be available for the other necessities of life even though the current income is zero.

In addition to retirement and temporary unemployment the family faces the potential for an even more serious problem. It is possible that the primary income earner may either be permanently disabled or die prior to the time when the family has either grown and moved on to their own lives or prior to the time when the primary income earner has been able to amass enough savings, retirement contributions, or insurance to provide for them.

The basic goal or objective of a family unit or of an individual is often considered to be the desire to obtain sufficient income or purchasing power over their *lifetimes* to insure that adequate goods and services can be purchased. This means that there are basically two separate and distinct problems to consider. The first problem is that of acquiring skills, placing these skills in the market, and obtaining in return for the services rendered a wage or salary for the factors of production offered to the market. This part of the problem is, in effect, the amassing or earning of a lifetime income. A lifetime income for most persons is earned between the ages of twenty to twenty-five and sixty-five, the age at which retirement affects most individuals. The factors which determine the aggregate amount of this flow of income and, to some extent, the flow of this income during the working years are employment or career decisions. The second part of the problem is to allocate this flow of income earned primarily between ages twenty-one and sixty-five over a lifetime which may extend beyond age sixty-five and to allocate the flow not only to the primary wage earner but also to his family and dependents. The primary income earner must be sure that:

    (a) he will have sufficient funds to allow for command over goods and services in retirement,

(b) he will have sufficient funds to meet periods of temporary adversity, either illness or temporary unemployment and

(c) he will have sufficient funds to meet responsibilities and to provide for dependents in the event of either disability or death prior to the normal retirement age.

How can the wage earner have such assurances? Basically the problems outlined above can be expressed as a problem of cash flow. The flow of income to the family or the income unit is not necessarily equal to the demands or flow of expenditures out of the unit for the purchases of goods and services. During the early years of a person's life he is dependent on the income earning power of the family or upon the state for transfer payments. In the early twenties most persons enter the world of work and establish a family relationship. At this time the flow of expenditure tends to be greater than the flow of income. The formation of a family and establishment of a household requires substantial outlay for "capital" goods—car, furniture, house, etc. These goods are frequently purchased on credit. In this case credit is used as an extension of income.

During the middle years earning power increases, and the demands for goods usually decline; as a result, the spending unit has increased savings. At retirement earned income declines, and the family must use savings to support consumption expenditures.

INCOME ALLOCATION DURING THE WORKING YEARS

The allocation of income and expenditures during the working years for a spending unit requires that cash flow and expenditure flow be matched in such a way as to provide the greatest level of overall enjoyment for that spending unit. It is convenient to think in terms of spending units as this eliminates the problem of talking in terms of families or separate individuals. The census defines the spending unit as a group of individuals living together, pooling their income and making common expenditures from that income. The most common spending unit, of course, is the family. In addition, however, spending units can be unrelated persons living together; persons living in a commune, for example, are a spending unit. Spending units must consider the possible interruption of the income flow resulting from unemployment, death, and risks associated with accidental loss and ill health. In addition to current considerations, it is important that the spending unit consider setting aside a portion of current income to provide for retirement.

PLANNING FOR RETIREMENT

When a wage earner retires after thirty to forty-five years of productive employment, he hopes and expects that his income level will allow him to enjoy the retirement years rather than cause them to be years of frustration and

FIGURE 9-1

Typical Lifetime Income, Expenditure, and Saving

deprivation. Partly in an attempt to insure that persons will have sufficient purchasing power, many firms have instituted pension and retirement systems. These systems collect contributions from the employee and the employer and are then frequently managed by an officer outside the firm for the benefit of the retired employees. This system of privately financed pensions is supplemented by the federally financed Social Security Administration. The Social Security funds are collected through taxes on both the employer and the employee and are, in effect, a means of transferring purchasing power from the working population to the retired population. When a worker retires he also should have the benefits of his savings program, whether this savings program be in the form of insurance of one form or another, or savings accounts, or the return on investments made with his savings. In addition, during the working years the retiree may also have engaged in part-time work.

Thus, the person needs to consider a package or combination approach. One needs to evaluate the sources of income flowing from insurance, investments, Social Security, and private pension funds and evaluate these in terms of the annual or monthly amount and expected duration of these payments. One should not consider that Social Security will be sufficient to maintain a reasonable standard of living in retirement nor that the returns from life insurance annuities will completely meet the needs of the retiree. One should consider that these several sources, in combination, have to serve a dual purpose. The insurance and saving programs during the working years must protect the income of the family or spending unit. At the same time it must be building toward a source of income for the retiree at the time when he is no longer gainfully employed.

The most important consideration that one has as a consumer is to combine current spending for goods and services and saving for the future. It is necessary to trade some present consumption for future consumption. This is an extremely difficult task since, as individuals, we value the present very highly and discount the future. That is, we would much rather have a new car today than to have it two, five, or ten years in the future, for each of us is unsure we will survive to enjoy it then. Furthermore, even if we were certain of being able to enjoy it in the future, we would much prefer the enjoyment today or as soon as possible. Hence we must encourage ourselves to think about planning for this package of needs—planning for needs during the working lifetime in terms of consumption versus saving.

In order to understand somewhat better the process of allocating income to current consumption, saving, or insurance against risk during the working years, it is appropriate to consider the following topics: savings and investment, life insurance and annuities, health and accident insurance, and transfer payments.

TRANSFER PAYMENTS

Transfer payments are payments made to individuals for which no productive service is rendered. In effect transfer payments are grants of purchasing power from one group within the economic system to another group. In some cases the transfer payment is not a transfer of purchasing power from one group to another but from one person within a particular group to another person within that group.

Members of a family transfer income from those working to those unable to work. The working generation usually transfers income to support children. This is the most frequent type of transfer. In the nineteenth and twentieth centuries the family transferred income to senior family members. This direct family support of the aged has, however, declined in the modern industrial countries. Declines in the portion of population on farms, a more mobile society, and a breakup of the extended family have all been important factors in bringing about the national system of social insurance in the United States.

UNEMPLOYMENT COMPENSATION

The rationale behind unemployment compensation is that at times individuals will find the market demand for their productive services has fallen. They may be temporarily laid off or in some cases permanently discharged from their positions. Unemployment compensation is designed to provide a short-run source of purchasing power for persons who have, for one reason or another, not continued in gainful employment. The typical structure is to provide payments on a weekly basis in some rough proportion to the income earned on the previous job. No attempt will be made here to be specific regarding the length, duration, or amount of payments. Suffice it to say that payments are approximately 80 percent of the prior earnings up to a maximum amount and that they continue if the person is unable to find gainful employment for approximately two-thirds of a year. At that time the payments terminate, and another source of income or transfer payment must be found to provide the person with income.

The funds for unemployment compensation are raised via a tax on employers. Each state administers the unemployment compensation system within federal guidelines and decides the amount and duration of compensation and assesses the employer tax. The tax on the employer is essentially a function of the frequency and duration of layoff in that firm and industry. Thus a firm or industry which has little seasonal variation in its employment patterns will generally be assessed at a lower rate than a firm which has high seasonal variations. In addition to the tax on employers there are funds provided by the federal government to sustain the program. Particularly in periods of recession and economic slowdown, it is necessary for the contributions of the federal government to increase in order that the program remain solvent. Unemployment insurance implicitly recognizes the interrelated nature of an industrial economy. The conventional wisdom argues that if a man is not working it is because he does not desire to work. This view came down from the Protestant ethic and the sayings of Benjamin Franklin. But in a modern world insufficient aggregate demand for final goods may make it impossible for large numbers of willing workers to find gainful employment. This is not because they are lazy but because there are no jobs available. Unemployment compensation recognizes this fact. It attempts to provide purchasing power for persons temporarily out of work.

WELFARE

For as long as man has maintained himself as a social animal, there have been transfer payments of a welfare type. Whether one considers tribal relationships or relationships of the extended family, one knows that the process of making transfer payments was done on a completely informal basis and was dependent on mutual respect and the ties of the family. In these cases the transfer payments were in effect food, clothing, and subsistence generated by the productive unit as a whole and allocated to the individuals on the basis of need. In effect the extended family and the tribe were communistic societies— from each according to his abilities, and to each according to his needs. As the market system grew and developed and as the technological revolution occurred, the extended family and tribal relations tended to break down and to be replaced by a market system of allocation. In the market system the process of allocation is from each according to his ability, to each according to his productivity. As a result, some participants in the system had little or no ability either owing to their health status or to their lack of skills and training; they would tend to earn relatively little.

As the Industrial Revolution progressed in the seventeenth and eighteenth centuries the people of England began to develop a formal system of welfare. It was reprehensible in the eyes of society in general to allow people to starve and to live in the extremely squalid conditions that were forced upon individuals who did not have the ability to contribute directly to the productive process. The widowed, the orphaned, the maimed, all were relatively undesirable in the eyes of employers. As a result of the work relief system, work houses and the poor laws of Great Britain arose. Their intent was to provide productive work opportunities for people and, in so doing, provide for the physical well-being of this group.

In many ways this approach was transferred to the United States, in that a system of relief for the poor, for dependent children, for the blind, and for the crippled was organized. This is our welfare system; it is dependent on tax monies from both state and local sources and from federal government sources. These funds are administered and allocated by local welfare departments to individuals on the basis of demonstrated need. The "means" test is generally applied: the persons must not have either capital goods, savings, or income property that will generate income if they are to receive welfare.

Families or individuals receiving welfare or unemployment payments can be classified into two major groups: (1) temporary recipients, and (2) permanent recipients. The problems, future expectations, and abilities of these groups are vastly different. The former includes persons who are temporarily disabled or out of work as the result of an economic condition. These persons expect to re-enter the working world as soon as conditions improve. They have, in most cases, some financial and real resources which can be used to reduce the suffering resulting from loss of income. The temporary recipients of transfer payments must consider how to utilize past savings and future earning power to be able to maintain an adequate standard of living. They can sell their homes, use life insurance as collateral for loans, and delay purchasing major items. These actions contribute to maintaining consumption at or near the accustomed level.

Persons who are permanently disabled or families receiving Aid to Dependent Children do not view their dependence on welfare as temporary but rather expect to receive payments for an extended period. The level of payment is such that there is little, if any, hope of saving, owning a home, or purchasing a car. Persons in this group are faced with the task of allocating their income in such a manner that they can continue to meet their most basic needs.

LIFE INSURANCE AND ANNUITIES

Life insurance as a term is a misnomer just as the phrase "death insurance" is a misnomer. Both titles miss the mark, for insurance on one's life serves two purposes. First, such insurance provides some amount of security for dependents of the insured person; and secondly, at retirement or some other specified time, the insured, if he has purchased a policy with a cash value, is able to use the money accumulated to purchase goods and services which he has foregone in previous time periods.

At present, Americans have over $1.1 trillion of life insurance, or over 155 times what it was in 1900. In 1900, only one out of every eight people in the U.S. had life insurance; today, two out of three people have life insurance in one form or another, with $23,000 of protection per family being average. Benefits have reached the rate of $14.4 billion a year, double that of a decade ago. In 1968, life insurance companies paid out benefits to the living in the amount of $8.2 billion in contrast to the $6.2 billion in payments to the families of those who died. This gives an indication of how important life insurance is to living policyholders as well as to beneficiaries.

Life insurance is based on the natural law of human mortality—the inescapable fact that as people grow older, an increasing proportion must die. Life insurance companies build up funds, in the form of premium dollars, for their policyholders to offset this increasing risk and eventual certainty. Additional funds must also be held in reserve for catastrophic or unexpected epidemics which could cause the mortality rates to rise. Part of the premium dollars, therefore, are set aside to allow for such eventualities. Until needed, these funds are put to work, to earn a return, to keep premium costs down, and to provide souces of capital to finance the nation's economic growth. The obligations of U. S. life insurance companies are backed by more than $188 billion, invested in a variety of ways as the figure below shows.

FIGURE 9-2

Percentage Distribution of Assets of U.S. Life Insurance Companies 1970

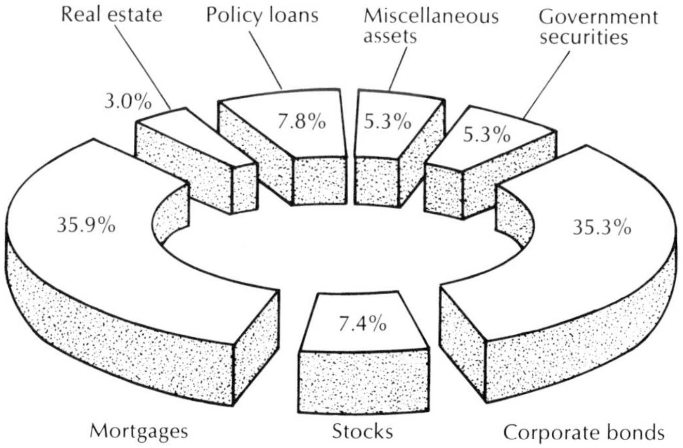

Source: *Life Insurance Fact Book, 1971,* Institute of Life Insurance, p. 71.

THE MANY FORMS OF LIFE INSURANCE

The essential differences between the various forms of insurance revolve around three variables—the amount of coverage, the savings element of the policy, and the number of years payments are to be made to the company. Term insurance usually has little or no savings element, whereas ordinary life and annuities have substantial savings aspects. Single-payment and twenty-pay life have a specified number of payments to the company, whereas ordinary life usually requires payments over the entire life of the policy. These factors must be evaluated carefully in the selection of a particular policy.

Term Insurance. Term insurance, as the name implies, is a temporary type of insurance; that is, it is for a specified period of time and provides protection only if the policyholder dies during the "term" of the contract. Most term policies cover a period of twenty years and must be renewed each year. However, a new medical examination usually is not required for renewal purposes. Some term policies are convertible; that is, they may grant the right to the policyholder to exchange them without proving his insurability for a whole life or endowment plan with, of course, a higher premium rate. If a policyholder decides to buy term insurance with a view toward exchanging it for some type of permanent insurance, he should do so as soon as his budget allows, since the premium rate will go up with each passing year because of the greater risk involved.

A term policy may also contain a renewal privilege, which is the right to renew the policy without providing insurability—without having a physical examination. A renewed term policy will also have a higher cost to the individual, again because of the passage of time and a corresponding higher life risk.

One of the uses of a term policy is to provide additional protection for an individual while his family is young, when persons usually need maximum insurance protection for the lowest possible premium outlay, (a major reason for term insurance—its low cost for a large amount of protection in relation to permanent policies). Another use of the term policy is to guarantee mortgage payments on the policyholder's home if he should not live to pay it himself.

Since the premium for a term policy pays only the cost of protection during the term of the policy, the policy seldom has any nonforfeiture value attached to it. That is, non-payment of the premium usually cancels the policy, and the insured has no further protection. Contrasted with this, all individual policies except term contain nonforfeiture values which give the policies greater flexibility in meeting changing needs. Basically, the nonforfeiture clause gives the insured the right to borrow on his policy (after a certain time period), or to stop paying premiums and (a) continue the insurance protection on a modified basis, or (b) receive cash or an income settlement and drop the coverage.

Ordinary Life Insurance. Ordinary life is a form of insurance which provides not only a sum of money to the beneficiaries to pay expenses and debts, but also provides a continuing income to a widow and children, making it possible to keep the home intact. In addition, it may provide income to the widow after the children are grown, and it can pay the children's way through college, retire the mortgage on the home, or any of several alternative electives.

Ordinary life insurance is used not only for protection in case of death, but also as a means of saving through cash values for use later in life. At that time the accumulated money may be taken either in one sum or in an income which will continue as long as the insured lives.

This type of policy is frequently used in the business world to insure the life of key men for the benefit of the business or to insure the life of a partner in a business, expediting the ability of the surviving partner or partners to pay the family of the deceased partner his share of the business.

Ordinary life insurance has many different uses, and a great many types of ordinary policies have been developed to meet individual needs for protection. Premiums for ordinary policies are usually paid directly to the insurance company annually, semi-annually, quarterly, or monthly. The policies are almost always issued in units of $1,000 or more (the average size ordinary policy in force in 1968 was $5,450), and a medical examination is usually required, although "non-medical" ordinary policies may be purchased in limited amounts.

Basically, there are only three types of individual insurance policies: term, whole life, and endowment. There are, however, several variations of each type; and a number of special purpose policies combine two or more of the three basic policies, with possibly an annuity element added. However, keep in mind that in each case the flexibility of the ordinary life insurance policy is being demonstrated; a new type of policy is not being introduced.

Annuities. A person who buys term insurance buys it with the thought that he needs protection for his family in the event of premature death. The person who buys an ordinary life policy wishes to combine a policy that insures against premature death with one that builds up a cash value. A person who buys an annuity wishes to place his greatest emphasis on the flow of cash received after retirement. He wants the insurance company to guarantee that he will receive monthly income payments throughout his entire retired lifetime; that is, he will never live so long that his savings will be depleted. This, in effect, is life insurance in reverse. When one purchases a term insurance policy, he purchases it in anticipation that he may not live long enough to support his family. A person who purchases an annuity-type program purchases it with the expectation that he will never run out of money.

Mortality tables are used in the calculation of annuities in the same way that they are used in the calculation of ordinary life and term life insurance policies.

SELECTING A LIFE INSURANCE PROGRAM

The reasons for purchasing life insurance are many and varied. Young families select insurance to protect the family, should the primary income earner die prematurely. Middle-aged families continue to purchase insurance plans as a means of insuring sufficient savings in their retirement years. Whatever the reason for purchasing or selecting insurance, one must consider the same kinds of questions that he faces in the purchase of an automobile or a consumer durable good. Insurance is a product; it is sold with the intent of providing a service to the purchaser. At the same time, the insurance industry provides employment for many people including the salesman, the office staff, the actuarial staff, and so on. As a wise purchaser one must consider a number of factors in selecting an insurance program.

First, the prospective purchaser must consider its cost in relation to the benefits to be accrued. The most simple case is the purchase of term insurance. When a person purchases $1,000 of term insurance at age twenty-two, he need only compare the monthly or annual rate for a $1,000 policy of several firms and select the one with the lowest cost. However, a consideration of ordinary life policies, family income protection policies, and annuities becomes much more difficult from the point of view of the purchaser. Rather than dealing with only two variables, the face amount of the insurance and the annual dollar cost, the purchaser must deal with all three of the basic variables—the amount, the buildup of cash value, and the annual premium payment. It is the second variable, the buildup of cash value, which causes the most difficulty in assessing costs and benefits. The various insurance companies and various plans within the same insurance company build up cash value at different rates during the life of the policy. This process of amassing cash value at differential rates means that the final amount of cash value may be substantially different for different policies carrying the same monthly premium. It thus becomes a difficult task for the consumer to purchase insurance on a price basis only, since the process requires that the consumer evaluate all of the variables and not just the face amount in relation to the annual premium.

It is, then, extremely important that the purchaser be careful and spend sufficient time analyzing the various alternatives in order that he may be able to obtain the most for his insurance dollar. The general principles of buying require that comparative shopping be undertaken, that the plans of various organizations be compared, and that the costs and benefits be evaluated. Since life insurance deals with our departure from this earth, it has often been associated with a certain aura that has made it difficult to consider the various alternatives rationally.

THE SPREADING OF RISK—
PURCHASE OF HEALTH, ACCIDENT, LIABILITY INSURANCE

The premiums of life insurance are based on the underlying fact that at some time everyone must die. In the area of accident and liability insurance, the same kind of basic assumption can be utilized. In this case, however, the assumption is that for a sufficiently large group of people there will be a given number of accidents and injuries during a period of time. Since each of us is unable or unwilling to assume the risk of our house burning down, of seriously injuring a pedestrian crossing a street, or of undergoing an extended period of time in the hospital, we average this risk over a large group of people. In this way each of us pays on an annual basis the expected cost of an accident which might occur to us.

The concept behind health, accident, and liability insurance assumes a known probability that a fire will strike a home, that a wind storm will blow away a roof, or that someone will have a collision with another automobile. Given the assumed probability of these events occurring, it is then merely necessary to divide the cost of these events by the number of persons desiring to be insured against them, to add a factor for sales and office management, and to add an additional amount for reserves and contingencies. Then one has an estimate of the premium to be charged for insuring against these risks. In the selection of insurance, it is important again to use wise shopping procedures and to select insurance as carefully as one would select an automobile. It is necessary that the coverage, the deductibles, the premium, and any extenuating circumstances concerning the policy be clearly understood. In comparing the policies of various companies, it is necessary to ascertain that the same benefits are being received before being able to determine the cost.

SAVING

In economics saving is defined as those funds or that portion of income which is not used for consumption. Our concern at this point is not how much will be saved, for that needs to be an individual decision in light of the individual's plans for the future, but rather the alternative uses of saving and the expected return and safety that are associated with these alternative uses.

Insurance. It has been previously shown that the purchase of insurance and annuities in effect has a saving element and that these savings earn an interest or dividend return as well as provide the insured or annuitant with protection in the event of death. This use of insurance has been, and is, one of the more important uses of saving in the United States and has provided many people with an outlet that is both safe and productive.

Banks and Savings and Loan Associations. Nearly all savers have from time to time placed money on deposit with a bank or a savings and loan in their local neighborhood. These financial institutions offer a very high degree of safety for the individual saver. Funds placed in a savings account or in certificates of deposit in these institutions are insured by agencies of the federal government. Each saver would be reimbursed for loss, should the institution fail, up to a maximum as stipulated by the Federal Deposit Insurance Corporation or the Federal Savings and Loan Insurance Corporation. Right now the maximum is $20,000 per account. Thus these accounts are very safe, and it is an unlikely event that one would find his savings unavailable in time of need. At the same time, savings deposited with these institutions earn a stipulated annual rate of return which allows the savings to grow and to increase in dollar amount as this interest return is applied and redeposited in the account. However, it is important to consider that, given the inflationary trend in the United States over the past several years, the interest return must be adjusted downward to compensate for the rate of increase in the price level; hence the true annual interest rate adjusted for price changes has been relatively low during the recent past.

Bonds. The saver who has amassed a substantial amount of funds can place savings in bonds of the local, state, or federal government or of private corporations. Investment in bonds insures that, unless the corporation goes bankrupt, the individual saver will receive his interest payments regularly and the principal will be repaid when the bond becomes due. It is unlikely that governmental institutions will default on their bonds and, from the point of view of most savers, there is small risk that the bonds of corporations will be defaulted upon as the result of bankruptcy. Thus in terms of comparative risk, the risks associated with the ownership of bonds as a form of saving is not much different from the ownership of saving accounts in either banks or savings and loans.

Common Stock. Common stock ownership offers the saver an opportunity to place savings in an outlet which offers growth as well as return. The saver who purchases stock in effect is becoming a part owner of the corporation. As a result he shares in the profits of the corporation; he also shares in its losses. Placing savings in common stock means that the saver is hoping for two events to occur: one, that he will receive annual dividends and thus earn a return on his savings; and two, that the value of the common stock will increase. The increase in value is associated with a capitalization of the increased profitability of the firm. However, should the saver select a stock in a firm that is about to incur losses or has been incurring losses, he may find that the dividend which he expects does not materialize and also that the value or price of shares of stock in the corporation will decline as people perceive a decline in the expected profitability of that firm. Hence the individual who invests his savings in the stock market must expect that he can suffer losses as well as earn profits.

Mutual Funds. Over the past several years the mutual fund industry has increased its activities significantly. The mutual fund offers the small investor an opportunity to buy into an organization which in turn uses his savings to purchase stock and bonds of many corporations. The mutual fund allows the small investor to average his risk over several firms by becoming a part owner of the mutual fund. This averaging of risk out over a number of firms is somewhat offset by the management fees charged by the mutual funds and the possibility that the fund selected may not be a well-managed fund.

In terms of safety, the placement of savings in the purchase of common stock must be considered less safe than insurance purchases, savings accounts, or bond purchases. However, the possibility of long-term capital gains and long-term increases in profits may be sufficient to offset the risk of capital loss.

It is extremely important that the saver balance these risks and opportunities. It is necessary that information be gathered so that a wise and rational choice of saving outlets can be made.

Real Estate. The typical consumer places a substantial amount of savings in owner-occupied housing. This process occurs as the mortgage is reduced via the monthly installment. Saving in housing is encouraged by the federal government by means of the income tax deduction for taxes and interest payments on housing.

In addition household units purchase and hold real estate for speculative purposes. In some ways the family home is a speculative venture. Given the tendency toward inflation, speculation in housing has been relatively risk free and often very profitable. Home ownership is not usually considered as a speculative venture, since all the virtues of thrift, hard work, and family stability are associated with it. Speculation frequently takes the form of holding vacant land, apartments, and farm land. These activities utilize the holding of a productive resource in the expectation that the price will rise in the near future. In some cases, the resource can be expected to yield sufficient current returns to cover the cost of holding the asset as in the case of a farm or apartment building. In others, all returns must be earned at the time of sale.

CONSUMER SAVINGS OUTLETS

Consumers in the American economy have been saving about 5 percent of disposable income since 1929. That year marks the beginning of regular data collection by the U. S. Department of Commerce. Prior to that date, the picture is less clear; but one can be certain that a savings rate of at least 5 percent had been maintained for a considerable prior period.

Tables 9-1 and 9-2 indicate the changes in real and financial wealth resulting from the savings of households in 1970. Inspection of the data provides some interesting insights into the financial-planning behavior of Americans. Households had a gross increase of $70.8 billion in financial assets in 1970 and $26.1

TABLE 9-1

FINANCIAL ASSETS AND LIABILITIES
OF INDIVIDUALS IN 1970
(Billions of dollars)

Financial Assets, Total	$1,883.0
Currency, Demand Deposits	121.9
Savings Accounts	407.0
U.S. Government Securities	95.9
Corporate Stock, Market Value	747.7
Insurance, Pension Reserves	361.0
Other Assets	149.5
Liabilities, Total	482.1
Mortgage Debt	293.5
Consumer Credit	126.8
Other Liabilities	61.8
Net Equity	$1,400.9

Source: Calculated from Federal Reserve data.

TABLE 9-2

SAVING BY HOUSEHOLDS IN 1970
(Billions of dollars)

Net Household Saving	$ 68.7
Increase in Financial Assets	70.8
Currency, Demand Deposits	3.4
Savings Accounts	34.5
Securities	4.6
Insurance, Pension Reserves	22.5
Other Financial Assets	3.9
Net Investment in:	
Owner-occupied Homes	9.5
Consumer Durables	9.0
Non-Corporate Plant and Equipment	7.6
Less: Increase in Debt	28.2
Home Mortgages	12.6
Consumer Credit	4.3
Other Debt	3.6
Non-Corporate Business	7.7
Discrepancy	− .6

Source: Calculated from Federal Reserve data.

billion net increase in real assets (housing, etc.). It is of interest to note that almost all of the increase in financial assets can be accounted for by dollar-denominated assets. All but $4.6 billion of the $70.8 billion are in fixed dollar value assets such as cash, savings accounts, life insurance and pension plans. The portion placed in securities includes bonds as well as stocks. The conclusion to be reached is that the great bulk of households do not have a significant hedge against inflation. They continue to place savings in the traditional outlets on a contractual-interest basis with only a modest 20 percent of savings being placed in housing and corporate stocks, which can be a hedge against inflation.

Inflation can destroy the value of savings placed at fixed interest rates. Consider the case of a family with a $10,000 savings account. In recent years this account could earn a return of about 5½ percent per annum. At the end of a year the dollar value of the account would be $10,550. But suppose prices had increased at a 6 percent annual rate during the year. It would require $10,600 to purchase the same quantity of goods $10,000 would have purchased at the beginning of the year. The real purchasing power of this family's savings account would have fallen by $50. Whenever the rate of price inflation exceeds the stipulated rate of return on dollar-denominated assets, the assets lose real value. This factor must be considered in the financial plan of each family with a careful balance of savings in dollar-denominated assets and equity assets (stocks, housing, plant, and equipment). In this way, there will be funds available for emergency use; and, at the same time, a portion of the portfolio will be in assets which will tend to increase with increases in the price level.

SUGGESTED READING

Personal Economics Readings

"Auto Insurance," *Consumer's Reports.* June, 1970, pp. 332-341, July, 1970, pp. 426-433.

Bernstein, M. C. *The Future of Private Pensions.* New York: Free Press, 1964.

Buckley, Joseph C. *The Retirement Handbook.* 3rd ed. New York: Harper and Row, 1967.

Cobleigh, Ira U. *All About Stocks.* New York: Weybright and Talley, 1970.

Consumer's Union. *Consumer's Union Report on Life Insurance.* Mount Vernon, N.Y., 1967.

Dervin, Brenda, et al. *The Spender Syndrome: Case Studies of 68 Families and Their Consumer Problems.* Madison, Wis.: Center for Consumer Affairs, University of Wisconsin Press, 1965.

Frank, Robert. *Successful Investing Through Mutual Funds.* New York: Hart Publishing Company, 1969.

Geier, Arnold. *Life Insurance: How to Get Your Money's Worth.* New York: Collier Books, 1965.

Institute of Life Insurance. *A Date with Your Future.* 277 Park Avenue, New York, New York, 1971.

——: *Decade of Decision.*, 1966.

——. *Life Insurance Fact Book, 1970, 1971.*

——. *Your Retirement.* 1970.

Insurance Information Institute. *A Family Guide to Property and Liability Insurance.* 110 William Street, New York, N.Y., 1967.

Margolius, Sidney. *Your Personal Guide to Successful Retirement.* New York: Random House, 1969.

Merrill, Lynch, Pierce, Fenner and Smith, Inc. *How to Invest in Stocks and Bonds.* 70 Pine Street, New York, N.Y., 1967.

——. *How to Read a Financial Report.* 1968.

Superintendent of Documents. *Are You Planning on Living the Rest of Your Life?* Washington, D.C.: U. S. Government Printing Office, 1969.

——. *Planning for Later Years.* 1969.

——. *Social Security Cash Benefits.* 1970.

——. *Social Security Cash Benefits for Students 18-22.* 1968.

——. *Social Security Information for Young Families.* 1968.

——. *Your Social Security.* 1970.

U. S. Department of Housing and Urban Development. *Home Mortgage Insurance.* Washington, D.C.: U. S. Government Printing Office, 1969.

Case Studies
in Family
Financial Planning

It should be clear that the process of allocating family income is extremely complicated and challenging. Income must be wisely spent in order to purchase goods of high quality at minimum cost. This portion of the allocation process is rather simple and straightforward compared to the process of allocating income over time. The purchase of a current good or service requires that data of costs and benefits be collected and choices be made based on these data. Decisions regarding saving, insurance, retirement planning, and investing require the same decision process, but the uncertainty of future events clouds the outcome. To illustrate the problems of allocating income over a period of time, two case studies will be presented. It is necessary to consider the family's goals, income, and current consumption needs, as well as expectations of future income.

The first case concerns the choices available to a family of three with an income of $12,000 a year. The second case will consider a family of four with an income of $18,000 a year. In these cases the consumption, saving, insurance, and investment considerations of family decision making will be examined. The income levels and allocations are only suggestive, but they reflect income levels of skilled workers. The actual spending decisions of each family must depend on its value structure and its expectations of future income.

CASE 1—THE ROGERS FAMILY

The Rogers are a young family with one child. Bill is twenty-four, his wife, Pat, is twenty-three and their child, Betty, is two. Bill and Pat have been married four years and live in a rental apartment. Bill earns $12,000 per year; Mary is not gainfully employed.

The decisions of the Rogers family regarding the allocation of income must be based on the current needs of the family for food, clothing, housing, and other necessary household expenses. In addition, savings to plan for future acquisitions and for retirement income are necessary. An income protection plan which will provide security for the family in the event that the primary wage earner, Bill, should either become disabled or die prematurely is also necessary.

In order to evaluate the budget of the family, consider the typical expenditures of a family earning approximately $12,000 (Table 2-1). The family must consider current expenditures for consumption purposes to cover the basic necessities of life. Total current consumption for the Rogers family amounts to $7,900.

In addition to the expenditures for current consumption, the Rogers family is amassing durable goods. During the first years following marriage, it is necessary to establish the household. This requires the purchase of furniture and appliances such as the refrigerator, washer, and dishwasher and in some cases necessitates the purchase of an automobile. These purchases of durable goods are relatively extensive during the early years of family formation. As a result, a separate item of $1,500 has been included in the budget for durable goods acquisition. It is expected that the amounts assigned to this category will decline in a few years as the stock of durables becomes sufficient to provide the family with the necessary household services.

The family pays $1,200 for personal taxes and $468 for Social Security contributions. The total amount of expenditures and taxes for the family are $11,068. This leaves $932 which can be used for life insurance programs and family savings for future consumption.

The Rogers family has made a fundamental choice at this point in that they have allocated the bulk of their income to current consumption and payment of taxes. Approximately $900 has been allocated to future consumption, either future consumption out of savings or the insurance of the ability to undertake future consumption in the event of a premature death. This choice should be conscious and rational. The budget figures for current consumption are derived from estimates of expenditures by many families shown in Table 2-1. If the Rogers family desired, as a matter of choice, to consume more now, they could reduce their life insurance coverage. On the other hand, the desire for saving on the part of the family might be higher. They could have a strong desire to move from the rented apartment to their own home; as a result, they might tend to reduce somewhat the expenditures for current consumption and durable goods and increase the total amount of saving necessary to purchase a home.

The rate of saving of the Rogers family is approximately 5 percent. This is a figure that is often considered a rule of thumb. It also corresponds closely with the savings ratio of all families in the U. S. on the basis of aggregate income data.

It is important that the family consider the outlet for these savings. If it is assumed that during the previous four years of marriage the family had been saving at approximately the same rate as this year, the family would have amassed a total liquid saving of approximately $4,000. Most family counselors urge that at least two- to six-month's salary be accumulated in readily available form prior to the consideration of a serious investment program. That is, during the next three to four years, the Rogers family would continue to save at the rate of about $400 or $600 a year. Then these savings should be placed in relatively liquid form. The family could decide to place this $500 a year in a savings and loan account or in a passbook account in a commercial bank; or after they have amassed a few thousand dollars they might purchase a Certificate of Deposit from a commercial bank or a savings and loan which pays slightly higher rates of return than do passbook savings accounts. However, the certificate of deposit has a specific maturity date and does tend to tie the savings up in a slightly less available form than passbook savings. For these reasons, the Rogers family has limited funds available for investment in mutual funds or stocks, which for them are considered speculative owing to the fact that they have not achieved the necessary cushion of liquid assets that a family should have to protect them from temporary adversity.

FAMILY INCOME INSURANCE

The responsibility of a head of household to his family has been modified slightly in the recent past. In years gone by, it was assumed that it was the responsibility of the family (either the individual's family or the extended family) to provide income insurance for children and wives in the event that a husband should die prematurely. Thus the family either obtained sufficient life insurance to meet this responsibility or expected that there would be sufficient income flow to maintain consumption purchases for the members of a fatherless family.

However, with the advent of modern industrialization, a part of the responsibility for providing income for one's family has been taken over by the government in the form of a Social Security program. As one assesses income insurance needs and requirements of the family, it is important that the individual consider not only private plans but public plans and benefits associated with the place of employment.

NEEDS

The needs for family income maintenance fall into essentially four categories. If the primary wage earner dies, funds are required to provide for immediate expenses and for the payment of any outstanding debts of the family. Second, emergency funds are required to accommodate the family during a transitional period of time. Third, funds are required for the education of the

TABLE 10-1

ROGERS FAMILY INCOME AND EXPENDITURES

Income			$12,000
Current Consumption:			
Food	$2,300		
Clothing	850		
Housing	2,000		
Other			
consumption	1,200		
Transportation	1,000		
Medical care	550		
		$ 7,900	
Durable Goods Purchases		1,500	
Taxes:			
Personal	$1,200		
Social			
Security	468		
		1,668	
Savings and Insurance:			
Life			
Insurance	$ 377		
Saving	555		
		932	
		$12,000	$12,000

TABLE 10-2

ROGERS FAMILY NEEDS IN THE EVENT
OF PREMATURE DEATH OF THE
PRIMARY WAGE EARNER

Cash Funds Needed:		
Last Expenses	$6,000	
Emergency Fund	5,000	
Education Fund	6,000	
		$17,000
Income Funds*		50,730
Total Needs		$67,730

*In addition to Social Security benefits.

children; and fourth, funds are required for income maintenance of the family over its lifetime.

If the Rogers family has $3,000 of outstanding bills, costs associated with Bill's death would be $6,000. Emergency funds required would be $5,000, and the family educational fund would be $6,000 (only one child). In addition, the wife and child would need approximately half the monthly salary of the working family thereafter. Thus from the present time through the age of eighteen for the child, the family would require $537 per month for living expenses. From the sixteenth year until the death of the wife, it is assumed that $250 of income would be required.

Thus the immediate need of the family is for $17,000 in the event of a premature death and an additional sum of money to meet the income needs of the family so long as obligations are present.

SOURCES OF INCOME

The first source which Bill should consider is the payment possible under the Social Security program.

Table 10-3 indicates the monthly income benefits available under Social Security. The average monthly wage of the insured determines the income benefits that a worker can expect to receive. In Bill's case the benefits of survivorship would accrue to the mother and one child until the child was eighteen years of age. Since Bill is earning and paying Social Security taxes on an amount

TABLE 10-3

EXAMPLES OF MONTHLY CASH PAYMENTS

Average yearly earnings after 1950	$923 or less	$1,800	$3,000	$4,200	$5,400	$6,600	$7,800
Retired worker—65 or older Disabled worker—under 65	70.40	111.90	145.60	177.70	208.80	240.30	275.80
Wife 65 or older	35.20	56.00	72.80	88.90	104.40	120.20	137.90
Retired worker at 62	56.40	89.60	116.50	142.20	167.10	192.30	220.70
Wife at 62, no child	26.40	42.00	54.60	66.70	78.30	90.20	103.50
Widow at 60	61.10	80.10	104.20	127.20	149.40	171.90	197.30
Widow or widower at 62	70.40	92.40	120.20	146.70	172.30	198.30	227.60
Disabled widow at 50	42.80	56.10	72.90	89.00	104.50	120.30	138.00
Wife under 65 and one child	35.20	56.00	77.10	131.20	181.10	194.90	206.90
Widowed mother and one child	105.60	167.90	218.40	266.60	313.20	360.60	413.80
Widowed mother and two children	105.60	167.90	222.70	308.90	389.90	435.20	482.70
One child of retired or disabled worker	35.20	56.00	72.80	88.90	104.40	120.20	137.90
One surviving child	70.40	84.00	109.20	133.30	156.60	180.30	206.90
Maximum family payment	105.60	167.90	222.70	308.90	389.90	435.20	482.70

Source: *Your Social Security*, U.S. Department of Health, Education, and Welfare (U.S. Government Printing Office, 1972) p. 12.

TABLE 10-4

BILL'S INSURANCE PROGRAM

Group term at place of employment		$12,000
Cost per year	$ 36.00	
Ordinary life		10,000
Cost per year	175.40	
Convertible term		45,000
Cost per year	166.05	
Total coverage		$67,000
Total cost per year	$377.45	

TABLE 10-5

Rogers Family Needs

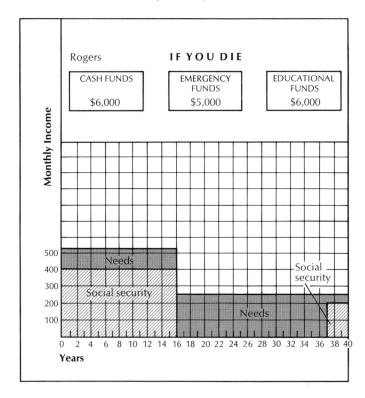

greater than the highest average monthly wage used for benefit calculation, his family would receive benefit payments based on the maximum average monthly wage. This amounts to $413 a month for the widow and one child for the years one to sixteen and $197 a month after age sixty. It is Bill's responsibility to provide sufficient resources so the family income during the first six years is

$537 and the income after that time is $250 per month, the amount needed to support Pat for the remainder of her life.

There is a need of $124 per month during the first sixteen years, $250 per month during the sixteenth through the thirty-seventh year, and $53 per month thereafter. The Rogers family requires a total of $67,000 of capital to provide this amount of income. The $17,000 would be payable at the time of death to cover expenses, and the remainder would be used to cover the monthly income required for the family.

This sample life insurance plan meets the needs of Bill's family during the time when the expenses will be highest and reduces the amounts when expenses decline.

OTHER INSURANCES

In addition to the basic insurance program providing for income maintenance, the costs of automobile, health, fire, and theft insurance are included in Bill's transportation and housing expenses. These programs provide a means of spreading risk so that, in the event of an accident, illness, or theft, the risk carried by Bill is an average risk. He would not then be required to meet the full cost of these events.

THINK IT OVER:

1. Why was Bill's primary income maintenance program composed of term insurance?
2. What will occur to the cost of this term insurance as Bill becomes older?
3. What are the advantages of term over ordinary life? What are the disadvantages?
4. Does this allocation of income between current consumption and future consumption meet the needs of the family? How would you alter it to meet the needs that you would expect in the near future?

CASE 2—THE SMITH FAMILY

The Smith family consists of a husband, Harvey, age thirty-eight; a wife, Hazel, age thirty-two; a thirteen-year-old boy, and an eight-year-old girl. The Smith family owns their home and conforms closely to the data presented for a family at the higher level of annual expenditure in Table 2-1. The total cost of this family's budget for consumption and taxes is $15,781. This is slightly higher than the figures for 1969, but it approximates the figures for 1971-1972 based on the increase in prices.

TABLE 10-6

SMITH FAMILY INCOME AND EXPENDITURES

Income			$18,000
Current Consumption:			
Food	$3,000		
Clothing	1,400		
Housing	3,689		
Other			
consumption	2,500		
Transportation	1,500		
Medical care	700		
		$12,789	
Taxes:			
Personal	$2,524		
Social Security	468		
		2,992	
Savings and Insurance:			
Life Insurance			
and disability	$ 736		
Saving	1,483	2,219	
Total		$18,000	$18,000

TABLE 10-7

SMITH FAMILY NEEDS IN THE EVENT OF PREMATURE
DEATH OF THE PRIMARY WAGE EARNER

Cash Funds Needed:			
Last Expenses	$ 3,000		
Mortgage Fund	21,000		
Emergency Fund	5,000		
		$29,000	
Income Funds Needed:*		80,000	
Total Needs			$109,000
Less cash and other assets			30,000
Income Maintenance Needs			$ 79,000

*In addition to Social Security benefits.

It should be noted that, in comparing the budget of expenditures of the Smith family with the Rogers family, there has been a tendency to expand all levels of current consumption as would be expected with a higher level of income. The one exception is the purchase of durable goods. By the time a wage earner has reached age 38 the family should have accumulated a sufficient stock of durables to use budget figures for current consumption that allow for replacement of those durables as they wear out. A sum of approximately $2,300 is left to be allocated between planning for retirement, planning for insurance against premature death, and planning for a savings program of investment or other savings alternatives.

THE SAVINGS, INSURANCE AND INVESTMENT PLAN

Life Insurance. The same procedures are used for the Smith family as were used for the Rogers family in selecting life insurance coverage. It is necessary to estimate family needs in terms of cash funds, emergency funds, and educational funds. For this family, the amount is $29,000: $3,000 for last expenses, $21,000 to pay off the mortgage, and $5,000 for the emergency fund. Educational funds are available from another source.

It is then necessary to determine the expected monthly needs of the family for the specified period of time. A total amount of coverage can then be calculated in relation to the total needs that might be expected by this family.

Income needs for the family amount to $80,000 in addition to those funds provided by Social Security. From this is deducted the cash and other assets of the family which could be used to support their consumption, leaving a net total of $79,000 needed to maintain income.

The Smith family has met these needs, as is shown in Table 10-8, with ordinary life insurance, group term insurance, term insurance paid for by the employer, and additional term insurance to total the required needs. The total cost of the income maintenance program is approximately $556 per year.

Saving. In addition to the savings aspect of the ordinary life insurance program, the family has $1,663 to use for college education and retirement planning. The bulk of this amount must be placed in a retirement or investment program which provides the family with income at retirement. The insurance program, at this point in time, is essentially an income-protection program with little consideration given to the retirement needs of the family. It is important, therefore, that the Smith family consider the ways in which their savings funds can be utilized to insure a comfortable retirement.

One alternative would be to use a retirement program based on an investment service. Another would be to use a retirement program based on the ability

TABLE 10-8

SMITH FAMILY INSURANCE PROGRAM

Type Policy	Amount	Premium
Ordinary life	$15,000	$360
Group term	40,000	130
Employer's term	10,000	——
Term	14,000	66
Total	$79,000	$556

TABLE 10-9

Smith Family Needs

of Mr. Smith to invest these funds so they would be secure in principal and would grow over the years. In either event, it is important that these funds be placed in reliable savings outlets in order to provide the necessary security for the Smith family at the end of the working years.

CONCLUSION

The case studies presented offer some insight into the problems of allocating income over time. A younger family has extremely high current demands on income. As a result, it spends substantial sums for durable goods and services. The older family has passed the years when the needs for durable goods are at their highest and is also approaching a period when family income is at its highest level. Therefore, the two families have different emphases with respect to current consumption. The Rogers family needs the benefits of current consumption and expects future income to rise. The Smith family has already amassed the ability to consume at a relatively high level, does not expect income to rise substantially in the future and begins to see the need for planning for family retirement.

Regardless of age or one's income level, it is extremely important for each person to take an inventory of his needs and his ability to satisfy these needs in terms of both current and future consumption.

It is not the intent here to provide specific guidelines nor to provide specific program alternatives for persons to use in making decisions regarding insurance and investment plans. It *is* the intent to encourage individuals to consider retirement and insurance questions in the same way they consider questions regarding the purchase of a car, house, or refrigerator. A rational decision-making process must be followed. Alternatives must be considered, and the cost of the various alternatives must be determined.

There is one very difficult aspect of planning for future income. Individuals tend to expect their incomes to rise more rapidly than they do. They tend to expect their consumption demands to be lower than they are. They tend to believe that they will live forever. Hence, it becomes necessary for all of us to consider our *real* opportunities in the future as well as our rose-colored expectations. The evaluation of the real events can best be handled by using actuarial tables, by comparing the trends in income with job classifications, and by relating these actual data to our own experiences.

Index